WITNESS TO THE REVOLUTION

WITNESS TO
THE REVOLUTION

*American and British Commentators
in France 1788–94*

PETER BURLEY

WEIDENFELD & NICOLSON
LONDON

This book is dedicated
to Jenny, Robert and Freya
for their forbearance
and support.

First published in Great Britain in 1989 by
George Weidenfeld & Nicolson Ltd
91 Clapham High Street, London SW4 7TA

ISBN 0 297 79546 5

Printed and bound in Great Britain by
Butler & Tanner Ltd
Frome and London

Contents

Illustrations

Thomas Jefferson (Museum of Fine Arts, Boston)
John Frederick Sackville (Mansell Collection)
William Eden (Mansell Collection)
George Granville Leveson-Gower (National Portrait Gallery)
Arthur Young (Mansell Collection)
The opening of the States-General (Mansell Collection)
Gouverneur Morris (Mansell Collection)
The sacking of the Hôtel de Ville (Bulloz)
The hanging of baker François (Bulloz)
William Short (Library of Congress)
The Marquis de Lafayette (Bibliothèque Nationale Estampes)
A local political club (Bulloz)
The second storming of the Tuileries (Bulloz)
Marie–Antoinette (Mansell Collection)
Louis XVI (Mansell Collection)
'The Zenith of French Glory – the Pinnacle of Liberty' (Mary Evans Picture Library)
'Les Journées de septembre' (University of London Library)

Preface

THIS project is unashamedly bicentennial in inspiration. It is also no coincidence that many of the sources upon which it has drawn were in fact researched and edited in the 1880s at the centenary of the French Revolution.

My own background is in research on the *ancien régime*. When working on that earlier period I became aware of, and increasingly impressed by, the English and American sources. They had a directness and insight into its politics which most native sources lacked. It was, therefore, a simple step to investigate whether the same quality of source material existed for the Revolutionary period. I have been able to use some of the results of my work on the *ancien régime* to help set the scene for the Revolution, and particularly (in the chapter on the context for the commentaries) to allow some ministers of state to explain to the modern reader how they understood and worked within a constitution in the *ancien régime*.

There have been several previous publications presenting contemporary and eyewitness commentaries on the Revolution. These have, however, tended to be more anecdotal than analytical. The reader has had to grapple unaided with substantial and unedited chunks of text. The aim of this book (which does also contain very substantial extracts from the authors quoted) is to present an analytical running commentary on the Revolution from a contemporary perspective, and to this end the material is more highly ordered and edited than in previous publications.

Any faults in the study are mine, and its strengths those of the commentators themselves, for the writings of the many authors consulted are in themselves a pleasure to read and work with. Arthur Young is the typical Englishman abroad, Gouverneur Morris has an unkind but irresistible wit, the British ambassadors are urbane fair-minded men, and Thomas Jefferson has a towering humanitarian intellect, combining compassion and insight. The extracts used for this study reflect only one small dimension of their work and personalities, and they deserve to be more widely read and known.

Peter Burley

1988

Outline Chronology of Events relating to the Commentaries*

1786–7

Dorset and Jefferson already in post; Short secretary to Jefferson and then to the American Legation; Huber working for the French East India Company; Miles gathering political intelligence on the Austrian Netherlands; Morris working in America on the constitution and then retiring from American politics; Young travelling in south-west France in 1787; Monro working as a secret agent for the British government – possibly in Turkey.

Calonne reveals size of debt (August 1786).
Assembly of Notables meets (February–May 1786).
Loménie de Brienne replaces Calonne (May 1787).
Programme of reform based on provincial assemblies.

1788

May	Lamoignon's 'May Edicts'.
June/July	'Revolt of the Nobility'.
July/August	Date of meeting of the States-General fixed.
August	Young arrives in Calais and travels to Brittany.
	Declaration of bankruptcy.
	Dismissal of Loménie de Brienne.
	Appointment of Necker.
September	Recall of the *Parlement* of Paris and ruling that States-General must adhere to 1614 constitution.
November	Assembly of Notables reconvened.
December	Decision to double the Third in the States-General.

1789

Winter/Spring	Elections to the States-General and Petitions of Grievance drawn up.
February	(Abbé Sieyès' *Qu'Est ce que le Tiers Etat*).
April	Réveillon riots.
May	Opening of the States-General.
	Obstruction of business by the Third Estate.
	Young and Morris arrive in Paris.
June	Death of dauphin.
	Constitutional crises, including Oath of the Tennis Court, leading to creation of the National Assembly.

* Events in brackets are those which went unnoticed by the commentators.

July	Dismissal and reappointment of Necker.
	Riots in Paris leading to the storming of the Bastille.
	Deaths of Foulon and Bertier de Savigny.
	Louis XVI ostensibly accepts Revolution.
July/August	Young in eastern provinces.
	Rural unrest: the 'Great Fear' and burning of the *châteaux*.
	First emigrations (Artois).
	Creation of municipalities and National and Bourgeois Guards.
August	Abolition of feudalism.
	Declaration of Rights.
	Young leaves for Italy.
September	Jefferson recalled to Philadelphia to become Secretary of State, Short becomes *chargé d'affaires* and acting American ambassador.
Autumn	Sections establish themselves in Paris.
October	March of the Women on Versailles.
	Royal Family forced to take up residence in Paris.
October 1789–September 1791	'Regeneration of France'.
November/December	Church lands sequestered for issue of *Assignats*. (Full civil rights for Huguenots.)
December	Young returns to France.

1790

January	Young arrives back in Paris, then returns to England.
May	Sections officially recognized.
	King's constitutional position regularized, renunciation of wars of conquest.
June	Abolition of nobility.
	Dorset recalled and replaced by Gower as British ambassador.
July	Civil Oath and *Fête de la Fédération*.
August	Miles arrives in Paris.
November	Decree to enforce Civil Oath on clergy.
	Looting of the Hôtel de Castries.

1791

February	Emigration of *Mesdames* and riots at Tuileries.
	Invasion of Luxembourg and Tuileries courtyard.
	Riots at Vincennes and outside Tuileries.
April	Mirabeau dies.
	Louis XVI attempts to go to Saint-Cloud, riots at Tuileries.

April	Miles leaves for London.
April/May	Huber serves as a Treasury Commissioner.
May	'Self-denying Ordinance'.
June	(*Loi Chapelier*).
	Flight to Varennes.
	Emigration of Provence.
July	*Fête de la Fédération.*
	Massacre of the Champs de Mars.
	Declaration of martial law.
August	Declaration of Pillnitz.
September	Annexation of Avignon.
	Louis XVI accepts constitution.
	National Assembly dissolved.
October	Legislative Assembly meets.
Autumn	Moves against *emigrés.*
	(Brissotins strengthen position against *Feuillants*).

1792	Publication of Arthur Young's *Travels in France* in Britain (published in France in 1793).
February	Morris appointed American ambassador.
March	Brissotin ministry formed under Dumouriez.
April (–September)	Declaration of war against Austria (succession of defeats leading to fear of occupation of Paris).
June	Ministerial crises leading to Dumouriez's resignation.
	First invasion of Tuileries.
	Lafayette fails to close Jacobin Club.
July	*'La Patrie en Danger'*
	Arrival of *Marseillais* in Paris.
	Duke of Brunswick's Manifesto.
August	Second invasion of Tuileries.
	Suspension of monarchy.
	Morris aids proscribed aristocrat(s).
	Recall of British ambassador.
	Sections gain ascendancy over Legislative Assembly.
	Lafayette defects.
September	Gower leaves France and Monro takes over gathering of political intelligence.
	Prison massacres.
	Cannonade of Valmy.
	National Convention meets.
September 1792–June 1793	Struggle between Brissotins and Jacobins.
November	French conquest of Austrian Netherlands.
December	Trial of Louis XVI.

1793
January   Louis XVI executed.
                                 Monro 'exposed' and leaves France.
                                 War declared on Britain.
March   Dumouriez defects.
April   Committee of Public Safety created.
June   Commencement of 'Terror'.
                                 Constitution of 1793.
July   Assassinaton of Marat.
                                 Impeachment of Brissot and his supporters.
October   Execution of Marie-Antoinette.
                                 Execution of Brissotins.

1794
March   Execution of Hébertists.
April   Execution of Danton.
July   *Coup d'état* of Thermidor.
                                 Recall of Morris.

Introduction

THE French Revolution attracts historians like bees to a honey-pot. Explaining this, and summing up the importance and impact of the Revolution, Gordon Wright, in his 'non-textbook' on modern French history, says:

> As tourists flock to Niagara rather than to Mud Creek Falls, so historians and readers of history have naturally been attracted to an episode that contains in concentrated form all the action, passion, color and drama that can be found in man's past. Excitement alone, however, does not explain the appeal of this monumental upheaval. As one of the few great political–social revolutions in modern history, it constitutes a rare laboratory for analysis and comparison. And by its very scope and depth, its impact was to shape the course of French development from that day to this.[1]

Norman Hampson, in a more recent and authoritative summation of the Revolution's importance, states:

> Its consequences to the life of France were immense but difficult to define with precision. As the men of the time realised when they invented the expression *ancien régime*, the Revolution put an end to a way of life. The old order implied divine-right monarchy, an autonomous Church actively involved in the administration of the country and a hierarchical society in which government was a matter of negotiation about precedents between royal Ministers and the various corporate bodies whose composition and claims were the living embodiment of tradition. For a society of Orders and a kingdom of provinces the Revolution substituted a unified state where property counted for more than birth or numbers, though birth still conferred respect and property in sufficient quantity always had done. Law was henceforth codified principle rather than local custom. The political legacy of the Revolution was constitutional government and an open society where rules, at least in theory, were the same for all. For the first time it was possible to think of the country as a nation state.[2]

What, though, creates the impact of the Revolution and makes it a perpetually current event? It is indeed still classified as 'current affairs' in French school curricula. The slick television advertising campaign which helped François Mitterand to retain the French presidency in 1988 featured a quick succession of snapshot images of the Revolution linking present-day French socialism with the storming of the Bastille and the constitutional achievements of the Revolution.

De Tocqueville, in his seminal non-ideological history of the Revolution, described the emotional impact of the events of 1789–94:

> No nation had ever before embarked on so resolute an attempt as that of the French in 1789 to break with the past, to make, as it were, a scission in their life line and to create an unbridgeable gulf between all they had hitherto been and all they now aspired to be. With this in mind they took a host of precautions so as to make sure of importing nothing from the past into the new order, and saddled themselves with all sorts of restrictions in order to differentiate themselves in every possible way from the previous generation; in a word, they spared no pain in their endeavour to obliterate their former selves.[3]

De Tocqueville's 'break with the past' (although he himself devoted the greater part of his work to disproving this thesis) is the dominant theme of this book. The people caught up in the events of the Revolution were unable to see beyond its novelty and drama and the creation of the new order on the ruins of the old. It is to their credit that they took this 'monumental upheaval' in their stride, and that this book can thus set before the present-day reader their impressions, commentaries, and analyses as a rational and ultimately sympathetic account of those tumultuous years.

The first chapter looks in detail at the commentators themselves, the context of their writings, and the way in which they reported events. The following chapter sets out the historical context for the commentaries, explains how the starting date of August 1788 (the declaration of a state bankruptcy and the fixing of a definite date for the summoning of the States-General) was chosen, and sets out Thomas Jefferson's account of the pre-Revolution up to that time. The succeeding chapters follow the course of events from August 1788 to August 1792 in chronological detail, as seen through the eyes of about a dozen witnesses. The final narrative chapter is in the nature of a postscript on events from August 1792 to July 1794, relying largely on only two fragmentary sources. The book concludes with a glossary of terms whose definition would otherwise burden the text.

Within the narrative chapters, the extracts from contemporary writers are presented in broadly chronological order, but grouped under headings to bring together relevant material by topics, as successive issues became the leading concern of the day. There is no special significance to the chronology of the chapters, or to the balance between them, which reflects the pace of the source material itself.

In the process of selection, material of an irrelevant, personal or trivial nature has been omitted, as have been long passages which are essentially only personal philosophizing. Also omitted are the very lengthy reports on the detail of official duties, such as the American embassy's interminable negotiations on the import duty to be paid on whale oil. Repetition between different commentators has been reduced to a minimum. Wholly factual accounts of well-known events which would add no new information or perspective to an understanding of them have been largely ignored. Two other very substantial topics dealt with in the despatches will also not feature in this study: these are the never-ending and virtually identical reports of *emigrés* massing on the borders from autumn 1789 onwards, and the second-hand reports of the diplomatic and military crises elsewhere in Europe, which often took up more space than reports on events within France.

The idea is to draw out from the commentators a first-hand report which sheds new light on an event or presents it in a new perspective. There are also eyewitness accounts of events which have remained controversial (e.g. the background to the Oath of the Tennis Court), and personal experiences which bring to life what living in Paris during the Revolution must have been like.

What do contemporary analyses add to an understanding of the period? First, they allow the people of the time to describe how they perceived, understood, and reacted to the events they witnessed. While the historian's task is to tell what really happened, part of that task is to communicate what contemporaries thought was happening in order to appreciate the basis for their decision-making then – however misguided it might later be proved to have been. An example of this is the reporting of the perennial rumour up to May 1789 that the government would find some way to prevent the States-General from meeting. They are one of the historian's primary sources of information, but historians write from hindsight. They may consciously, or unconsciously, present a teleological interpretation of the period. Contemporary commentators were unable to do that; they could only judge events from their own experience and perspective, which were those of the *ancien régime*.

This book, therefore, is a history of a specific group of people's experiences, reporting, and assessment of the period 1788–94, and is dependent on them for its content and perspective. It is not a comprehensive history. Some events will be missed entirely and others misinterpreted in contemporary judgements – one correspondent, for example, reports the Cannonade of Valmy as a French defeat.

Intended primarily as a political study, the text does however follow the commentators into the social and economic issues as they themselves tackled them. It pays little more than cursory attention to the *sans-culottes* or to the peasantry, because the commentators only rarely met and talked with them, but it puts across the ideas of disinterested but intelligent and informed people, sympathetic to the creation of a new order in France, bringing to life and making sense of events as they unfolded, and hoping with optimism and trepidation for the emergence of a happier society.

Maps

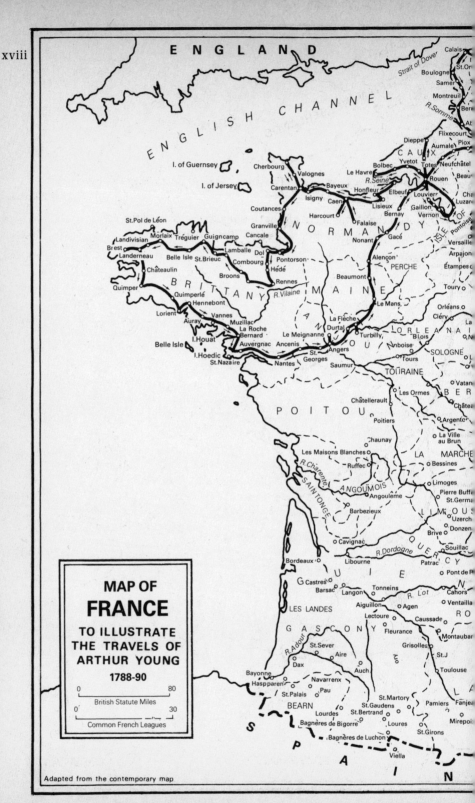

MAP OF FRANCE

TO ILLUSTRATE THE TRAVELS OF ARTHUR YOUNG 1788-90

0   80
British Statute Miles

0   30
Common French Leagues

Adapted from the contemporary map

Map of the *ancien régime* Provinces and Arthur Young's travels in France 1788–90 (only the journeys to the South-West fall outside the period covered by this book)

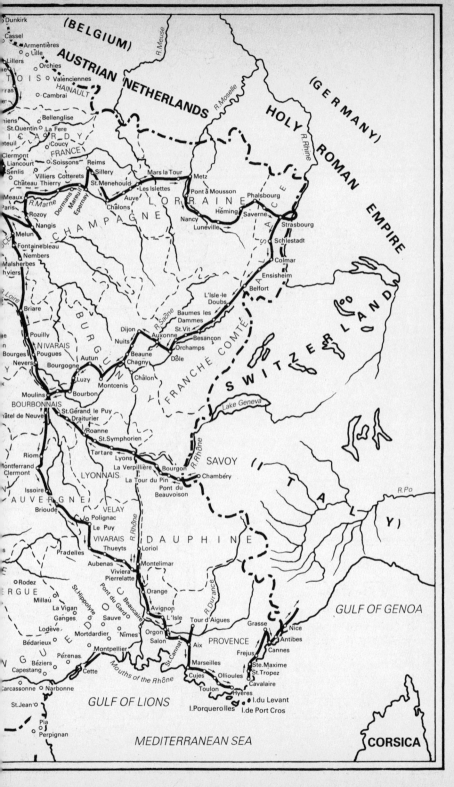

Map of the Departments from the *Almanach National* for 1793.

MER MÉDITERRANÉE

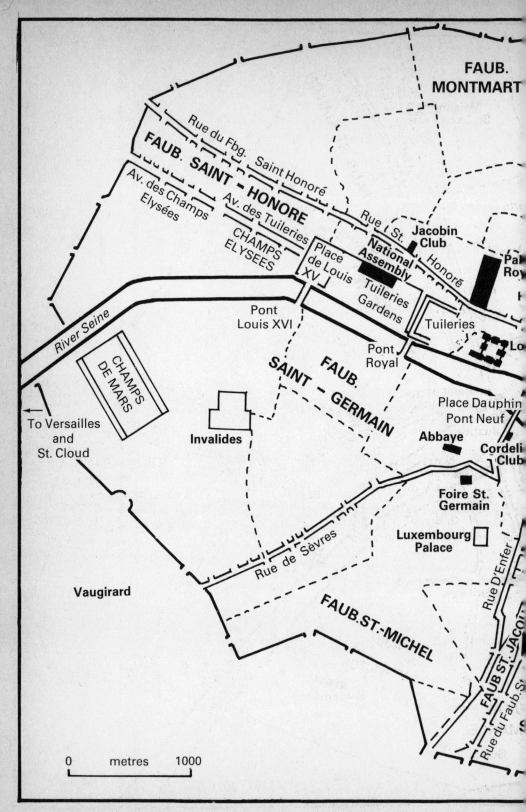

Paris 1788–94 (without the Feuillant Club which moved too often to be shown here)

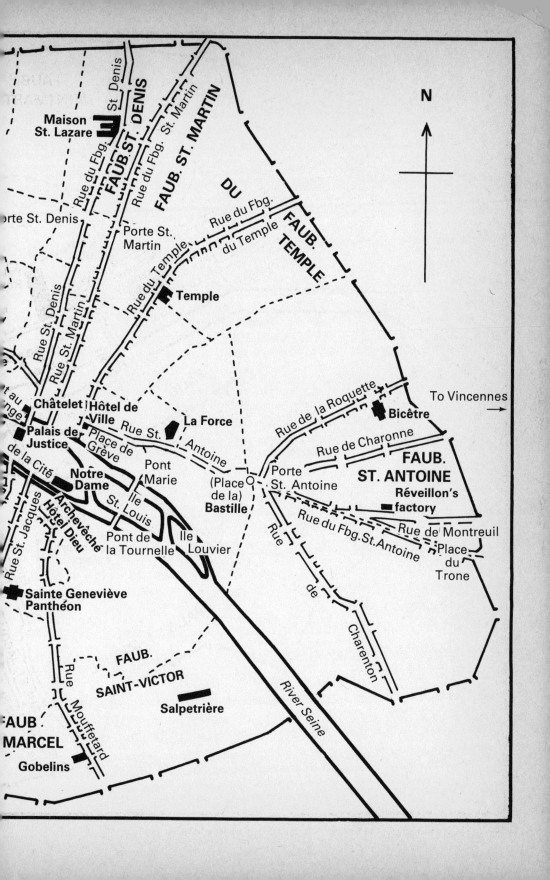

CHAPTER 1

The Commentaries and Commentators

'. . . to glide unnoticed through a silent execution of duty'

THE extracts chosen seek to present a first-hand account of the day-to-day experience of living through, and operating within, the politics of the French Revolution. The choice of a starting point has been made on the basis of historiographical merit, and the commentary begins in August 1788, with Thomas Jefferson's assessment of the pre-Revolution and the government's options as it faced up to the reality of a state bankruptcy. The significance of this moment and the constitutional ramifications of the bankruptcy will be explored in the next chapter.

The point of conclusion is dictated by the sources, and the date when a continuous and broadly-based account has to end is August 1792, when Louis XVI was deposed as head of state. The commentators saw it as a watershed, and felt that after this time France no longer possessed within its internal political resources the ability to turn back away from democracy and egalitarianism. This they predicted would lead, if not to anarchy, then to certain conflict with the surrounding *ancien régime* monarchies.

On a more practical level, the British government – in line with most other European governments – refused to accept the legitimacy of the new republican regime, and broke off diplomatic relations. This in turn made the position of foreigners – even accredited diplomats – in France much more difficult, and any despatch ran the risk of being treated as a secret agent's report which could bring instant arrest and implicate anyone else named in it. Gouverneur Morris, for instance, was unable to send more than a handful of despatches out of France during the Terror.

But there was still useful material being written after this date, from Morris's increasingly guarded despatches and from British travellers and agents remaining in Paris or reporting their experiences on return. The book, therefore, follows events through, in an abbreviated form, to the fall of Robespierre. This is one of the other widely accepted watershed events of the Revolution, and makes a logical and convenient finishing point. It is also, by coincidence, the time when Morris was recalled from Paris. With the end of his reportage the last thread of continuity with the commentaries of earlier years is broken.

The book is based on the writings of around a dozen people, the more important of whom are described below.[1] Between them they covered a wide spectrum of political views, from the Jacobin sympathies of Jefferson to the

royalism of Gouverneur Morris. Most of the British correspondents fall some-
where in between, having little sympathy for the *ancien régime* (largely
because of what today would be called its 'human rights' record) but being
wary of radical change. They all welcomed the moves towards more constitutional government up to autumn 1789, and then condemned the
Revolution later on for its treatment of the royal family.

The British and American commentators shared a number of common
features. The first was that they were all people who spent prolonged periods
in France and were expected either already to have a thorough knowledge
of French politics and society, or else to be able quickly to acquire one. This
puts them into a different category from the many British visitors to France
who were political tourists coming to marvel or scoff at the novelty of a
democratic regime so suddenly springing up in the heart of *ancien régime*
Europe, or who, like the otherwise estimable English tourist, Dr Edward Rigby,
were just passing through and patently had no prior knowledge of or interest
in French politics and society. While some of Lord Auckland's correspondents
may have spent little time in France, their role as gatherers of intelligence for
the British government (even if retrospectively) qualifies them for inclusion
in this book.

Other features they shared were that they were all to a greater or lesser
extent witnesses to the events they described, and that they wrote for an
Anglo-Saxon readership. This meant that from time to time they had to
provide definitions, explanations, and thumb-nail sketches of the institutions,
events, or personalities mentioned in the despatches. That almost all the
material was written in English gives an obvious immediate advantage for
an English-speaking reader, but it carries other more important benefits in
the context of reporting on Revolutionary France.

The British and American observers were familiar with representative
government and mixed constitutions, and the processes by which they operated. This gave them a political experience and vocabulary to draw upon
when reporting on the birth of a constitutional regime and then a democratic
republic in France. They were not so overwhelmed by events as were the
French themselves, and could look on, and even participate to a small extent,
while remaining disinterested. Jefferson above all was able to sympathize with
the Revolution while still being able to see the wood for the trees. The acid
test was the ability to predict the course of events, and this Jefferson was able
to do on several occasions, showing that he was ahead of events and not
always being surprised by them.

Most of the correspondents were accredited diplomats, and the others had
either official business in France (even if clandestinely) or authority from a
high level for their presence there. This gave them immunity from most
immediate personal dangers, other than that of being mistaken for a spy. It

also gave them the freedom to write as they pleased (so far as their French hosts were concerned) until the late summer of 1792 and still, on occasion, after that. Their status placed the diplomats – more than it does for their counter-parts two centuries later – at the centre of events and enabled them to discuss political issues freely and informally with government ministers and subsequently with deputies to the States-General/National Assembly. On occasion their advice and help was actively sought. A British embassy ball, for example, was used to lobby candidates for election to the States-General; Jefferson used his good offices to reconcile factions in the National Assembly; and Morris and Short were officially asked to help with drafting some parts of the new constitution.

The commentary is very consciously limited to Paris (and Versailles) and to national issues, except where it follows Arthur Young into the eastern and southern provinces. All the other correspondents were based full-time in Paris. The commentary also makes only passing references to the progress of the Revolutionary war. None of the correspondents visited the front line, and the real value of their reports is in charting the changing mood in Paris. Because of their perspective, the commentators are not a comprehensive source for information on the shifting interplay of factions in the National Assembly or in the various ministries, where they dealt almost exclusively with the Foreign Ministers.

There are several advantages in using despatches and diaries over con-temporary newspapers. First, there was no necessity to write a report if the correspondent did not feel he (or in a few cases, she) had news worth communicating. Second, the reports were written while events were still freshly in mind but not usually to a specific deadline. This had the advantage that facts could be checked, or a sequence of fast-moving events allowed to run its course before pen was put to paper. This was particularly evident in Jefferson's very cool reporting of the constitutional crises of June 1789. Third, there was no popular readership to be appeased with moralizing, novel, or jingoistic asides. *The Times*, for example, took the view that the whole Rev-olution was a well-deserved come-uppance for French involvement in North America (1777–81), and that a Frenchman's greatest misfortune was not to have been born a Briton. This editorial approach permeated the factual reportage and is an impediment to gaining a long-term understanding of – or sympathy with – the events being described.

In terms of style and language, the diaries and despatches as quoted required no re-editing to make them intelligible. Their language is often a model of direct and concise writing. This is in sharp contrast, again, to *The Times*, which adopted an archaic and overblown style which interposes a barrier between the events reported and the latter-day reader. The only real work of editing has had to be in integrating the extracts into the study as a whole and in standardizing references to people and institutions.

The commentators did not share the concerns and perspectives of the modern historian when viewing the events of the Revolution. It is, therefore, useful to sketch in their intellectual milieu. They had all, to a greater or lesser degree, received a conventional classical education, which, it was assumed, would have produced an orderly and logical mind. They would have supplemented this basic general education with a working knowledge of current politics and political theory. Their perspective on the Revolution was shaped by two political traditions: their knowledge of classical history (with particular reference to episodes of 'democracy' in ancient city states), and their reading of such authors as Montesquieu or Locke. They might further (confirmed in Morris's case) have added knowledge of the writings of men such as Thomas Paine or the abbé Sieyès (but not of Rousseau, whose political theories at this time were unknown outside a very restricted French intellectual élite). All of them were aware of Edmund Burke's speeches and publications.

Only Arthur Young would have had any real concept of an economic or social dimension to history – he was one of the pioneers of economic history. All of the commentators (Young included) subscribed to the 'great man' school of history, and awaited – disappointedly – for his emergence from the Revolutionary crowd. Despite these limitations, the reader should be pleasantly surprised by how much social and political analysis is contained in their writings.

The commentators wrote without the benefit of hindsight. This means they were absent from Paris at seminal moments in the Revolution, or that they failed to perceive the significance of measures which have since come to dominate historiography. As the Revolution progressed, the ability to comment was itself restricted. An event entirely missing from the commentaries, for example, is the assassination of Marat. An issue, the importance of which was scarcely grasped, is the Revolution's relationship with organized labour. There cannot be, therefore, a comment for every historiographically-important aspect of the Revolution. On a more mundane level, some comments were expressed in such complex, ambiguous, or indirect ways as to render them valueless for this study. Conversely, some events which have faded into relative obscurity made a profound impact at the time, and deserve recording for that reason. The clearest example of this is the looting of the Hôtel de Castries in November 1790.

The Commentators

Arthur Young (1741–1820)

Arthur Young became a commentator on French politics and society from a background in agricultural and British parliamentary reporting. He had fancied himself as something of a dandy, and tried in his earlier life to cut a dash in London's literary society. He failed, but the experience of this milieu stood him in good stead when he came to mix in French provincial and Parisian society. While living near London he took up a post of parliamentary lobby correspondent (1773–6), which gave him an experience of journalism and of politics.

Young is best known, though, as an agriculturalist and leading figure in the English 'agricultural revolution'. He was a working farmer, experimenter, researcher, editor, and estate manager. As a researcher he undertook 'travels' first around the British Isles (starting in 1768) and then around Europe and conducted comparative analyses of rural economies and agricultural techniques.

For much of the period 1787–90, he was travelling in France. His record of the journeys is both meticulous and stimulating. He had introductions to courtiers on the one hand, and on the other was prepared to stop his horse or carriage to question casual day-labourers about their work and their political views.

His political stance was typically British. He deplored the abuses, inequalities, and inefficiencies of the *ancien régime*, but in the end deplored even more the excesses, as he saw them, of the Revolution. He admitted to editing his diary at the time of publication (1792) to make it less critical of the *ancien régime*, but these changes are likely to have been more in the nature of restraining his personal comments than of removing factual observations.

His work is detailed, objective and of a high standard. Its importance was soon recognized by historians on both sides of the Channel, and his even-handed treatment of the pre- and early Revolution has made a particular impression on British historiography.

William Augustus Miles (1753?–1817)

William Miles was a (sometimes political) pamphleteer by profession, but he enjoyed a quasi-diplomatic career from the mid-1780s to the mid-1790s. He travelled extensively on both sides of the Atlantic before taking a special interest in conditions in the Austrian Netherlands in the 1780s. In 1790 he was recruited personally by William Pitt the Younger to act as his agent in Paris in a separate capacity from the embassy and specifically to try to detach the French from the Family Compact with Spain.

Miles performed this mission from August 1790 to April 1791, and his daughter, who had accompanied him, continued gathering political intelligence during the summer of 1791. Miles joined the Jacobin Club and lobbied quite openly there for British interests. He harangued deputies to the National Assembly on their shortcomings and on the faults of the Revolution. Although Miles had 'no communication' with the embassy, his mission could not be described as clandestine (even if Pitt had hoped it could), and he was known as 'Pitt's secret agent' in Paris. He returned to London in April 1791 for further instructions, but was never sent back to France. Instead he was retained by the British government to write on their behalf as a journalist and pamphleteer. He worked strenuously through the contacts he had built up in the Revolutionary administration to avert war. Like Auckland (see below), he acted as a clearing house for correspondence from Paris, although most of this was from French writers and falls outside the scope of this book.

Miles had hoped that this work would lead to a more formal diplomatic career, but this was not forthcoming, and he turned instead to attacking the government. Although he wrote anonymously, his authorship was suspected, and Pitt withdrew his patronage. He returned to a full-time freelance writing career. After the Restoration he returned to France to research a book on the Revolution. He died there in 1817 and one of his friends from America and Paris – Lafayette – attended his funeral.

Miles's chronicle of his time in Paris was in the form of letters to various people in the Foreign Office in London. Few of the originals ever reached London, but Miles had made copies and these were edited in 1890. (Miles himself claimed that most of his original letters had been confiscated by the French censor.) Overall, the bulk of his correspondence about the Revolution was written from London, and only a year's worth (including his daughter's), reporting on the Revolution as a witness and participant, was written from Paris. The letters are biased towards reports on his specific mission and his opinions on the Revolution, but do still contain some genuine insights.

Like the correspondence addressed to Auckland, Miles's despatches parallel those of the embassy. His most impressive achievement was a prediction (made in March 1791) of Robespierre's rise to power. There are obvious similarities between his position and Monro's (see below), but Monro had a much wider brief and gave vent to fewer personal feelings. In all, Miles's letters have had to be used sparingly, but they are an extraordinary record of someone working openly within the Revolution and playing an active part in the Jacobin Club.

Miles was closest in his politics to Gouverneur Morris (see below). He did not remain as objective about the Revolution as did the embassy staff, but was overtly royalist and anti-Jacobin in his writings. The most succinct account of his position he gave in a letter on 27 November 1790: 'As a friend to liberty, I rejoice in the Revolution that destroyed the systematic tyranny by which France had been oppressed for ages; but as an enemy to anarchy, dissimulation, and public rapine, I detest the conduct of those whose temporary popularity alone preserves them from the halter.'[2]

The British Embassy and Foreign Office

The British embassy in Paris and the Foreign Office in London provided a number of correspondents with first-hand accounts of events in France. Together they shared a broadly similar outlook and the objective of keeping the British government informed generally about the state of affairs in France, and specifically about issues affecting British interests. It is the former objective which provides the most important correspondence. Perhaps the most typical British reaction to witnessing the events of the early Revolution was one given by a Channel Islander in late 1790: 'I am now neither aristocrat nor democrat.... More violence must yet be committed, however, before the late system can be regretted.'[3]

The embassy and Foreign Office staff and agents tended to be well-informed, and to report in a restrained and balanced manner. They had no specific axe to grind until the Revolution began to threaten the position of the royal family. They seemed to welcome the moves in 1788–9 towards what appeared to be a constitutional monarchy. As with other ambassadors, they enjoyed easy and informal relations with French ministers. One of the instructions from the Foreign Office to Lord Gower on how he should conduct his embassy was prefaced with the statement: 'As it must ever be essentially necessary to our service at all times to be as accurately informed as possible on the interior state of France.'[4] The embassy despatches carried out this request.

Diplomatic relations between Britain and France were severed (by Britain) in August 1792, and the ambassador withdrawn. It took, however, a month for Lord Gower to be able to leave France, during which time he continued to report on events. After his departure the embassy was kept open very briefly with a skeleton staff, ordered to keep a watch on developments. This, however, proved impractical. From September 1792 to January 1793, Colonel George Monro, a secret agent who had been infiltrated into the expatriate Jacobin community, continued clandestinely to gather political intelligence.[5] At the same time the Foreign Office continued to receive reports from secret agents or travellers from inside France, including one of the last accounts of Marie-Antoinette before her execution.

There were five principal correspondents associated with the embassy and Foreign Office during the period 1788–92. John Frederick Sackville, Duke of Dorset (1745–99) was ambassador from 1783 to 1790. He was a well-mannered, softly-spoken, dignified man, very much at ease in the courtly ceremonial world of the *ancien régime*. He quickly acquired a comprehensive grasp of French politics and institutions, and sent back illuminating reports of the pre-Revolution. This embassy was the only post of significance he held outside the world of cricket.

His successor was George Granville Leveson-Gower, Earl of Gower and Duke of Sutherland (1758–1833). After completing his education with a prolonged visit to France, Gower took up an academic career. He then became a Member of the House of Commons, and soon after inherited the first of his titles which took him to the House of Lords. In a complete change of career he was unexpectedly appointed to the embassy in France and held the post for two years (1790–92), at a time when it was the most difficult diplomatic assignment in Europe. He retired from public life for health reasons for some years after his recall, but later re-entered politics. Thereafter he inherited a number of family titles and estates, becoming one of Britain's leading land-owners and patrons of the arts in his later years.

One of the Foreign Office's most useful correspondents was Monsieur Huber (and, on occasion, Madame Huber). Huber was born in France of French parents, but was a Swiss subject by this period and had married an English wife. He was a long-standing friend of Necker and of William Eden (see below), with whom he corresponded. He had followed a career in banking and in 1788 was working for the French East India Company. He participated in political life in the pre- and early Revolution, and served briefly as a Treasury Commissioner for the Revolutionary government in 1791.[5]

Back in London, much work in the nature of political intelligence was carried out for the Foreign Office by William Eden, Baron Auckland (1744–1814). He was a close friend and supporter of William Pitt, and had served in France attached to the embassy from 1785 to 1787, negotiating a series of commercial treaties which bear his name. Although appointed ambassador to Spain (1788–9) and the Netherlands (1791–3), he continued to gather French political intelligence, and forwarded to Whitehall either agents' and travellers' own accounts of events in France or else despatches based on interviews with them.

Colonel George Monro (for whom there are no general biographical details known) was a secret agent reporting through the British embassy. He was employed to infiltrate and report on the activities of British, Irish, and American republicans living in Paris. When the embassy closed down he was asked to take on their political intelligence gathering work. As an 'accredited' Jacobin he could venture much closer to the heart of Revolutionary political events than could the embassy staff and managed, for example, to enter one of the prisons where the 'September massacres' took place while the killing was still in progress. He had to leave Paris in January 1793 after his cover had been 'blown' and he was recognized as a spy.[7]

American Embassy and Correspondents
Unlike their British counterparts, the Americans in Paris did not take a broadly similar view of the Revolution, and they need to be treated as separate correspondents.

Thomas Jefferson (1743–1826)

Thomas Jefferson came from a line of wealthy, well-established, Virginia squires. He received a thorough classical education and was admitted to the Bar in 1767. He was elected to the Virginia House of Burgesses in 1769 and then played one of the leading roles in the American Revolution, drafting the Declaration of Independence and being elected governor of Virginia.

In 1784 he went to Paris, to join the American Delegation there, and he was appointed ambassador later that year, a post he held until the close of 1789. On his return to America he was appointed Secretary of State, then served as vice-president (1797–1801) and president (1801–9), when he retired from politics to complete the work of founding the University of Virginia.

Jefferson was unusually tall for the age and was of pleasant appearance. He was a highly articulate and literate polymath, well-connected and at ease in French society both before and during the Revolution. Politics was just one of his many interests and activities, his motivation for which, and his encouragement of the Revolution in particular, he ascribed to his 'love of mankind'.[8] He took pains to understand all the complexities of the *ancien régime* and fully understood its predicament. However, he welcomed and encouraged the moves towards constitutional change, and his sympathies lay wholly with the Revolution, even as it evolved towards a democratic and egalitarian regime. As Secretary of State he pursued a pro-Jacobin foreign policy and kept very closely in touch with events in France.

Morris was critical of Jefferson's approach to the Revolution for two reasons. First, he did not – Morris believed – think that anyone could be as clever as he was: 'I think he does not form very just estimates of character but rather assigns too many to the humble rank of fools.'[9] Second, he had 'too sanguine expectations of a downright republican form of government'.[10] Morris probably meant by this that Jefferson both assumed too quickly that a republic was inevitable in France and that he overestimated the potential benefits it would bring, being predisposed towards a republican form of government. Morris later elaborated: 'He, with all the leaders of liberty here, is desirous of annihilating distinctions of order.'[11]

Morris wrote of Jefferson's general standing in Paris in July 1789: 'He commands very much respect in this country, which is merited by good sense and good intentions.' He accused him of 'originality' in his social graces, however, implying that unconsciously or deliberately he cultivated a colonial style, which the French – fortunately – found appealing, especially when combined with Jefferson's 'good table and excellent wines, which he distributes freely'.[12]

Jefferson himself was modest about his role, which he saw as being 'to glide unnoticed through a silent execution of duty'.[13]

William Short (1759–1849)
William Short was a minor career diplomat from Virginia. He spoke perfect French and possessed an easy charm which greatly assisted him in his diplomatic work. He joined the American embassy staff in 1785 as Thomas Jefferson's secretary. In 1789 he was promoted to secretary to the legation (i.e. the embassy), and promoted again that year (on Jefferson's recall) to being the chargé d'affaires. He was never promoted to ambassador in France, but in effect discharged all the duties of an ambassador until Gouverneur Morris was appointed to the post in 1792. He had shared Jefferson's enthusiasm for the Revolution in its early stages, but had become increasingly doubtful of its benefits as the Jacobins gained ground. He was admonished by Jefferson as Secretary of State for his anti-Jacobin sentiments.

Jefferson wrote to him on 3 January 1793, explaining his previous dissatisfaction and stating the political differences between them:

> The tone of your letters had for some time given me pain, on account of the extreme warmth with which they censured the proceedings of the Jacobins of France. I considered that sect as the same with the republican patriots, and the *Feuillants* as the monarchical patriots, well known in the early part of the Revolution, and but little distant in their views, both having in object the establishment of a free constitution, and differing only on the question whether their chief executive should be hereditary or not. The Jacobins (as since called) yielded to the *Feuillants* and tried the experiment of retaining their hereditary executive. The experiment failed completely, and would have brought on the re-establishment of despotism had it been pursued.[14]

Morris was, and remained, on very good terms with Short. They still corresponded after they had left Paris. Morris passed no judgements on Short, but he did record that Jefferson had discussed Short's merits with him. According to Morris, Jefferson had never considered Short equal to the post of full ambassador. Knowing this, Morris records that on a number of occasions he tried to prevent Short holding unrealistic expectations about his chances of promotion under Jefferson as Secretary of State.[15]

Later in his career Short was moved to Madrid and then to the Hague, but he never became an ambassador.

Gouverneur Morris (1752–1816)
Gouverneur Morris was a French-speaking American of Huguenot descent and education from a family well established in the New York squirearchy. In the American Revolution the family were divided, though he was himself a Patriot. He followed two quite separate political careers. In his early life he played an active part in the American Revolution and helped to draft the

American constitution. He then retired in 1787 having acquired 'a cynical contempt for democracy'. His second career was in commerce, and led him back into politics. He was appointed an agent in Europe for the American tobacco exporters, and based himself in Paris. Although not an accredited diplomat, he enjoyed close links with the American embassy and was to all intents and purposes a commercial attaché. He was appointed ambassador in 1792 in succession to Jefferson (there having been the interval during which William Short, as chargé d'affaires, had carried out the duties of ambassador). Alone of the ambassadors of major powers he stayed in Paris throughout the Terror. He was not, however, able to report freely on his experiences then for fear of implicating either himself or others.

Some explanation is required of Morris's diplomatic role running in parallel with the official duties of the embassy staff, and of why he, as a royalist, was chosen as ambassador when the Secretary of State's (Jefferson's) sympathies were Jacobin. Morris was operating (1789–92) in the capacity of an agent of the President, and was carrying out commissions on Washington's behalf. This separate presidential role in foreign affairs was allowed for in the (new) American constitution, and, in this case, was conducted with the full knowledge and support of the State Department. Morris enjoyed Jefferson's confidence as a diplomat, and he was very much Washington's man in Europe. He did not interfere with Short's work at the embassy, and given that Short forfeited Jefferson's confidence (if he had ever truly held it), then Morris represented a continuity of diplomatic presence in Europe when made ambassador. His appointment was hotly disputed in Congress, but that was a battle internal to American politics.

Although he was a wealthy man, an aristocrat by American standards, and a royalist in French politics, he was very much a man of the people. He had a wooden leg (the result of jumping out of a lady's window in an amorous escapade) but disdained the use of a carriage for any business within the confines of Paris. He also paid little attention to his dress, and must have cut a somewhat eccentric figure, stomping through the streets in shabby clothes, with no entourage, and turning up unannounced for official engagements. He gave a thumb-nail sketch of his demeanour and impact on others: 'Go to dine with the Keeper of the Seals. His domestics know not what to make of me, a thing which frequently happens at my first approach, because of the simplicity of my dress and equippage, my wooden leg, and tone of republican equality.'[16]

He had an immediate *entrée* to French politics and society, both from friendships made during the American Revolution and from introductions he obtained for his official duties. He had the ear of French ministers (because of the customs revenue his tobacco could raise) and discussed informally with them all aspects of political life. His own politics were by the 1790s anti-

democrat and royalist in French terms, to the point where he tried to help
the royal family. He had no sympathy for the directions the Revolution took,
but his ability to survive the Terror speaks for his suitability for the post and
the very real talent he must have possessed.

When, in October 1791, Short first got wind of the possibility that Morris
might be promoted (over Short's head) to the post of ambassador, he wrote
what can only be described as a character assassination in order to pre-empt
the appointment. The relevant extract from this despatch is reproduced in
full. It has to be said that, on the one hand, it is an interested and partisan
assessment of one career diplomat competing with another for the same post,
but, on the other, that it confirms an impression of Morris which he himself
does nothing to contradict in his own private writings.

Short wrote back to Jefferson:

[It] would seem to render it my duty to inform you in what light he is
considered at this place ... his aristocratical principles, his contempt of
the French revolution and of the French nation expressed in all societies
without reserve, and his dogmatizing manner and assumed superiority
has exposed him generally to ill will and often to ridicule. For some time
he was a favorite among the aristocratic party, but even that is now
worn off, and as the French have no measure in their expressions of
people they dislike they say of Morris the most disagreeable things, many
of which I know he does not deserve, but it produces the same effect. As
he is engaged in commercial affairs it is in that way they attack him. He
told me himself of a report which circulated here, that he was an enemy
to the revolution because under the ancient system he had had an
exclusive contract with the ministry etc. As he is a very active talking
forward man and goes about a good deal he has established generally
and particularly in the *corps diplomatique* who see him at the Count de
Montmorin's [the Foreign Minister] that he is *un intriguant* [*sic*].[17]

Finally, it is interesting that Morris is very much *persona grata* with the Fifth
Republic, and one of the official French commemorations of the bicentenary of
the Revolution is a television series dramatizing his life.

CHAPTER 2

The Context for the Commentaries
and Jefferson's Account of the Pre-Revolution

'Temporary annihilation in the political scales of Europe'

THE historical point at which the contemporary commentary on the Revolution is picked up will need to fulfil four criteria: it must match up to the source material available, it must give a context to the start of the story of the Revolution, help to create an understanding of the commentators' own perspective of events, and have some historiographical meaning.

On the first criterion, the material available would enable a detailed commentary to be picked up at any time after the restoration of normal diplomatic relations between Britain, France, and the United States of America in 1783.

The other criteria are interlinked. It would be impractical to take the study back too far in the direction of seeking the origins of the Revolution, not least because this quest has led some historians as far back as 1715, and also because the material would be more of an investigation into the *ancien régime* than a study of the Revolution. The book however must open at a date before 14 July 1789 in order to explain how the regime had come to lose control to such an extent over politics and public order and why the Parisians had reached the point where they were prepared – with confidence – to assault a major fortress.

Some help in fixing a date for the start of the demise of the *ancien régime* can be obtained from authors within the regime, who noted a sea-change in political life after the mid-century. After this date, it was recognized, the regime could not avoid undertaking some major reforms if it were to be able to defeat the Prussian army, the British navy, and the spectre of insolvency at home.[1] Successive Controllers-General wrestled with the problem of the mounting deficit, but it was not until 1786 that the government broke its public silence on the issue with Calonne's stark announcement that bankruptcy was imminent without immediate structural reform of a type not previously contemplated by a Bourbon sovereign.

The response to Calonne's announcement was the convening of the Assembly of Notables in February 1787. The Notables began a process of debate on how the regime might extricate itself from its problems without undermining the monarchy. For all their apparent novelty, the Notables were meeting within a wholly *ancien régime* constitutional framework. They looked back to the many seventeenth-century precedents when they had been called on to advise the crown in order to avoid the necessity of summoning a session of the States-General. If the *ancien régime* could see its way out of its difficulties without declaring a bankruptcy or having to summon the States-General it would survive essentially unchanged and intact. This outcome remained the expectation – if not necessarily the hope – of most people in France from February 1787 to May 1788.

Between May and August 1788, however, these expectations were ended for the regime by the need to take both the measures (declaring a bankruptcy and summoning the States-General) so long avoided. Their effect, added to a cumulative weight of more minor reform, was such as to transform the regime into a new political entity. It was this changed regime, albeit a very transitory one, which gave the context to the Revolution and provides a starting point for the commentaries. (For complete accuracy, the date for the summoning of the States-General was set in July 1788, but it did not pass into the domain of public awareness and debate until August.)

From the commentators' perspective this date has some real meaning. With no foreknowledge of their outcome, the commentators found the events of 1787 interesting but not unduly unusual. The regime had experienced financial crises before (in 1768, for instance), had endured determinedly reforming ministers (e.g., Turgot, 1774–6), and had even seen a coherent programme of provincial reform through local assemblies (1778–9).[2] The real discontinuity came during May–August 1788, with the bankruptcy and calling of the States-General, and from this time the commentators used the term 'revolution' (to indicate a change in the constitutional relationship between the king and his subjects) with increasing frequency.

The reason for defining the regime after August 1788 as something different from the *ancien régime* is that so many of its basic aspects had now been lost. The *ancien régime* is traditionally defined as 'Catholic, corporate, and customary'.[3] To take these in order: 'Catholic' meant not only that Roman Catholicism was the 'established church' but that it was the only imaginable church. The king styled himself 'His Most Christian Majesty' – and meant it. He also held himself accountable only to God.

'Corporate' meant that, theoretically, every subject enjoyed membership of some organization which could mitigate the impact of royal absolutism upon him or her. This came about because the corporations enjoyed the 'privilege' of assembling and regulating their internal affairs without the need for recourse to outside authority, or the threat of interference, and of dealing as a body with the royal administration.

The corporations ranged from the village assemblies, where collective decisions were taken about the *taille*, to the *parlements* with their unique privilege of acting as intermediaries between the crown and subjects in the implementation of laws. Members of many of the more powerful corporations, and the *parlements* above all, were able to buy and own their 'offices' in them as private property. Prompted by Montesquieu, the monarchy chose to regard private property as inviolable, and any regime which attacked it a 'despotism'.

This meant that the corporations were an effective impediment (but not bar) to royal authority. There were so many corporations that any reform anywhere in the administration was sure to infringe some corporate privilege or prerogative. Any move against the members of a corporation had to be handled very carefully unless the government were prepared to risk a constitutional crisis, as in 1771–4 when Chancellor Maupeou suspended all the *parlements*. All this made the *parlements*, and the *Parlement* of Paris above all, the focal points of *ancien régime* political life, and the one area where royal power might be tempered. In the last resort, however, the *parlements'* power was illusory, as the regime demonstrated in its draconian suppression of them in 1771–4. The other corporations also existed only on sufferance, as demonstrated by Turgot's abolition of the guilds in 1776.

The three juridical Orders of society (the Clergy, or First Estate; the Nobility, or Second Estate; and the Commons, or Third Estate), by contrast, could only assemble and enjoy a political existence at the behest of the king. This existence was denied to the Second and Third Estates, but the First enjoyed the unique benefit of being simultaneously an Order and a corporation. What was left to the second juridical Order was privilege and opportunities attached to accident of birth. These served to reinforce their position in society. Such privileges were exemption from direct personal 'ordinary' taxation, guaranteed access to certain professions, and legally enforceable social precedence.

'Customary' is the term with the widest meaning in this definition. It meant that the regime did things the way they had always been done. To paraphrase a letter sent under the Duc de Choiseul's name, in answer to an enquiry if the entry qualifications to the Order of St John of Jerusalem could be reviewed, the old regulations were the best regulations because they were the old regulations.[4] This attitude permeated all levels of society, and finally saw its obverse in the Revolution when, as Gouverneur Morris commented: 'Those who rule the roost here seem to think that because the old government was sometimes wrong, everything contrary to what they did must be right.'[5]

In the context of this book the most important aspect of the customary nature of the regime was the way in which the Bourbon monarchs chose to exercise their power. The first cornerstone of the Bourbon monarchy was Catholicism. A second was that, accountable only to God, the monarchy did not share its power. The conduct of government was the prerogative solely of the king. While ministers might advise, and comment from autonomous corporations might be tolerated, there was no obligation on the king to heed them, Frenchmen were never allowed to feel that they participated in the exercise of royal power or that the king might in any way be accountable to fellow mortals. To take an interest in politics if not invited by the king was, in effect, *lèse-majesté*. If the British constitution was unwritten, then the French constitution, between Frenchmen, was unspoken.

Linked to power not being shared was careful management of the corporations and administration to ensure that they did not form alliances or perceive communities of interest beyond simple loyalty to the king. In this the monarchy was supremely successful, and even Louis XV exerted himself on this front with the famous *Séance de Flagellation* in 1766 to keep the *Parlement* of Paris in line. The *séance* quashed the pretension of the '*unité des classes*' whereby the *parlements* nationally sought to set themselves up as a 'congress' (to use a term which became current in French politics after 1775) with the implication of participating in the exercise of power.

The benefits the monarchy derived were that opposition only arose piecemeal and could be dealt with as such. This reinforced the monarchy's view of society as a wheel with the king as the hub, the corporations as spokes, and the nation as the rim. By this analogy several spokes could be damaged before the integrity of the wheel would be impaired. (The *parlements*, by contrast, saw society as a chain with the links stretching from king to peasant. In this model every link was vital, and the first break would destroy the monarchy.) The price the monarchy paid for preventing alliances between corporations was that in 1787–90 there was no effective conservative opposition to reform and revolution. Not even the army perceived a community of interest with endangered institutions or even with the monarchy itself.

A third cornerstone was the belief that the king ruled with regard to fundamental laws and with the willing (and enlightened) obedience of his subjects. The term which characterized this aspect of the regime, and extended further to the social relations between more and less privileged members of society, was *douceur de moeurs*. This was not entirely a fiction. When Saint-Germain, as Secretary of State for War, introduced a Prussian drill book and corporal punishment into the army (in 1776) a wave of revulsion was felt, his career never prospered thereafter, and the measures were quietly dropped a year later.

The *ancien régime*'s fundamental laws have warranted a study of their own.[6] In this context their importance is that the king took it upon himself not to rule above the law. In almost the only example of the French constitution being explicitly discussed by a government minister in a public forum in the *ancien régime*, the Secretary of State without Portfolio, Bertin (standing in at the time for the Foreign Secretary), explained to the British ambassador that Louis XVI could not, as the English press and public so readily assumed, simply order a merchant who had been arrested to be freed from jail, because of 'the impossibility of the king's interposing his authority, to over-rule any legal decisions ... were he to make that use of his power, he would not be a monarch but a despot'.[7]

The fourth, and last, cornerstone was that custom be respected. Existing institutions were not abolished, vested interests not antagonized, and previous practice was honoured. On these cornerstones rested a complex relationship between the monarchy, nobility and clergy whereby the privileged Orders were allowed great latitude within various corporations and institutions (e.g., the army or law courts), were granted fiscal immunities and were paid pensions from state funds, all in return for the First and Second Estates remaining social and not political groupings.

The system functioned from 1614 (the last meeting of the States-General prior to 1789) to c.1750, because the government was able to run the administration on the basis of working with and within the institutions inherited from the sixteenth century, allowing some to lapse and bypassing others, and instituting minor reforms where needed. After that date, however, the system as it stood could not deliver enough fiscal revenue to meet the monarchy's outgoings. At the same time the interaction of the different features of the Bourbon monarchy prevented effective action being taken.

The regime had two solutions to its indebtedness. It could declare a bankruptcy or raise more taxes. The *ancien régime*, however, could not tolerate the implications of either alternative. Whichever it chose would alter it out of all recognition. In the circumstances it chose to muddle through for as long as possible, hoping for a miracle which never came.

Bankruptcy was so hard an option for moral as well as practical reasons. Reneging on debts honestly contracted was dishonest and dishonourable. It was also unChristian. If the king were to default on his debts, but expect his subjects to continue to pay theirs (e.g., in taxes), that implied rule by coercion. The *ancien régime* did not have the resources to impose its rule on its subjects against their will, nor did it wish to. The two most obvious practical objections were that the regime would have to live without loans or the possibility of increased future tax revenues. (Against this, in the very short term, there would be the windfall of not having to repay the crippling interest charges on the existing debt.) Loans were then, as now, an essential tool in public finance to allow sudden increases in expenditure (e.g., a war) to be met without an equal immediate rise in taxation. The Duc de Choiseul explained the effect of bankruptcy: 'The Controller-General may by a bankruptcy, raise the revenues to be equal to the king's expenses; but ... if the king should hereafter happen to stand in need of a loan, nobody would ever advance a *livre* upon the public faith.'[8]

The scenario of the regime living within a more realistic budget was also unacceptable. The previous level of pensions could not be paid, the court would not glitter so brightly, the army would have to be reduced, and the king would have to allow financial stringency to be seen to be a factor in policy-making. The loss of pensions and reserved careers would break the customary relationship between crown and nobility, with the risk that they might seek political outlets.

In one field the regime was already being overtaken by indebtedness by the late 1780s. In foreign policy France dared not intervene in the Russo-Turkish War of 1787–90, the Prussian invasion of the United Provinces in 1787, or the rebellion and civil war in the Austrian Netherlands (1788–90). In previous decades each would have provoked some military response from France, but now, with no money to refit the fleet or mobilize the army, France was suffering a 'Temporary annihilation in the scales of Europe'.[9] The monarchy could not afford to let the same annihilation affect domestic administration.

The other side of the equation – raising additional taxation – posed equally insurmountable problems. This was because of the monarchy's professed respect for legitimate and customary government. By custom only the States-General had the constitutional authority to ratify new 'ordinary' taxation. This constitutional position of the States-General was usually left implicit by *ancien régime* writers, but G-F Letrosne, the late *ancien régime*'s leading authority on provincial administration and its reform, did touch on it as a preamble to his treatise. He wrote, prophetically in 1779, that, if the regime, as it stood, ever had to initiate sudden fundamental fiscal reform without the monarchy being prepared to act 'despotically' in terms of implementing a pre-planned comprehensive programme of political and administrative restructuring (i.e., Letrosne's own proposals), then it would have no choice but to rely on the tender mercies of the States-General for its constitutionality.[10] To return to the term 'ordinary', it was used by Necker in the *Compte Rendu* deliberately to confuse the financial picture, and historians since have rightly commented that it has no meaning in accounting terms. The distinction, however, between 'ordinary' and 'extraordinary' taxation lies at the heart of the *ancien régime*'s constitutional difficulties over taxation. The principal 'ordinary' tax was the *taille* (poll-tax) which fell at a flat rate within each province on all members of the Third Order. All other personal taxes were in some way limited in their scope or duration, but they had the inestimable advantage of being collected through up-to-date tax rolls and being linked to the taxpayer's financial resources.

The whole tax system needed overhauling to make the basic personal tax both more equitable and more productive. No one doubted that France properly taxed could meet all its commitments. The proof of this was held to be self-evident by contemporaries in the comparison between Normandy and Languedoc. Normandy came under the direct rule of the central government (a *pays d'élection*) and was accounted potentially one of the richest provinces.

Languedoc was a *pays d'états* with a doubled Third Estate and its own autonomous machinery for collecting taxation kept up to date and in line with social and economic changes in the provinces, but it was accounted one of the poorest regions. The two areas generated approximately the same level of tax revenue, with visible social strain in Normandy and apparent acquiescence in Languedoc. This observation formed the basis of the single most influential and beguiling study of provincial reform under the *ancien régime* written by Mirabeau's father.[11]

In very broad terms, in the late 1780s the government was spending 700,000,000 *livres* per annum, but raising only 600,000,000 l per annum. Contemporary analyses put the potential tax base at 1,000,000,000 l per annum.[12] The missing 400,000,000 l per annum could not, though, be tapped by any constitutional means customary to the regime. Fiscal reform on that scale would have to be ratified by the States-General or undertaken through an exercise of 'despotism'. The various initiatives towards fiscal devolution from 1768 (when Corsica was made a *pays d'états*) to the provincial assemblies of 1787–8 could only be half-measures and experiments without national coherence. For the government to ride rough-shod over this problem and grant all provincial assemblies the right to revise tax-rolls, reassess the *taille* and turn it into an income tax would have brought it back to the problems of despotism and coercion.

In February 1787, the regime found itself forced to address the issue of potential bankruptcy in the semi-public forum of the Assembly of Notables. One of the cornerstones of Bourbon rule had been broken. While the Notables were only a debating forum with no executive powers, their meeting in the circumstances of financial crisis, together with the agenda before them, threw open to the public gaze the monarchy's failure to keep its own house in order and invited comment on political issues. The concomitant was a relaxation of the laws restricting the publication of political material, which culminated in the full debate of the nation's ills in the drawing up of the Petitions of Grievance in 1788–9 and the publication of works such as the abbé Sieyès' *Qu'Est-ce que le Tiers Etat?*.

The Notables produced a host of ideas and schemes for reform. The government found it could not resist this tide of reform and bowed to it. Among these reforms were many affecting the law, and the most important of these was an edict of toleration for Protestants. This did not grant freedom of worship, it only de-criminalized Protestantism, but it had a number of practical and humanitarian advantages (e.g., Huguenots could now more easily be taxed and their children ceased to be illegitimate). Its overwhelming importance is that it broke the exclusively Catholic nature of the regime.

All the Notables' debates still could not tackle the central issue of reforming 'ordinary' taxation. By May 1788 the monarchy admitted to itself that the summoning of the States-General was unavoidable. The edict of May 1788 to call the States-General gave no commitment on a specific date for the meeting, and the government still hoped at this stage to be able to borrow on the confidence and expectations raised by the act of summoning the States-General in order to avoid ever having to name a specific date and convene an actual assembly. None the less, the principle of needing to rule through representative and participative machinery had been accepted. After May 1788, in theory if not yet in practice, the *ancien régime* had become a limited monarchy.

Other edicts in May 1788 reformed the law courts and – yet again – exiled the recalcitrant counsellors from the *Parlement* of Paris, setting up new legal structures to replace them. This was the monarchy in stern reforming mood not seen since 1771, and it constituted as serious an attack on corporate powers and privileges as witnessed at any time under the *ancien régime*. The monarchy had been seen to be acting despotically against its more customary desire to be seen to respect corporations. The Duc d'Orléans in one debate during the pre-Revolution provoked Louis XVI to say, from the throne: '*C'est la loi parce que Je le veult.*'[13] This was a more extreme statement of royal prerogative than any made by Louis XIV, and, although it was based more on petulance than on considered policy, it was a profoundly disturbing remark.

Many historians (but not contemporaries) have made the mistake of believing that the States-General was a defunct medieval relic, a political dinosaur with no place in the world of 1788–9. This is not the case. Although the States-General had not met since 1614 it was still a living part of the *ancien régime*'s constitution. Not a decade had passed since 1614 when there had not been some serious call for its assembly. The strongest patrons had been the Duke of Burgundy's Circle – a group of reformers around Louis XIV's grandson in the 1690s – who in effect drew up the political agenda for the *ancien régime* in the eighteenth century.[14] For its part the government could never ignore the States-General, and had always to take care not to venture into its areas of prerogative when drafting regulations to be laid before the *parlements*.

The local machinery for assembly had been maintained throughout France. In every province there were officials in 1788 already prepared to set in motion the elections and drawing up of the petitions of grievance.[15] The proof of the States-General's survival as a living institution is the ease with which the elections were conducted. Although the very out-of-date constituencies gave problems, only the French West Indies – which had not, of course, existed in 1614 – experienced any real difficulty in returning deputies. The problems associated with the States-General were political not practical.

By summer 1788, therefore, the regime had ceased to be exclusively

Catholic, and had adopted a measure of public debate on political issues. The beginnings of a programme of reform in the direction of civil liberties protecting the subject from arbitrary royal (or other privileged) power had been instituted, and the principle of representative and participative institutions in government accepted. The regime had already begun to experience the humiliation of having policy dictated by financial stringency, and had been prepared to accept the opprobrium of despotism in its dealings with obstructive corporations. The regime which had convened the Assembly of Notables was recognizably the regime bequeathed by Louis XIV, the regime by August 1788 was not.

In August 1788 the crisis of indebtedness caught up with the monarchy in the form of all the government's cash and credit running out. The problem had to be tackled immediately if – for example – the army were to be paid. The time for debating had passed: from August onwards only actions would count. The commentaries begin here with the government having to decide how best to present to the public the previously unthinkable policies of bankruptcy and naming a specific day for the States-General to assemble.

Later in the autumn of 1788 Thomas Jefferson was asked to set out how France had come to this point. His resulting account, of what, unbeknown to him, would be termed the pre-Revolution, sets the scene for the start of the day-to-day narrative in the following chapters:

Having been on the spot since [the present struggle's] first origin and watched its movements as an uninterested spectator, with no other bias than a love of mankind I will give you my ideas of it.... the American war seems first to have awakened the thinking part of this nation in general from the sleep of despotism in which they were sunk.... The press, notwithstanding its shackles, began to disseminate [common sense and common right]: conversation too assumed new freedoms; politics became the theme of all societies, male and female, and a very extensive and zealous party was formed, which may be called the Patriotic party, who sensible of the abusive government under which they lived, longed for occasions of reforming it. This party comprehended all the honesty of the kingdom, sufficiently at its leisure to think: the men of letters, the easy bourgeois, the young nobility, partly from reflection partly from mode.... Happily for the nation, it happened that at the same moment, the dissipations of the court had exhausted the money and credit of the state, and M. de Calonne found himself obliged to appeal to the nation and to develop to it the ruin of their finances. He had no ideas of supplying the deficit by economies; he saw no means but new taxes. To tempt to consent to these some douceurs were necessary. The Notables were called in 1787. The leading vices of the constitution and administration

were ably sketched out, good remedies proposed, and under the splendour
of these propositions a demand of more money was couched. The
Notables concurred with the minister in the necessity of reformation,
adroitly avoided the demand of money, got him [Calonne] displaced,
and one of their leading men [Loménie de Brienne, the Archbishop of
Toulouse] placed in his room. The Archbishop of Toulouse by the aid of
the hopes formed of him, was able to borrow some money, and he
reformed considerably the expenses of the court. Notwithstanding the
prejudices since formed against him, he appeared to me to pursue the
reformation of the laws and constitution as steadily as a man could do
who had to drag the court after him, and even to conceal from them the
consequences of the measures he was leading them into. In his time the
criminal laws were reformed, provincial assemblies and states established
in most of the provinces, the States-General promised, and a solemn
acknowledgment made by the king that he could not impose a new tax
without the consent of the nation. It is true he was continually goaded
forward by the public clamours excited by the writings and workings of
the Patriots, who were able to keep up the public fermentation at the
exact point which borders on resistance without entering on it. They
had taken into their alliance the *parlements* also, who were led by very
singular circumstances to espouse, for the first time, the rights of the
nation. They had from old causes had personal hostility against M. de
Calonne. They refused to register his loans or his taxes, and went so far
as to acknowledge they had no power to do it. They persisted in this
with his successor, who therefore exiled them. Seeing that the nation
did not interest themselves much for their recall, they began to fear that
the new judicatures proposed in their place would be established and
that their own suppression would be perpetual. In short they found their
own strength insufficient to oppose that of the king. They therefore
insisted the States-General should be called. Here they became united
with and supported by the Patriots, and their joint influence was
sufficient to produce the promise of that assembly.[16]

Jefferson seemed unaware that the *Parlement* of Paris had since 1775 been
calling for the States-General to meet – though in the certain expectation
that the government would never call their bluff.[17] The monarchy, for reasons
outlined above, never had the option of enforcing a reform of the tax system
ignoring *both* the *Parlement* of Paris *and* the States-General. The government
had made a real show of strength against the *parlements* in May 1788 with
Keeper of the Seals Lamoignon's 'May Edicts' reforming the judiciary, as
Jefferson states. What Jefferson could not see was that this action, followed
by the summoning of the States-General, effectively ended the period of the

pre-Revolution now known as the 'Revolt of the *Parlements*'. The period after May 1788 was the 'Revolt of the Nobility'.[18] Lastly, Jefferson may have underrated the effect of the impending bankruptcy on the decision to summon the States-General on a specific date.

The government had to choose between despotism, the *parlements* and the States-General as the only paths out of the financial crisis, and the making of this choice is the point at which the commentary begins in the next chapter.

CHAPTER 3

From the Declaration of Bankruptcy and the Summoning of the States-General to its Assembly (August 1788 to May 1789)

'The total incompetency of a single head to govern a nation well ...'

THE day to day commentary cannot do better than start with Arthur Young, who landed at Calais on 30 July and travelled thence to Brittany. On 13 August he reached Rouen (the Manchester of the *ancien régime*) and 'inquired much into the common sentiments of the people, and found that the king personally ... is more popular than the [*parlement* of Rouen], to whom they attribute the general dearness of everything'.[1]

Immediately, therefore, Young has echoed Jefferson's remarks about the *parlements*, drawn up the battle-lines for the politics of the autumn, and thrown into the political arena the issue of food prices.

By coincidence, a few days later Jefferson elaborated a very similar view about Louis XVI, describing him as

> the honestest man in his kingdom, and the most regular and economical. He has no foible which will enlist him against the good of his people; and whatever constitution will promote this, he will befriend it obstinately.... I believe he will consider the opinion of the States General as the best evidence of what will profit and please the nation and will conform to it.[2]

This is a very generous assessment, but it was true to say over the span of his reign and period as dauphin that it was hard to shake his resolve to follow a policy if he thought it would be popular.

The Summoning of the States-General

Although Loménie de Brienne had agreed in principle to the assembly of the States-General, in the edict of 1 May 1788 this was still an abstract gesture until a commitment to a specific date was given. After this the States-General was placed firmly on the regime's political agenda, and the monarchy had to begin to adjust its behaviour to take account of the new constitutional scene. Once the date was fixed, people's minds became focused on the institution: its composition, proceedings and potential effects on French politics. The mechanisms for generating this debate were the election promises of the candidates, the plethora of publications exhorting the potential deputies to follow particular policies, and the drawing up of the petitions of grievance.

The British embassy set the scene: 'We are in daily expectation of an *arrêt* of the Council of State to fix the convocation *des Etats Généraux* for May 1789: It is become very necessary to name a period for that important assembly, was it only to raise the public credit which at present is much on the decline.'[3] The embassy reported that until the publication of this *arrêt*, the edict 'hitherto seems to have operated very little in favour of government, for the funds, which is the only criterion of public faith, rose only two per cent on the first day, and have continued sinking ever since'.[4]

After the *arrêt*'s publication Jefferson analysed the issue which would be dominating political life for the rest of the autumn:

> The interesting question is how the States General shall be composed. There are 3 opinions: (1) To place the three estates, Clergy, Nobles, and Commons, in three different houses. The clergy would probably like this, and some of the nobility. But it has no partisans out of those orders. (2) To put the Clergy and Noblesse into one house, and the Commons into another. The *Noblesse* will be generally for this. (3) To put the three Orders into one house, and make the Commons the majority of that house. This reunites the greatest number of partisans.[5]

The account of reactions to the summoning of the States-General has, however, to end on a more cautious note. After a day's reflection the British embassy wrote, 'the nation will never be satisfied or give faith to anything the Council issues', now that the assembly was imminent. The embassy went on to give a cogent warning against judging the 1789 assembly on the evidence of sixteenth- and seventeenth-century States-Generals: '... [it] cannot be expected to bear much resemblance to those convened formerly ... when great ignorance prevailed with respect to all matters of Government'.[6]

The Declaration of Bankruptcy

For perhaps the last time an *ancien régime* ministry had shown real political acumen in announcing the date for the assembly of the States-General before it was forced into declaring the bankruptcy and recalling the *parlements* (see below). Had the bankruptcy been declared first it would have pushed the government into an almost immediate assembly of the States-General with no opportunity to exercise any initiative over the elections. The *parlements* with their 'told you so' attitude would have been the only institutions with any credibility. Instead, the government gave at least the appearance of retaining the initiative. If the bankruptcy was a 'problem', then the States-General was the 'solution', and the government provided the solution before admitting the scale of the problem. This effectively harnessed the States-General to the government's cause. The loss of face caused by the declaration of bankruptcy destroyed the ministry (see below) but not the monarchy. The bankruptcy was very much a Parisian event, and no news of it reached Arthur Young in Normandy or Brittany.

On 14 August the British embassy predicted that only a 'subterfuge'[7] could avoid the declaration of a bankruptcy, and on 18 August the government duly had to announce a rescheduling of the national debt, a suspension of some repayments, and an adjustment of other state outgoings. Jefferson's account and comment leaves little more to be said:

> the want of money has in fact over-borne all their resources, and ...
> they published an *arrêt* suspending all reimbursements of capital, and
> reducing the payments of the principal mass of demands for interest to
> 12 *sous* in the *livre*, the remaining eight *sous* to be paid with
> certificates.... The consternation here is as yet too great to let us judge
> the issue. It will probably ripen the public mind to the necessity of a
> change in their constitution and to the substituting the collected wisdom
> of the whole in the place of a single will.... It is a remarkable proof of
> the total incompetency of a single head to govern a nation well, when
> with a revenue of six hundred millions they are led to a declared bank-
> ruptcy, and to stop the wheels of government, even in its most essential
> movements, for lack of money.

More tersely, he added a few days later: 'The treasury became literally moneyless, and all purposes depending on this mover came to a stand.'

The most striking effect of the bankruptcy and ensuing lack of funds was felt in foreign affairs. France was powerless to intervene in either the Austrian Netherlands, Eastern Europe, or the Near East. This led Jefferson to speak of France's 'temporary annihilation in the political scales of Europe'.[8]

Fall of Loménie de Brienne

The immediate consequence of the declaration of bankruptcy was the res-ignation of Loménie de Brienne. The period of his ministry had brought the regime to the point where noble disaffection had brought several provinces to near secession, a bankruptcy, with all its consequences, had been declared, the government had had to surrender the monarchy's constitutional lead to the States-General, and there could be no avoiding the recall of government's old adversaries, the *parlements*. Added to all this, the harvest had been poor and food prices were rising. Necker (see below) was recalled.

Jefferson wrote: 'The public joy on this change of administration was very great indeed. The people of Paris were amusing themselves with trying and burning [Loménie de Brienne] in effigy.'[9] The British embassy confirmed that 'The public ... have let loose their rage on him.'[10]

The Recall of Necker

Necker had enjoyed a long relationship with the *ancien régime*. He had been its philosophical and literary hero in 1773 and its Director-General (i.e., Controller-General in all but name) from 1776 to 1781. From 1781 to 1789 he had been a constant thorn in the side of successive ministries, maintaining a running commentary on their shortcomings and offering himself as the only man who truly understood the regime's finances and how to reform them. The longer he was out of office, the more popular he became.

The British embassy noted 'The predilection of the public or rather of the people is so great for M. Necker that he was received on his return from Versailles with the loudest acclamations, and it is expected that there will be illuminations this evening.'

The embassy continued, though, in a more cautious tone: 'Many, however, less sanguine, are apt to consider this elevation of the favourite of the people, either as temporary resources of credit till the convocation of the States General, or else as an expedient to put it off, and even perhaps to prevent that assembly's taking place.' Necker 'had no plan forward before he came into office'. 'As yet no minister, even in the tranquillity of the closet, has been found equal to the management of this disordered empire.'[11]

The Recall of the *Parlements*

One of Necker's first acts seems to have been to insist on an immediate recall of the *parlements*,[12] perhaps realizing that they had already lost the political initiative to the forthcoming States-General. The *Parlement* of Paris re-entered the capital in triumph on 23 September and immediately threw down the gauntlet by insisting, on the 25th, that the States-General assemble in the same form as at its last meeting in 1614.

The British embassy assessed the position of the *Parlement vis-à-vis* the government at the moment of recall, and before their ruling on the States-General:

> What degree of moderation will be shewn by them after so complete a victory, and at the moment when they see the fate of the kingdom depending (at least until the meeting of the States) upon themselves, is a matter of very curious speculation. Certain it now is that those bodies which the government has so long affected to despise, have at least raised themselves to a degree of consequence, from their negative authority, that if they choose to continue to display it, nothing can withstand.[13]

After the ruling Jefferson reported: 'Their first *arrêté* has been to demand the *Etats Généraux* in the form of 1614. Here the cloven hoof begins to appear. While the existence of *Parlement* itself was endangered by the royal authority, they were calling for the *Etats Généraux*: now they have obtained a kind of victory, they see danger to themselves.'[14]

The *Parlement's* fears were well grounded. Taking stock of the period of electioneering for the States-General, Jefferson later wrote: 'We hear so little of the parlements for some time past that one is hardly sensible of their existence. This unimportance is probably the forerunner of their total remodification by the nation.'[15]

The background to the *Parlement's* use of the States-General, in its absence, as a stick with which to beat the government has been explored in the previous chapter, but some explanation of why the *Parlement* adopted its position with regard to the elections and representation is required. Their ruling immediately forfeited them all the public good will they had enjoyed during exile, but it represented their last desperate gamble to retain some political initiative once the government had called their bluff by actually summoning the States.

The States-General would eclipse the *parlements* and relegate them to a purely legalistic role. The only way the *parlements* could limit the damage would be to ensure that as many deputies to the States as possible, in every Order, would represent their interests and could be drawn from magisterial families. This control was effectively exercised in the several provincial assemblies of States, where there was a long-standing (but wholly particularist) alliance of local institutions against the central government.

This was probably a realistic objective if the elections could be kept low-key, and particularly if the structure of the assembly could be kept to its traditional – numerically limited – form. There was, however, a substantial body of public opinion, which soon turned into a landslide, in favour of adopting the precedent set by the States of Languedoc of doubling the representation of the Third Estate to reflect, however crudely, changes in society since 1614. These additional deputies to the States-General would place control of the Third Estate beyond the magistracy's grasp, and they fought to prevent it. In doing so their self-interest was exposed and they became a marginalized, but still dangerous, political force. The Assembly of Notables' debate on the detail, and the form, of the assembly became the focus of political attention in the autumn of 1788.

Debate on the States-General by the Assembly of Notables

The government's reaction to the *Parlement's* ruling on the composition of the States-General was to turn again to the Assembly of Notables. The Assembly was summoned to meet in November to debate the constitution of the States. This led to renewed public debate and lobbying for a doubling of the Third Estate.

The commentators were sceptical for two reasons about this decision to recall the Notables. In the first place they lacked confidence in the Notables as an effective or useful institution. A contemporary British pun called them the 'Not-Ables', and Jefferson expected little of these 'privileged characters' when it came to debating the best interests of commoners.[16] In the second place the government's underlying motives were suspect: 'there are many who think this step has been taken in order to gain time, and ... to retard very much, and, perhaps, to get rid altogether of the States'.[17]

This climate of speculation helps explain the public disquiet and scepticism about royal intentions from September 1788 onwards, and the very real fear that at any moment the government would opt for 'despotism' and abandon a constitutional solution to its problems.

At the same time the government and the *parlements* had constantly to be reviewing where their true interests lay and how they would best be served in relation to the form of the States-General. In November the British embassy detected *Parlement* seeking to ingratiate itself with the government for the reasons outlined earlier: 'those *Corps* have much to apprehend from the numerous body of the States General and who, it may be expected, will aim some fatal blow at the over-grown authority and influence of the parlements; ... the magistrates ... endeavour to ingratiate themselves with their sovereign and the nobility, as their only support in case they should be driven to extremities'.[18] The government and nobility, however, were not prepared to respond.

Administration

Despite the constitutional crisis, life had to go on. The imminent prospect of credible and effective fiscal reform had steadied the domestic political situation: 'to the credit of their country ... the public seem disposed to submit to any inconvenience for the moment', but troops were being moved into Paris in case of violent demonstrations against the *Parlement*.[19] Jefferson wrote optimistically on 18 November 1788: 'I am in hopes [that the convoking of the States General] will end in giving a good degree of liberty to this country. They enjoy at present the most perfect tranquillity within'; and on 4 December: 'As soon as the convocation of the States General was announced, a tranquillity took place thro' the whole kingdom. Happily no open rupture had taken place in any part of it.'[20]

Huber spoke at the end of the month of the 'dawn of a new constitution', adding, 'don't laugh ... the constant existence of the States General must prevent future depredations'.[21]

Price of Bread and Adverse Weather
Of growing concern to all parties was the rising price of bread, following the poor harvest, and the exceptionally severe winter, whose story can be followed in the British embassy's despatches through to spring floods after the thaw. The first symptoms of real problems began to show at the end of November when forty bakers had to close and 'The price of bread has again been raised.' It was raised again a fortnight later and the weather had become 'unusually severe'.

One effect of this was an increase in street crime: 'It is by no means safe to walk the streets late in the evening', and carriages were being attacked. By the middle of December, water mills, essential for milling the grain, were frozen up. By the new year the frosts had hardened, and charity could not keep pace with the demand for it. People were being found frozen to death. The final blow came in late January when a thaw caused floods.[22]

The British embassy reported further that some northern ports had frozen over, preventing even the import of grain.[23]

Jefferson reported that the temperature had reached twenty degrees below zero (Fahrenheit), and, describing the winter to a friend, said:

> We have such a winter Madame, as makes me shiver yet whenever I think of it. All communications almost were cut off. Dinners and suppers were suppressed, and the money laid out in feeding and warming the poor, whose labours were suspended by the rigour of the season.... It gave occasion for a display of the benevolent character of this nation, which, great as I had thought it, went beyond my expectations.[24]

Some of this charity was dispensed by Louis XVI personally, and as a part of the hagiography of the martyr king produced under the Restoration, memorable prints of a pre-Raphaelite character were produced showing the benevolent monarch comforting the deserving poor huddled round royal bonfires.

To bring this weather and the issue of food prices back into the political arena, Jefferson recorded that Necker had approached him personally to secure shipments of American grain.[25] The effects of unemployment, scarce food supplies and high prices were greatly to exacerbate the government's problems in preserving law and order in Paris in the spring and summer of 1789.

Jefferson's Assessment of the State of the Nation, 19 November 1788
Jefferson took stock of the political state of the nation, drawing various threads together. His observations serve to set the scene for the debates in the Assembly of Notables on the forms and procedures for the forthcoming States-General. In the same report he went on to speculate on an agenda for the States-General arising from the concerns of the moment, and warned that

the possibility of royal despotism could still not be discounted.

The internal tranquillity of this nation is perfect. Their stocks however continue low; and the difficulty of getting money to face current expenses, very great. In the contest between the king and *Parlement*, the latter, fearing the power of the former, pressed the convoking the States-General. The government found itself obliged by other difficulties also, to recur to the same expedient. The *Parlement* after its recall, shewed that it was now become apprehensive of the States-General; and discovered a determination to cavil at their form, so as to have a right to deny their legality if that body should undertake to abridge their powers. The court thereupon very adroitly determined to call the same Notables who had been approved by the nation the last year, to decide on the form of convoking the States-General: thus withdrawing itself from the disputes which the *Parlement* might excite, and committing them with the nation. The Notables are now in session. The government had manifestly discovered a disposition that the ... Commons, should have as many representatives in the States-General, as the nobility and clergy together.... It is doubted whether the States-General can be collected so early as January, tho' the government, urged by the want of money, is pressing for their convocation. It is still more incertain what the States-General will do when they meet. There are three objects which they may attain, probably without opposition from the court: (1) a periodical meeting of the States-General, (2) their exclusive right of taxation; (3) the right of enregistering laws, and proposing amendments to them as now exercised by the *parlements*. This would lead, as it did in England, to the right of originating laws. The *Parlement* would by this last measure be reduced to a mere judiciary body, and would probably oppose it. But against the king and nation their opposition could not succeed. If the States-General stop here for the present moment, all will probably end well, and they may in future sessions obtain a suppression of *lettres de cachet*, free press, a civil list, and other valuable mollifications of their government. But it is to be feared that an impatience to rectify everything at once, which prevails in some minds, may terrify the court and lead them to appeal to force, and to depend on that alone.[26]

The Debate in the Assembly of Notables on the Form of the States-General
On 20 November the British embassy gave a very similar account of the background to the debates in the Assembly of Notables, concluding that there was 'great temper' and 'differences of opinion' there. On 27 November the embassy assessed that the Assembly of Notables was embarrassing the government, which might have done better to have accepted the *Parlement* of Paris's

original judgement and lived with the consequences, instead of stirring up a
public debate and exposing divisions within the political establishment. Too
lengthy a debate might actually delay the meeting of the States-General and
still produce an outcome unfavourable to the Third Estate's representation.
The embassy warned: 'The body of the people are by no means disposed in a
matter of such consequence to them, to submit quietly to the decision of
certain individuals, styled Notables, assembled by government and acting
under its influence, to the great detriment, as the people conceive, to their
natural rights.'[27]

The progress of the debate can most profitably be followed in Jefferson's
despatches, with their acute analysis of the implications of events as they
developed:

> five bureaux of the Notables have voted by very great majorities that
> [the Third Estate] should have only an equal number with each of the
> other orders singly. One bureau, by a majority of a single voice, had
> agreed to give the Commons the double number of representatives. This
> is the first symptom of a decided combination between the nobility and
> clergy, and will necessarily throw the people into the scale of the king.

> the Notables ... have deservedly lost their popularity. ... There is a great
> outcry against [the bureaux's 5:1 vote], and the friends of the people
> and of justice will try the question over again in an assembly of all the
> bureaux, but there seems no hope of success. ... This may end in liberty
> or despotism at [the king's] will. I think that both he and his ministry
> are in favour of liberty, and that having 23 and a half million on their
> side they will call the other half million to order, and show them
> that instead of being two thirds of the Nation they are but the forty-
> eighth.

> [The Notables] ... have proved themselves a mere combination of priests
> and nobles against the people.

> The stream of public indignation, heretofore directed against the court,
> sets strongly against the Notables.

There was then an unexpected intervention from the *Parlement* of Paris which
pointed to a way out of the crisis:

> The Notables are not yet separated, nor their treasonable vote against
> the people yet consolidated. ... The *Parlement* have taken up the subject,
> and passed a very laudable vote in opposition. They have made it the

occasion of giving sketches of what should be a bill of rights. Perhaps this opposition of authority may give the court an option between the two.

Finally, on 23 December 1788, Jefferson was able to report: 'the great decision of the court [is] that the *Tiers Etat* shall elect a moiety of the States General'.[28]

This was the last occasion on which the *Parlement* was to hold the political limelight, but its concession on doubling the Third Estate carried a sting in the tail. The *Parlement* insisted that voting continue to be by Order rather than by head, in other words that although the Third Estate had as many deputies as the other two Orders combined, they could still be outvoted 2:1 by them.

Situation between Settling the Form of the States-General and their Elections and Jefferson's Predictions for the States-General

Jefferson stood back from immediate events to write to Thomas Paine, the English radical who had played a prominent part in the American Revolution and who would shortly offer his services to the French Revolutionary government. He sketched out the issues which had been raised and how they would form the battle-ground for the politics of the next few months:

> The clergy will move heaven and earth to defeat the effect of this [just] representation. They will endeavour now that the votes shall be by Orders, and not by persons. The Princes of the Blood (Monsieur and the D. d'Orléans excepted) have threatened scission and if the clergy can bring over a majority of the *noblesse* to the same sentiments, a scission may be effected. But the younger part of the nobility are in favour of the *Tiers Etat*, and those more advanced are daily coming to them. So that I am in hopes, by the meeting of the States General, there will remain against them only those whom age has rendered averse to new reasons and reformations.

> Upon the whole it has appeared to me that the basis of the present struggle is an illumination of the public mind as to the rights of the nation, aided by fortunate incidents; that they can never retrograde, but from the natural progress of things must press forward to the establishment of a constitution which shall assure them a good degree of liberty. They flatter themselves they shall form a better constitution than the English. I think it will be better in some points, worse in others. It will be better in the article of representation which will be more equal. It will be worse, as their situation obliges them to keep up the dangerous machine of a standing army. I doubt too whether they will obtain the trial by jury, because they are not sensible of its value.[29]

(Jefferson's prediction here was wrong, as trial by jury was to be one of the Revolution's judicial reforms, though not in the immediate future.)

The Elections to the States-General and the Procedures for the Petitions of Grievance

Once the form of the assembly of the States-General had been fixed the election of deputies and drawing up of the petitions of grievance could proceed. It is a credit to the *ancien régime* that these processes – which had not been used since 1614 – functioned at all.[30]

Leaving aside Jefferson's comment that overall the representation in the States-General would be fairer than it was for the contemporary British House of Commons, the procedure for the elections took many forms depending on local custom. Some deputies in the nobility simply assumed they had a God-given right to represent their district, while the clergy held elections only for the *curés* – the bishops already knowing which of them would sit in the States-General. Most of the deputies were selected by electoral colleges, and the electioneering revolved around the choice of the members for the college – wherever, again, the membership was not an automatic right vested in certain individuals – and the choices made by the colleges. Jefferson, the British embassy and M. Huber commented very little on the procedural details, but watched carefully the results from some of the more interesting noble electoral colleges whence 'tomorrow's men' were expected to emerge.

The same variation in procedures applied to the process of drawing up the petitions of grievance. Some were anodyne professions of loyalty to the crown, while others were bitter attacks on the regime voicing peasant anguish. A great deal of debate and lobbying attended their preparation, and the correspondents were privy to some of the detail of this activity. The correspondents wanted both to report on the more interesting detail of the elections and on their overall conduct. Huber picked on the former Controller-General, Calonne's, attempt to become a deputy as being the election of greatest interest both to himself and to English readers: 'Calonne ... presented himself for the *bailliage de* Bailleul near Douai. At first the murmur was only *sound*, but soon broke out into such a flame as made him think an immediate retreat advisable; he afterwards tried Dunkirk, where he met with a worse reception.' The attempt to be elected was pure 'bravado' and only earned him a warrant for his arrest. According to Huber, Necker interceded on his behalf and he was able to leave France safely and became an exile in England.[31]

The British embassy noted Mirabeau's candidacy in Provence. Details were also given in a fuller report on this, and other, local campaigns by Jefferson: 'Mirabeau has been declared in his province not to be a noble, whereupon he offered himself for the people.'[32] 'All the world is occupied here in electioneering, in choosing or being chosen', he wrote in March 1789.[33]

The British embassy surveyed the general conduct of the elections with optimism:

> A number of people leave Paris every day to go to their several estates in order to assist at the elections: the most satisfactory accounts have been received from many of the *bailliages*, mentioning that the utmost harmony subsists there amongst the three Orders.

> The elections have in general been carried on more quietly than might have been expected.

> As far as any judgment can be formed from present appearances [in the elections] there is every reason to expect that the operations of the States General will turn out favourably for the country.

The embassy added a shrewd comment, which could only have been made by someone versed in the workings of a mixed constitution: 'a great deal of intrigue is employed in the different *bailliages* to make the elections as favourable as possible to the wishes of the government and no pains have been spared to endeavour to secure a majority in its favour'.[34]

Jefferson also seems to have given some candidates advice and help during their campaigns. In a remarkable letter to Lafayette on his election he wrote: 'You will in the end go over wholly to the *Tiers Etat*, because it will be impossible for you to live in a constant sacrifice of your own sentiments to the prejudices of the *noblesse*. Suppose a scission should take place. The priests and nobles will secede, the nation will remain in place, and, with the king, will do its own business.'[35] Thus did Jefferson foresee not only the moves towards the nobility and clergy joining with the Third Estate in a unified National Assembly, but also the emigrations which would follow it.

What this letter also shows is that there were people in France in 1789, before the storm broke, who fully understood the political situation and all its implications. When he entered the States-General, therefore, Lafayette had a course of action – which he took – already sketched out for him, and as the pace of events quickened he was riding on the crest of their wave instead of being swept along by them.

The Preparation and Politics of the Petitions of Grievance

In practice, the processes of electing deputies to the States-General and drawing up the petitions of grievance were inseparable. The correspondents took a keen interest – and perhaps part – in the policies being debated. The novelty of an uncensored public debate on the state of the nation and the abuses of its government were a heady novelty for Frenchmen, but the Anglo-Saxon commentator could remain more aloof. Jefferson quipped: 'Everybody here is trying their hands at forming declarations of rights.'[36]

Part of the electioneering process was the publication of a flood of pamphlets analysing the regime and exhorting the States-General to reform it. Historically, the most significant was the abbé Sieyès' *'Qu'est ce que le Tiers Etat?'*, but it went unnoticed at the time. The only pamphlet which did attract comment was Mirabeau's *'L'Histoire Sécrète de la Cour de Berlin'*. Huber described it as 'diabolical', and the British embassy predicted it would 'be burnt by the common hangman', which was the customary fate of seditious literature under the *ancien régime*.[37]

In their coverage of this aspect of the elections, the correspondents noted a few maverick elements, which caused more amusement than concern. The British embassy recorded that 'the demands of the *Tiers-Etat* are extraordinary beyond measure, not to say ridiculous: at Tours in particular the people went so far as to require an equal partition of property'.[38]

Huber gave one of the best general descriptions of conduct and policy discussions in the electoral assemblies: *'Les élections des bailliages* go on vigorously and very well. In most places they begin on the part *du Tiers Etat* with violent complaints and expressions against the *noblesse*. In every such place it has hitherto produced a most conciliatory deputation from the *noblesse* to the *Tiers*; a renunciation of the first two Orders of the *privilèges pécuniaires*, and a handsome acknowledgement in return from the *Tiers*. In a great many and important places the unanimity of the three Orders has shown itself instantly; nowhere has the proportion been disputed of two to two' (i.e. the doubling of the Third), and Huber held out real hope that the States-General would offer solutions to the national crisis.[39]

The British embassy confirmed this general mood of altruistic self-sacrifice for the national good in the Paris elections, which, 'have not caused much external sensation but ... the three Orders are united upon the principal object, that of sacrificing their property and interests for the good and prosperity of the nation'. This generosity of spirit was to be a feature of the Revolution, and no amount of cynicism can detract from its importance. The embassy also noted from Normandy the emergence of an issue which was crucially to affect the early course of events in the States-General: 'The *bailliage* holding at Caen is attended with no small degree of fermentation the consequence of the extreme distress to which the lower sort of the clergy have been exposed.' The bishop was 'loaded with abuse' by the *curés*, and 'a similar spirit of opposition to the dignified clergy prevails throughout the kingdom'.[40]

Huber, in one letter, lets the reader see into the lobbying behind the drawing up of the petitions of grievances at both the *bailliage* and national levels:

What would make me think the sensible abbé Cérutti cannot be the *'directeur spirituel du Duc d'Orléans'* is, that in his pious holiness's instruc-

tions *'à ses représentants aux bailliages',* he requests that they will demand
the liberty of divorce of the States General. Madame de Staël very
pleasantly thanked him for it yesterday at the Duke of Dorset's ball, *'au
nom des femmes'.*[41]

This passage shows the existence of a women's lobby, albeit led by a foreign
Protestant (Madame de Staël, who was Necker's daughter and married to the
Swedish ambassador, and was therefore Swiss by birth and Swedish by
nationality). Because of Madame de Staël's involvement, it is likely that the
policy had Necker's support. The employment of the abbé Cérutti also opens
a window on the harnessing of the intelligensia to the elections and petitions.
The abbé was a leading Catholic religious popularizer. There is more pessimistic a footnote to add to the women's lobby from Jefferson: 'In my opinion
a kind of influence, which none of their plans of reform take into account,
will elude them all; I mean the influence of women in the government.'[42]

To return from the realms of high policy to the nitty-gritty of workday
detail, Huber commented that the States-General faced a huge agenda simply
to transact all the business arising from the petitions. By mid-January some
800 had already been received and a whole new bureaucracy was having to
be set up to service the assembly.[43]

Young's Analysis of the Petitions of Grievance

Arthur Young made it his business to read and analyse all the petitions,
which were printed and on sale in 1789, and in 1791 he wrote this account
(for comparison with the National Assembly's legislative programme):

Before the Revolution is condemned in the gross, it should be considered
what extent of liberty was demanded by the three Orders in their *cahiers*;
and this in particular is necessary, since those very *cahiers* are quoted to
show the mischievous proceedings of the National Assembly. Here are a
few of the ameliorations demanded; to have trial by jury, and the *habeas
corpus* of England; to deliberate by head, and not by Order, demanded *by
the nobility themselves*; to declare all taxes illegal and suppressed, but to
grant them anew for a year; to abolish for ever the *capitaineries*; to
establish a *caisse nationale séparée inaccessible à toute influence du pouvoir
exécutif*; that all the Intendants should be suppressed; that no treaties of
commerce should be made but with the consent of the States; that *all*
monks be suppressed, and their goods and estates sold; that tithes be for
ever suppressed; that salaries be paid to the deputies; that the permanence
of the National Assembly is a necessary part of its existence; that the
Bastille be demolished; that the duties of *aides*, on wine, brandy, tobacco,
salt, leather, paper, iron, oil, and soap, be suppressed; that the domains
of the king be alienated; that the king's studs (*haras*) be suppressed; that

the pay of the soldiers be augmented; that the kingdom be divided into districts, and the elections proportioned to population and to contributions; that all citizens paying a determinate quota of taxes vote in the parochial assemblies; that it is indispensable in the States General to consult the Rights of Man; that the deputies shall accept of no place, pension, grace, or favour.

Young went on to observe that the petitions did not seek a republic, but did very clearly intend the States-General 'to be a body *solely* possessing the legislative authority'.[44]

Young drew the conclusion that the National Assembly had done very little which had not often been demanded by the nobility before even the States-General had met. This confirmed for him the fundamental rightness of the Revolution, whatever its future excesses.

The Dauphin

While the debates progressed, a minor theme of political life was being picked up by the British embassy, who, perhaps, realized that it could interact at a later date with the more important political events of the day. This was the failing health of the dauphin. The first word of this came on 1 January 1789, when it was reported that the dauphin had, a 'deformity of his body'. At the end of the month Dorset wrote: 'I conceive that little hopes are entertained of his arriving at years of maturity.' A month later he was 'in an almost hopeless state'. And he continued thus for a month, by which time he was in a 'very dangerous and precarious state of health'. At the end of April 'The dauphin had a very alarming crisis.'[45] Thus the royal family faced a domestic as well as a national political crisis on the eve of the assembly of the States-General.

Popular Disturbances

The political fermentation of the elections and petitions of grievance, combined with rising food prices, almost inevitably led to popular unrest. There was a steady flow of reports of riots and disorder in various provinces, and Brittany in particular, but more seriously the disturbances began to move towards Paris: 'Disturbances in the neighbouring villages (to Paris) increase, and are likely to become still more alarming, for the scarcity of corn is general throughout the country.' Even more worrying was the news that the government's stockpile of corn in Paris was running out, with some months before the next harvest, and that the stocks in the provinces had been raided in the previous autumn to keep Paris fed during the winter.[46] Jefferson summed up the mood: 'The want of bread is very seriously dreaded thro' the whole kingdom.'[47]

These disturbances culminated inside Paris in an episode known as the Réveillon riots, when a wallpaper factory was burned down and troops called in to fire on the crowd. The British embassy called it 'a very serious tumult' and went on to give a very full (albeit second-hand) account concluding: 'No other motive than the dearness of bread has been assigned to by the unhappy wretches who were engaged in these excesses ... though some are disposed to suspect that the friends and supporters of the *Parlement* have secretly fermented the disturbance.' Two hundred were reported dead.[48] Jefferson reported in very similar terms: 'We have had in [Paris] a very considerable riot in which about 100 people have been probably killed ... nor did the wretches know what they wanted, except to do mischief. It seems to have had no particular connection with the great national questions now in agitation.'[49]

Gouverneur Morris had discussed the public order problems in the capital with Lafayette on 17 April 1789: 'We consider a revolt in Paris, and agree that it might occasion much mischief but would not produce any good.'[50]

Preparations for the Assembling of the States-General
The actual opening of the States-General was to be a public event on the scale of a coronation or royal wedding. The deputies inevitably would have to arrive at, and hence attract their first public attention in, Paris. A great deal of thought was given to how the capital would behave. The government had first, however, to choose where the meetings of the assembly would take place. A number of large adjoining buildings were needed, and the obvious choice was Versailles, but this was not a customary location, the palace having not even been projected at the time of the States' last meeting. 'Necker wished [they] should be held at Paris, but his opinion was over-ruled by the rest of the ministers who conceived that there might be a great danger of disturbance from the ungovernable spirit of the populace of the city, and Versailles is therefore the place finally decided upon.'[51]

Once the decision was taken, preparations were put in hand as early as February: 'It is the intention of the court to prepare every kind of amusement for the members of the States General during their residence at Versailles, and orders have already been given to the directors of the public theatres at Paris.' The embassy staff saw a street carnival, also in February, in honour of the forthcoming event, where people were dressed up in the prescribed formal dress (which was mandatory) for the three different Orders.[52]

In early May troops were drafted into the capital 'to check the slightest appearance of commotion among the people'.[53]

The government had decided on a policy of bread, circuses and military force. The bread it could no longer deliver, the circuses were well prepared, and, as yet, no one doubted that the army could be relied on to fire on the crowd just as it had done outside Monsieur Réveillon's factory.

Morris's Impressions on the Eve of the States-General
This chapter opened with Arthur Young's comments on arriving in France: we may conclude it with Gouverneur Morris's initial assessments of the politics in the run-up to the States-General, as he saw them on his arrival in February 1789:

> I find on this side of the Atlantic a strong resemblance to what I left on the other – a nation which exists in hopes, prospects, and expectations – the revenue for ancient establishments gone, existing forms shaken to the foundation, and a new order of things about to take place, in which perhaps even to the very names, all former institutions will be disregarded.

Morris realized that 'the most important scene enacted for many years on the European theatre, will in the next few months be displayed at this place'.[54]

CHAPTER 4

From the Opening of the States-General to the Storming of the Bastille (May to July 1789)

'A great opportunity, but lost'

THE opening of the States-General was marked by two ceremonial events. On 4 May 1789 there was a procession of the court – including all the government ministers and as many deputies as had managed to reach Versailles in time – through the town of Versailles to attend a mass. On 5 May there was an opening session of the States presided over by the king, at which he formally welcomed the deputies and at which Necker gave a three-and-a-half-hour-long speech on the theme of the state of the nation. All concerned with both events were meant to wear their appropriate ceremonial robes, and they were both glittering spectacles.

The ambassadors had seats of honour reserved for them on 5 May, but do not seem to have attended the procession and mass on 4 May. Morris made the effort to watch the procession, but forgot to take his hat and was sunburnt for his pains. He left this description: 'The procession is very magnificent.... Neither the king nor queen appears too well pleased ... the latter meets not a single acclamation. She looks, however, with contempt on the scene.'

Morris then spent a frustrating afternoon trying – unsuccessfully – to cadge a ticket for a seat at the opening session from various courtiers only to find that Jefferson had had a spare one all the time (reserved for the absent William Short) and had sent it to Morris's home during the day. On 5 May Morris arrived at the Salle des Menus just after 8 a.m., and

> I sit there in a cramped situation till after twelve, during which time the different members are brought in and placed, one *'bailliage'* after the other. When M. Necker comes in he is loudly and repeatedly clapped, and so is the Duke of Orléans; ... An old man who refuses to dress in the costume prescribed for the *Tiers*, and who appears in his farmer's habit, receives a long and loud plaudit. M. de Mirabeau is hissed, though not loudly. The king at length arrives, and takes his seat; the queen on his left, two steps lower than him. He makes a short speech, very proper, and well spoken or rather read. The tone and manner have all the *fierté* which can be expected or desired from the blood of the Bourbons. He is interrupted in the reading by acclamations so warm and of such lively

affection that the tears start from my eyes in spite of myself. The queen weeps or seems to weep, but not one voice is heard to wish her well.

Morris tried, but failed, to persuade some of the Frenchmen sitting next to him to applaud her. He then watched a whispered altercation between the king and queen on what Louis XVI should do with his hat, which in turn led to the deputies wondering what they should do with theirs. (Contemporary representations of the session show Louis XVI retaining his hat while the deputies are bare-headed.) Morris finished the day – having sat through Necker's speech – falling in with a group of Third deputies and having dinner with them in a nearby inn. The group included a liberally-minded Breton noble who had deliberately stood for election to the Third. Morris advised them to seek a constitution, but one in which voting should remain by Order rather than by head.[1]

Jefferson had more of a bird's-eye view of proceedings, and stood back from the ceremonial detail:

The States-General were opened the day before yesterday. Viewing it as an opera it was imposing; as a scene of business the king's speech was exactly what it should have been and very well delivered, not a word of the [Keeper of the Seals] was heard by anybody, so that I have never heard a single guess at what it was about. M. Necker's was as good as such a number of details would permit it to be. The picture of their resources was consoling and generally plausible. I could have wished him to have dwelt more on ... great constitutional reformations.

He later went on to analyse Necker's speech in more detail:

M. Necker stated the real and ordinary deficit to be 56 millions, and that he shewed that this could be made up without a tax by economies and bonifications which he specified. Several articles of the latter are liable to the objection that they are proposed on branches of the revenue of which the nation has demanded a suppression.... On the whole his discourse has not satisfied the patriotic party.[2]

Arthur Young gave his reaction to the speech after reading a printed version: 'a great opportunity, but lost; no great leading or masterly views; no decision on circumstances in which the people ought to be relieved, and new principles of government adopted; it is the speech you would expect from a banker's clerk of some ability'.[3]

The British embassy concentrated on purely factual reporting of the content of speeches, but then set opening sessions into a wider context a few days afterwards: 'The attention of the public being wholly engrossed by the States

General, nothing that has not some relation to that is at present the subject of conversation.'[4]

At first, then, all seemed to be going well for the government. There were, though, clouds on the horizon, as Huber analysed. The first was the palpable hostility to Marie-Antoinette, the second the division between the Duke of Orléans and the rest of the Princess of the Blood (who had been hissed), and third was Huber's fear of the mischief which the 'many *mauvaises têtes*' might cause, and Mirabeau above all.[5]

Early Proceedings of the States-General – Impasse

Necker's most optimistic scenario had been for a quick session of the States-General which would ratify his fiscal programme undebated, for no discussion of constitutional issues (which he had so assiduously avoided in his opening speech), for the remaining business (e.g. the petitions of grievance) to be transacted as a formality, and a speedy dissolution with no need for a recall.

This hope was dashed by a succession of procedural and ceremonial wrangles, starting with the farce over Louis xvi's hat and leading, as time went on, to more and more attention being paid to the structure of the assembly, its relationship to the 'nation', and the fullest role it might play: 'the affairs of the nation are not at all advanced since last week owing to the differences subsisting between the nobility and the Third Estate [over the verification of deputies' credentials]. . . . The disorder and confusion that have prevailed are scarcely to be imagined.'[6] (The Third were deliberately delaying verification to buy time to lobby for the Orders to merge into a single chamber (or National Assembly) *before* the transaction of any substantive business began.)

One result of this delay in being able to get down to business was that the more radical of the noble and clerical deputies were also able to carry out serious lobbying within their own Orders for a joining with the Third to form a National Assembly. Jefferson, however, was not optimistic that this could be achieved easily if at all:

The *noblesse* on coming together shew that they are not so much reformed in this principle as we had hoped they would be. In fact there is a real danger of their totally refusing to vote by persons. Some found hopes in the lower clergy which constitute four fifths of the deputies of that Order. If they do not turn the balance in favour of the *Tiers Etat*, there is real danger of a scission. . . . If the king will do business with the *Tiers Etat* which constitutes the nation, it may be well done without priests or nobles.

It is now for the first time that their revolution is likely to receive a serious check, and begins to wear a fearful appearance. The progress of light and liberality in the Order of the *noblesse* has equalled expectation in Paris only and its vicinity. The general mass of deputies of that Order which come from the country shew that the habits of tyranny over the people are deeply rooted in them. They will consent indeed to equal taxation. But five sixths of that chamber are thought to be decidedly for voting by Orders.... Some aid however comes in from a quarter where none was expected ... the lower clergy have obtained five sixths of these deputations. These are the sons of peasants who have done all the drudgery of the service for 10, 20, 30 guineas a year, and whose oppressions and penury contrasted by the pride and luxury of the higher clergy had rendered them perfectly disposed to humble the latter.[7]

Jefferson had little faith in the committee set up to seek an agreed solution to the problem, but on 20 May – fifteen days after the session had opened – he saw the glimmerings of a way out of the impasse:

Another hypothesis ... is that ... the *Tiers* will invite the other two Orders to come and take their seats in the Common chamber. A majority of the clergy will come, and a minority of the nobles. The chamber thus composed will declare that the States General are now constituted, will notify it to the king and propose to do business.

I think that in the end the nobles will be obliged to yield to the vote by persons, because the *Tiers* are more unanimous, more inflexible, and more formidable.[8]

Meanwhile, this impasse was having serious repercussions for the government, particularly in terms of its effect on public opinion in Paris:

It is scarcely possible to give ... an adequate idea of the confusion that prevails at present at Versailles owing to the dissentions, hitherto fruitlessly, carried on by the several Orders.... In the meantime the public is dissatisfied and becoming very impatient of delay occasioned by the disunion of the Orders at a time when the nation has flattered itself that some salutary measures would have been adopted.

More troops were moved into Paris, perhaps to stave off the public disorders which could be expected if the worst possible outcome came to pass: 'It is not easy to foresee how these difficulties will terminate ... the dismission of the States General appears to be inevitable.'[9]

Arthur Young's Assessment of the Political Situation

Arthur Young had arrived in Paris on 8 June 1789, and immediately set about acquainting himself with the mood of the capital. His reports have the strength of emanating from Paris at a time when the diplomatic correspondents were spending most of their time in Versailles: 'Paris is at present in such ferment about the States General ... that conversation is absolutely absorbed by them.'

Young then described the dispute between the Orders, continuing

> Those who are warm for the interest of the people declare that it will be impossible to reform some of the grossest abuses in the state, if the nobility, by sitting in a separate chamber, shall have a negative on the wishes of the people, and that to give such a veto to the clergy would be still more preposterous.... The most prominent feature that appears at present is, that an idea of common interest and common danger does not seem to unite those, who, if not united, may find themselves too weak to oppose the common danger that must arise from the people being sensible of a strength the result of *their* weakness.The king, court, nobility, clergy, army, and *Parlement* are nearly in the same situation. All these consider, with equal dread, the ideas of liberty now afloat; except the first, who, for reasons obvious to those who know his character, troubles himself little, even with circumstances that concern his power the most immediately. Among the rest, the feeling of danger is common, and they would unite, were there a head to render it easy, in order to do without the States at all.... the Commons themselves look for some such hostile union.

Young took a particular interest in the press:

> The business going forward at present in the pamphlet shops of Paris is incredible. I went to the Palais-Royal to see what new things were published. ... Every hour produces something new. Thirteen came out today, sixteen yesterday, and ninety-two last week.... Nineteen-twentieths of these productions are in favour of liberty, and commonly violent against the clergy and nobility.... It is easy to conceive the spirit that must thus be raised among the people.... I am all amazement at the ministry permitting such hotbeds of sedition and revolt.[10]

Agitation for the Creation of a National Assembly

Two steps were needed to break the deadlock preventing the creation of a single-chamber national assembly. The first was the Third deputies' declaration that they were the voice of the nation and constituted in themselves a national assembly which deputies of the other Orders were invited to join (as Jefferson had predicted), and the second was the substantial defection of clerical deputies to the Third.

With hindsight, the historically significant decision was taken by the Third deputies on 10 June, but for the commentators at Versailles this day's events were just some among many in a confused jumble. On 11 June the British embassy was still speculating on the possible consequences of such a step, should it be taken in the future: 'it is therefore the intention of the *Tiers Etat* ... in the course of a few days to constitute themselves ... as representatives of the nation, and qualified to act as such independent of the other Orders.... [This] extraordinary resolution [will] be productive of infinite confusion and insurmountable embarrassment to ministers'.[11]

Young, however, viewing it from Paris, had no difficulty in assessing its importance:

Yesterday [i.e. 10 June] the abbé Sieyès made a motion in the House of Commons, to declare boldly to the privileged Orders, that if they will not join the Commons, the latter will proceed in the national business without them; and the house decreed it with a small amendment. This causes much conversation on what will be the consequence of such a proceeding.... In these most interesting discussions, I find a general ignorance of the principles of government; a strange and unaccountable appeal, on the one side, to ideal and visionary rights of nature; and, on the other, no settled plan that shall give security to the people.... But the nobility, with the principles of great lords that I converse with, are most disgustingly tenacious of all old rights, however hard they may bear on the people; they will not hear of giving way in the least to the spirit of liberty.... The popular party, on the other hand, seem to consider all liberty as depending on the privileged classes being lost.... I am always told, that the first object must be for the people to get the power of doing good; and that it is no argument against such a conduct to urge that an ill use may be made of it.[12]

The attempt to give reality to the declaration of a national assembly seemed, at first, to be a damp squib: 'a few of the lower clergy appeared amongst them, but have since retired to their own Order ... violent language was held against the clergy and nobility'.[13]

Jefferson waited a few days to obtain a clearer picture, and then described the events of the past week and predicted their likely outcome.

The clergy have as yet given no answer. The nobility adhered to their former resolutions [to remain a separate chamber]. An intrigue was set on foot between the leaders of the majority in that house, the queen and princes [to preserve the nobility as a separate chamber]. The Commons

having verified their powers, a motion was made the day before yesterday
to declare themselves constituted and to proceed to business. I left them
at two o'clock yesterday, the debates not then finished.... Their next
move I fancy will be to suppress all taxes, and instantly reestablish them
till the end of their session in order to prevent a premature dissolution:
and then they will go to work on a Declaration of Rights and a constitution.[14]

Morris had met Talleyrand, the bishop of Autun who led the clergy in their
defection to the Third, on 6 June, and found him 'a sly, cunning, ambitious,
and malicious man'. Morris reported on the clergy's defection and its consequences, and was, for once, in agreement with Jefferson:

The clergy have this day by a small majority determined to join the *Tiers*.
This stroke is fatal to the *noblesse,* for the *Tiers* having already constituted
themselves the National Assembly as representing 96 per cent of the
nation, they will now have the claim to be a majority of Orders as well
as heads. Unless the royal authority will be imposed to save the nobles,
they are gone.[15]

Inertia of the Government
Throughout the period of the disputes between the Orders, leading to the
declaration of the National Assembly, the government remained 'supine',[16]
and exercised no discernible influence on events beyond the rumours of
Marie-Antoinette's supposed meddling. The ministry had, in retrospect,
irrevocably lost the initiative to the Third – and to those in the other Orders
seeking a national assembly – as soon as it had failed to railroad its business
through in early May. Young wrote: 'Everyone agrees that there is no ministry
... everything is in confusion.'[17]

On 28 May the British embassy had pinpointed the reason for this inertia.
There was no provision for government ministers to sit in, let alone speak at,
the States-General either separately in their Orders or collectively. The type
of communication (or control) a British ministry could establish in the Houses
of Parliament with the Members was wholly lacking from the constitution of
the States-General. By 11 June the embassy realized that the government
could only control the Third through 'violent measures'. A week later
the army was thrown into the political scales, with the prediction that they
would support the king if he stood firm on behalf of the nobility and their
privileges.[18]

Young's Report on the States-General

Young finally went out to Versailles on 15 June and attended a session of
the States-General. His skills as a parliamentary correspondent stood him in
good stead, and his description of the chamber and the detail of proceedings
was the first of many during the course of the Revolution. He captures
the atmosphere in the chamber throughout the period, whether the
assembly was the States-General in Versailles or the National Convention in
Paris:

> at Versailles by eight in the morning. We went immediately to the hall
> of the States to secure good seats in the gallery; we found some deputies
> already there, and a pretty numerous audience collected. The room is
> too large: none but stentorial lungs, or the finest clearest voices can be
> heard; however the very size of the apartment, which admits 2,000
> people, gave a dignity to the scene. It was indeed an interesting one. The
> spectacle of the representatives of twenty-five millions of people, just
> emerging from the evils of 200 years of arbitrary power, and rising to
> the blessings of a freer constitution, assembled with open doors under
> the eye of the public, was framed to call into animated feelings every
> latent spark, every emotion of a liberal bosom; to banish whatever ideas
> might intrude of their being a people too often hostile to my own country,
> and to dwell with pleasure on the glorious idea of happiness to a great
> nation; of felicity to millions yet unborn. M. l'abbé Sieyès opened the
> debate. He is one of the most zealous sticklers for the popular cause;
> carries his ideas not to a regulation of the present government, which
> he thinks too bad to be regulated at all, but wishes to see it absolutely
> overturned; being in fact a violent republican.... M. de Mirabeau spoke
> without notes, for nearly an hour, with a warmth, animation, and
> eloquence, that entitles him to the reputation of an undoubted orator....
> M. Barnave, a very young man, from Grenoble, spoke without notes
> with great warmth and animation.
>
> In regard to their general method of proceeding, there are two cir-
> cumstances in which they are very deficient; the spectators in the gal-
> leries are allowed to interfere in the debates by clapping their hands, and
> other noisy expressions of approbation. This is grossly indecent; it is also
> dangerous; for, if they are permitted to express approbation, they are, by
> parity of reason, allowed expressions of dissent; and they may hiss as
> well as clap; which it is said, they have sometimes done:– this would
> be, to overrule the debate and influence the deliberations. Another
> circumstance, is the want of order among themselves; more than once
> today there were an hundred members on their legs at a time, and M.

Bailly absolutely without power to keep order. This arises very much from complex motions being admitted.[19]

Death of the Dauphin and Oath of the Tennis Court

On 4 June the dauphin's condition deteriorated so much that the arrangements for the court to go into mourning were put in hand. He died later that day.[20]

In any other circumstances such an event would have brought all public affairs to a halt, but it seems to have passed almost unnoticed against the backdrop of the constitutional crisis in the States-General. It did, though, create an atmosphere of confusion at Versailles itself, to the point where it has been alleged that the locking of the States-General meeting hall on 20 June was a part of the funeral arrangements. Morris and Lord Dorset, however, were both quite clear that the chamber had been locked on specific royal instructions as the first step in a belated move to regain the political initiative, restore royal authority, and knock heads together in a session deliberately postponed from 20 to 22 June. The mechanism to be used would be a *séance royale* whereby the king could state his position personally, in the theory that any political opposition would constitute the unthinkable crime of *lèse-majesté*. This initiative was being taken to halt 'the progress the *Tiers Etat* have made towards effecting a complete revolution in this empire'.[21]

Jefferson picked up his narrative of events on 19 June with the formulation of the government's strategy:

> On the 19th a Council was held at Marly in the afternoon. It was there proposed that the king should interpose by a declaration of his sentiments in a *séance royale*. The declaration prepared by M. Necker, while it censured in general the proceedings both of the Nobles and Commons, announced the king's views such as substantially to coincide with the Commons. It was agreed to in Council, as also that the *séance royale* should be held on the 22nd and the meetings till then be suspended. These proceedings ... were kept secret from everybody.[22]

The secrecy was to prove a fatal flaw to the strategy, as it predisposed the Third deputies to fear that any government proposals would be detrimental to them and because it led to the very provocative circumstances of the Third deputies' first discovery that the government had decided to flex its muscles:

> The next morning, (the 20th) the members repaired to the House as usual, found the doors shut and guarded, and a proclamation posted up for holding a *séance royale* on the 22nd and a suspension of their meetings till then. They presumed in the first moment that their dissolution was decided, and repaired to another place where they proceeded to business.

They there bound themselves to each other by an oath never to separate of their own accord till they had settled a constitution for the nation on a solid basis, and if separated by force, that they would reassemble in some other place.[23]

Jefferson's 'another place' was, of course, the royal tennis court. The proof that the government was taking concerted action was given by the British embassy who, after reporting that the news of the lock-out had caused 'consternation' and 'marked anxiety' in Paris, précised the orders given to the *Intendant* of Paris: 'It is essential ... that you assure everyone in Paris that His Majesty continues to work at restoring unity and peace for the happiness of his people and that the sessions will resume'.[24]

Young described the episode in detail, and called the lock-out an 'ill-judged act of violence'. He analysed the Oath of the Tennis Court and its implications by analogy with British parliamentary history:

The step the Commons have taken of declaring themselves the National Assembly ... is in fact an assumption of all the authority in the kingdom. They have at one stroke converted themselves into the Long Parliament of Charles I. It needs not the assistance of much penetration to see that if such a pretension and declaration are done away, king, lords, and clergy are deprived of their shares in the legislature of France. So bold, and apparently desperate a step, full in the teeth of every other interest in the realm, equally destructive of the royal authority, by *parlements* and the army, can never be allowed. If it is not opposed, all other powers will lie in ruins around that of the Commons. With what anxious expectation must one therefore wait to see if the crown will exert itself firmly on the occasion, with such an attention to an improved system of liberty, as is absolutely necessary to the moment! All things considered, that is, the characters of those who are in possession of power, no well-digested system and steady execution are to be looked for.[25]

On 21 June the Third deputies,

met in a church, and were joined by the majority of the clergy. The heads of the aristocracy, that is to say *the queen, Count d'Artois and Prince de Condé* saw that all was lost without some violent exertion. The king was still at Marly. No body was permitted to approach him but their friends. He was assailed by lies in all shapes. He was made to believe that the Commons were going to absolve the army from their oath of fidelity to him and to raise their pay. *The queen abandoned herself to rage and despair.*[26]

The session of the States-General scheduled for 22 June was further delayed (because of dissentions between those counselling the king) to 23 June. Young had made a special effort to attend on 22 June, and was personally inconvenienced by Louis xvi's actions. He made the best of his trip to Versailles, though, and: 'To the ... church of St Louis ... and were in time to see M. Bailly take the chair, and read the king's letter, putting off the session till tomorrow. The spectacle of this meeting was singular; the crowd that attended in and around the church was great; and the anxiety and suspense in every eye.'[27]

Young returned to Versailles on 23 June to watch the preparations for the twice postponed session:

> In the morning Versailles seemed filled with troops; the streets, about ten o'clock, were lined with the French guards, and some Swiss regiments, etc. The hall of the States was surrounded, and sentinels fixed in all the passages, and at the doors; and none but deputies admitted. This military preparation was ill-judged, for it seemed admitting the impropriety and unpopularity of the intended measure, and the expectation, perhaps fear, of popular commotions. They pronounced, before the king left the *château*, that his plan was adverse to the people, from the military parade with which it was ushered in.[28]

Jefferson described what happened at and after the session, where Louis xvi had been persuaded by his advisers at court to oppose the demand for a single-chamber national assembly:

> [At the session on 23 June Louis xvi] was about an hour in the house delivering his speech and declaration.... On his coming out, a feeble cry of *'vive le roy'* was raised by some children, but the people remained silent and sullen. When the Duc d'Orléans followed however their applauses were excessive.... He had ordered in the close of his speech that the members should follow him, and resume their deliberations the next day. The *noblesse* followed him, and so did the clergy, except about 30 who, with the *Tiers*, remained in the room and entered into deliberation. They protested against what the king had done, adhered to all their former proceedings, and resolved the inviolability of their own persons. An officer came twice to order them out of the room in the king's name, but they refused to obey. In the afternoon the people, uneasy, began to assemble in great numbers.[29]

In retrospect the *séance* can be seen as having great constitutional significance. The concessions made by Louis xvi would have created a limited monarchy legitimized by the king's consent. Louis himself remained prepared to honour them throughout the Revolution. In practice the commentators noted the *séance*'s effect on the pretensions of the Third and on the mood of the capital.

The failure of the attempt to cow the Third deputies, led Morris to make a grim prediction: 'as the king is extremely timid, he will of course surrender at discretion. The existence of the monarchy therefore depends on the moderation of the assembly.'[30]

Young, back in Paris, reported the mood of the capital on receiving the news of the day's events:

> The ferment at Paris is beyond conception; 10,000 people have been all this day (24 June) in the Palais-Royal; a full detail of yesterday's proceedings was brought this morning, and read by many apparent leaders of little parties, with comments, to the people. To my surprise the king's propositions are received with universal disgust ... the people seem, with a sort of frenzy, to reject all idea of compromise, and to insist on the necessity of the Orders uniting.[31]

Jefferson commented in similar terms, adding: 'As soon as the proceedings at Versailles were known in Paris, a run began on the *caisse d'escompte*, which is the first symptom always of the public diffidence and alarm.'[32]

On 24 June Jefferson recorded: 'nothing remarkable past except an attack by the mob at Versailles on the archbishop of Paris'.[33]

Young took a more serious view of this attack and its implications:

> Yesterday at Versailles the mob was violent; they insulted, and even attacked all the clergy and nobility that are known to be strenuous for preserving the separation of Orders.... The confusion is so great, that the court have only the troops to depend on; and it is now said confidently, that if an order is given to the French guards to fire on the people, they will refuse obedience.[34]

On 25 June Jefferson reported:

> forty-eight of the nobles have joined the *Tiers*. Among these is the Duke d'Orléans.... There are with the *Tiers* now 164 members of the clergy, so that the Common chamber consists of upwards of 800 members.... I found the streets of Versailles much embarrassed with soldiers.... Instead of being dismayed with what has passed [the Third deputies] seem to raise their demands, and some of them to consider the erasing [of] every vestige of a difference of Order indispensable to the establishment and preservation of a good constitution. I apprehend there is more courage than calculation in this project.[35]

Young commented on this development: 'The conduct of the court is inexplicable, and without plan; ... and, what is equally a proof of the unsteadiness of the court, the Commons are in the common hall of the States, contrary to the express command of the king.'[36]

The heightening of political tension, the increasing radicalization of popular demands on behalf of the Third deputies, and the government's unwillingness to give force to its desire to exert its authority were noted by Arthur Young on 26 June:

Every hour that passes seems to give the people fresh spirit: the meetings at the Palais-Royal are more numerous, more violent, and more assured; and in the assembly of electors, at Paris, for sending a deputation to the National Assembly, the language that was talked, by all ranks of people, was nothing less than a revolution in the government, and the establishment of a free constitution. What they mean by a free constitution is easily understood – *a republic*; for the doctrine of the times runs every day more and more to that point; yet they profess, that the kingdom ought to be a monarchy too; or, at least, that there ought to be a king. In the streets one is stunned by the hawkers of seditious pamphlets, and descriptions of pretended events, that all tend to keep the people equally ignorant and alarmed. The supineness and even stupidity of the court is without example; the moment demands the greatest decision, and yesterday, while it was actually a question whether he should be a doge of Venice or a king of France, the king went a hunting! ... It is now understood by everybody, that the king's offers in the *séance royale*, are out of the question. The moment the Commons found a relaxation, even in the trifling point of assembling in the great hall, they disregarded all the rest, and considered the whole as null, and not to be taken notice of, unless enforced in a manner of which there were no signs.[37]

The Crisis Breaks: Recognition of the National Assembly
On 27 June the crisis broke. The remainder of the noble and clerical deputies joined the Third and the National Assembly had been created *de facto*. From this moment the government could no longer procrastinate nor hope to reverse the collapse of the customary constitution of the States-General. Jefferson's prediction had been borne out. The importance of the transition from States-General to National Assembly cannot be exaggerated. It dispensed, at the highest political level, with the juridical Orders of society, and presaged the elimination of privilege and social distinction. In immediate procedural terms it removed the privileged Orders' in-built majority. For the longer term it moved the focus of attention away from the monarchy's fiscal problems as the assembly's most important agenda item and towards the need to draw up a written constitution to regularize the new order.

The government accepted the *fait accompli*, and now – nearly two months after the States-General had first met – it had a body with which it could transact business. It seemed to those observing events that the crisis which had started in August of the previous year was, to all intents and purposes, over. Jefferson rashly informed his Secretary of State on 29 June: 'This great crisis being now over, I shall not have matter interesting enough to trouble you with as often as I have done lately.'[38]

On 26 June Young had been fearful of 'confusion, and even civil commotion' because of the crisis, and had determined to leave Paris for his own safety. On 27 June he felt he was right to be leaving, but for the opposite reason:

> The whole business now seems over, and the revolution complete. The king has been frightened by the mobs into overturning his own act of the *séance royale*, by writing to the presidents of the Orders of the nobility and clergy, requiring them to join the Commons, full in the teeth of what he had ordained before. [Because of] this step ... he will never know more where to stop, or what to refuse; or rather he will find, that in the future arrangement of the kingdom, his situation will be very nearly that of Charles I; a spectator, without power.... The joy this step occasioned was infinite.

> At all events however, the tide now runs so strongly in favour of the people, and the conduct of the court seems to be so weak, divided, and blind, that little can happen that will not clearly date from the present moment.

> At night the fireworks, and illuminations, and mob, and noise, at the Palais-Royal increased; the expense must be enormous; and yet nobody knows with certainty from whence it arises.... There is no doubt of it being the Duc d'Orléans's money; the people are thus kept in a continual ferment, are for ever assembled, and ready to be in the last degree of commotion whenever called on by the men they have confidence in. Lately a company of Swiss would have crushed all this; but, let it last a fortnight longer, and an army will be wanting.

> I shall leave Paris, however, truly rejoiced that the representatives of the people have it undoubtedly in their power so to improve the constitution of their country, as to render all great abuses in future, if not impossible, at least exceedingly difficult, and consequently will establish to all useful purposes an undoubted political liberty; and if they effect this, it cannot be doubted but that they will have a thousand opportunities to secure to their fellow-subjects the invaluable blessing of civil liberty also. The state of the finances is such, that the government may easily be kept virtually dependent on the States, and their periodical existence absolutely secured. Such benefits will confer happiness on 25 millions of people.[39]

The British embassy was less enthusiastic, but still spoke of 'a complete revolution ... in this powerful and extensive kingdom without recourse being had to violence'.[40]

The embassy was concerned about the royal family, who were 'no longer secure from outrage even in the Palace'.

The nobility were also only prepared to go along with the National Assembly, 'when it was seen that the king's personal safety was actually endangered.... Nothing can equal the despondency of the nobility ... forced as they have been ... to sacrifice in one moment every hope they had formed.'[41]

Like Young, Huber's enthusiasm for the 'revolution' was tempered by his disquiet over the power which had been exercised by the crowd: 'Paris is in an alarming state of agitation. The novelty of the situation has turned the brains of the people; each thinks himself a Brutus, and sees a Caesar in each noble.'[42]

Public Order

While the constitutional crisis was being played out at Versailles, a crisis of a very different kind, but equally alarming to the monarchy, was developing in the countryside. The peasantry were starting a national, if uncoordinated, revolt.

On 4 June the British embassy had added, almost as an afterthought to reports of a good harvest in prospect: 'yet a report prevailed yesterday that ... at Lagny the peasants had assembled and destroyed great quantities of standing corn'.

On 18 June news was filtering through of a grain convoy from America being late and of famine taking hold in some provinces. The countryside around Versailles was becoming unsafe, and this was linked to wider peasant grievances: 'The peasants [around Versailles] have committed great outrages in the king's forests in defiance of the game keepers ... one of whom was shockingly butchered a few evenings since.'

The king and queen had had to return to Versailles for fear of being attacked themselves.[43]

Young linked the course of this peasant unrest with the course of the constitutional crisis. One of the reasons why Louis XVI had acceded to the demand for a National Assembly was that:

It was represented to him, that the want of bread was so great in every part of the kingdom, that there was no extremity to which the people might not be driven; that they were nearly starving, and consequently ready to listen to any suggestions, and on the *qui vive* for all sorts of mischief; that Paris and Versailles would inevitably be burnt; and in a

word, that all sorts of misery and confusion would follow his adherence
to the system announced in the *séance royale.*[44]

On 2 July the British embassy reported that 'disturbances' were continuing,
that around Loudon the authorities had confiscated all civilian firearms, and
that the unemployed in Paris had been drafted into road building, 'in order
to draw them off from joining in the disaffection which is industriously
encouraged in the capital'.

The corn which had been stockpiled in Paris was being sent back to the
provinces. This was having a disastrous effect: 'The scarcity of bread grows
every day more alarming....'[45]

Necker's Position and Dismissal

The government from 5 May to 13 July 1789 had made no impression on
events other than to exacerbate them and provoke trials of strength, from
which they backed down. The leading minister was, of course, Necker.
His role was pivotal, but his position ambiguous. Louis XVI found he was
encumbered by a minister who inspired almost Messianic confidence in the
public at large but whose parliamentary skills were nil. Louis could not run
the administration of the realm without him and he could not manage the
court or the States-General with him.

On 13 June Young reported the precariousness of Necker's position *vis-à-
vis* the court, and the opinion being formed of him by those holding out
against the creation of a National Assembly:

> It is said that M. Necker is alarmed for his power, and anecdote reports
> things to his disadvantage ... that, as the Count d'Artois, Mme de
> Polignac, and a few others were, but two days ago, walking in the private
> garden of Versailles, they met [Madame de Staël], and descended even
> to hissing her; if half this is true, it is plain enough that this minister
> must speedily retire. All who adhere to the ancient constitution, or rather
> government, consider him as their mortal enemy; they assert, and truly,
> that he came in under circumstances that would have enabled him to
> do everything he pleased; he had king and kingdom at command; but
> that errors he was guilty of, for want of some settled plan, have been the
> cause of all dilemmas experienced since. They ... assert that his letting
> the king go to the States General, before their powers were verified, and
> the necessary steps taken to keep the Orders separate, after giving double
> the representation to the *Tiers* to that of the other two Orders, was
> madness; that he ought to have appointed commissaries to have received
> the verification before admittance. They accuse him further of having
> done all this through an excessive and insufferable vanity, which gave

him the idea of guiding the deliberation of the States by his knowledge and reputation.[46]

On 19 June Jefferson passed on an equally unflattering character sketch, and made a pessimistic forecast of Necker's political future:

It is a tremendous cloud indeed which hovers over this nation, and he at the helm has neither the courage nor the skill necessary to weather it. Eloquence in a high degree, knowledge on matters of account, and order, are distinguishing traits in his character. Ambition is his first passion, virtue his second.... His judgement is not of the first order, scarcely even of the second, his resolution frail, and upon the whole it is rare to meet an instance of a person so much below the reputation he has obtained.... If the *Tiers* separate, he goes at the same time: if they stay together and succeed in establishing a constitution to their mind, as soon as that is placed in safety, they will abandon him to the mercy of the court, unless he can recover the confidence which he has lost at present, and which indeed seems to be irrecoverable.[47]

On 24 June Young heard that Necker had made an offer to resign, bowing to pressure from the court (i.e. specifically Marie-Antoinette, the Comte d'Artois, and the Princes of the Blood other than the Duc d'Orléans). Young, however, cast this offer in the light of the national financial situation:

But the stumbling-block to this and every plan that can be devised, as the people know and declare in every corner, is the situation of the finances, which cannot possibly be restored but by liberal grants of the States, on one hand, or by a bankruptcy on the other. It is well known, that this point has been warmly debated in the Council. M. Necker has proved to them, that a bankruptcy is inevitable, if they break with the States before the finances are restored; and the dread and terror of taking such a step, which no minister would at present dare to venture on, has been the great difficulty that opposed itself to the projects of the queen and the Count d'Artois. The measure they have taken is a middle one, from which they hope to gain a party among the people, and render the deputies unpopular enough to get rid of them; an expectation, however, in which they will infallibly be mistaken.[48]

The next day Young continued, in a very critical mood:

The criticisms that are made on M. Necker's conduct, even by his friends, ... are severe. It is positively asserted, that abbé Sieyès, Messieurs Mounier, Chapelier, Barnave, Target, Tourette, Rabaut, and other leaders, were almost on their knees to him, to insist peremptorily on his

resignation being accepted, as they were well convinced that his retreat
would throw the queen's party into infinitely greater difficulties and
embarassment than any other circumstance. But his vanity prevailed
over all their efforts, to listen to the insidious persuasions of the queen,
who spoke to him in the style of asking a request that would keep the
crown on the king's head; at the same time he yielded to do it, contrary
to the interests of the friends of liberty, he courted the huzzas of the mob
of Versailles, in a manner that did much mischief. The ministers never
go to and from the king's appartment on foot, across the court, which
M. Necker took this opportunity of doing, though he himself had not
done it in quiet times, in order to court the flattery of being called the
father of the people, and moving with an immense and shouting multitude at his heels.[49]

In fairness to Necker, the British embassy report of the same scene reads
as if Necker's presence alone calmed an already gathered mob and defused a
dangerous situation. The moral of both versions, though, was the same –
Necker could command the loyalty and power of the crowd, and the king
had better heed it.[50]

There had been no love lost between Necker and all those at court with
the right to informal access to the king – despite the contradictory indications
of Marie-Antoinette's attitude to Necker's resigning. Louis XVI was content
to let this hostility smoulder until July, when he came down against Necker
and dismissed him on 11 July. What may have laid the groundwork for this
was a dispute between Necker and the army on its use as a police force; he
was thought to have expressed 'uneasiness at the appearance of so large an
army [in and around Paris and Versailles]'.[51]

The news of Necker's dismissal was received with even more hostility
in Paris than the government had feared: 'Paris is in the utmost confusion
and ... full of troops, but notwithstanding every possible precaution is
taken to prevent disorder, it will be very difficult to check the frenzy of the
mob.'[52]

Jefferson reported on 12 July: 'M. Necker was dismissed from office on the
evening of the 11th and set out for Geneva.... The mobs immediately shut
up all the playhouses. The foreign troops were advanced into the city. Engagements took place between some of them and the people.'

This episode had culminated with German cavalry charging a crowd in
the Place Louis XV.[53]

Morris gave an even more vivid account ending with a prediction of more
trouble to come:

Much alarm here. Paris begins to be in commotion....

The people are employed in breaking open the armourers' shops, and presently a large body of the *Gardes Françaises* appear, with bayonets fixed, in the garden, mingled with the mob, some of whom are also armed. These poor fellows have passed the Rubicon....

If the representatives of the *Tiers* have formed a just estimate of their constituents, in ten days all France will be in a commotion.[54]

The government could only wait to see if this new storm would blow itself out.

CHAPTER 5

The Fall of the Bastille
and the Burning of the Châteaux
(July (to September) 1789)

'The intrepid champions of twenty-five millions of people'

THE government had hoped that the disturbances in Paris in early July were only minor footnotes to Necker's dismissal and the setting up of the National Assembly. Arthur Young, sharing this belief, had packed his bags and set off for Alsace (travelling so fast that he kept ahead of the news from Paris until 19 July).

Morris passed on this interpretation of events a seen from Versailles: 'the fashion at court is to believe that the disturbances at Paris are very trifling'. His own concern on the evening of 13 July was to be seen wearing the appropriate cockade to please the crowds roaming the streets: 'after dinner go to the Louvre, having previously ornamented my hat with a green bow in honour of the *Tiers*, for this is the fashion of the day, which everybody is obliged to comply with who means to march in peace'.[1]

Like Morris, Huber felt that the focus of attention remained firmly in Versailles, and could write on 14 July:

> Twenty-four hours have made a total change – a mixture of *Gardes Françaises* and *Gardes Bourgeoises* have patrolled and guarded Paris; ... this excellent conduct will strengthen and facilitate that of the States General, who behave like Romans; words could not do them justice ... intrepid champions of twenty-five millions of people.[2]

Jefferson was also concentrating on Versailles, but his comments to Tom Paine on 11 July foreshadow a revolution driven by public ferment,

> The National Assembly ... having shewn thro' every stage ... a coolness, wisdom, and resolution to set fire to the four corners of the kingdom and to perish with it themselves rather than to relinquish an iota from their plan of a total change of government, are now in complete and undisputed possession of sovereignty. The executive and the aristocracy are now at their feet: the mass of the nation, the mass of the clergy, and the army are with them. They have prostrated the old government, and are now beginning to build one from the foundation.[3]

Continuing Public Unrest

The riots at Necker's dismissal marked, in fact, a significant quickening of the pace of growing popular unrest. Morris has already been quoted to the effect that crowds would set on passers-by not wearing the colours of the Third Estate, but into this atmosphere of political violence came the peasant and – a term still to be penned – *sans-culotte* disturbances over shortages and high prices of food. Some members of the National Assembly were suspected of rabble-rousing, and the Palais-Royal was notorious as a focus for anti-government publishers and orators, who enjoyed effective immunity from the police there.

Despite his general optimism about the political scene, Huber was all too well aware of the breakdown of public order on the streets. On 12 July several of his own friends had almost been killed by either the foreign troops trying to restore order, who had fired on and charged crowds, or by the mobs of 'poor deluded Parisians' and French troops who had mutinied. He was with Necker, his wife and daughter, the archbishop of Bordeaux (one of the liberal bishops), and others when this news arrived. He wrote to Eden, 'We are all going out of Paris till the darkness is cleared up', adding that they would be taking their gold and silver with them.[4]

On 12 July the British embassy had reported: 'Paris is in the utmost confusion ... full of troops. Almost every day produced some act of violence.'

As well as the extra troops being drafted into the Ile de France, Paris and Versailles had effectively been cordoned off from the rest of the country, and food supplies were not passing through the local customs barriers.[5]

Unreliability of the Army

For the government the most worrying feature of the public order crisis was the unreliability – and even outright mutiny – on the part of some regiments. The *Gardes Françaises* had refused to patrol Paris, fire on crowds, or take orders which they felt might put them in opposition to the civilian population. Some of them deserted – with their weapons – and were prepared to fight against the regiments brought in to replace them.

As Jefferson put it: 'Paris and Versailles were thrown into tumult and riot [by the creation of the National Assembly]. The soldiers in and about them, including even the king's own life guard, declared themselves openly for the Commons, the accounts from the soldiery in the provinces was not more favorable.'[6]

The military commander of the province of the Ile de France, the Duc de Broglie, took the two obvious steps of withdrawing suspect units and bringing in more reliable ones over the first two weeks of July. He also separated out loyal troops into armed camps and allowed no fraternization with civilians or other regiments. Three factors heightened tension. The first was that the loyal troops tended to be Swiss or German – in other words foreigners who, quite incidentally, spoke the same language as the queen but often did not speak any French. The second was an order given by the War Ministry, who enjoyed some specific jurisdictions within Paris, to make ready the weapons in the armouries under its control (the Arsénal and Invalides). The third was a rumour that once the harvest was in, a great many more troops would be released from elsewhere in the country to police the Ile de France.[7]

To these sober facts Morris added one of the rumours prevalent in Paris on the eve of the storming of the Bastille, that Marie-Antoinette, the Comte d'Artois, the Duc de Polignac and two loyal regiments would 'reduce Paris to famine, and take two hundred of the National Assembly prisoners'.[8]

Jefferson described the military build-up and the army's disaffection to Tom Paine:

> It was discovered at length that great bodies of troops and principally of the foreign corps were approaching Paris from different quarters. They arrived in the number of 25,000 or 30,000 men. Great inquietude took place, and [on 9 July] the Assembly voted an address to the king for an explanation of this phenomenon and removal of the troops. His answer has not been given formally, but he verbally authorised their president to declare that these troops had nothing in view but the quiet of the capital; and that being once established they should be removed. The fact is that the king never saw anything else in this measure; (but those who advised him to it, assuredly meant by the presence of the troops to give him confidence, and to take advantage of some favorable moment to surprize some act of authority from him. For this purpose they had got the military command with the Ile de France transferred to the Marshall de Broglie, a high flying aristocrat, cool and capable of every mischief). But it turns out that these troops shew strong symptoms of being entirely with the people, so that nothing is apprehended from them.[9]

The Storming of the Bastille and the Events Leading up to it

Jefferson has already mentioned the National Assembly's request for troops to be withdrawn from Paris, the British embassy elaborated in their report that the resolution had carried an implicit threat that the Assembly might move itself to another location – Orléans, Blois or even Paris itself. This would force Louis xvi to chose whether to base his authority on the Assembly or the army.[10] As has been seen, the army may well not have possessed the military capacity to occupy and pacify Paris against the kind of opposition experienced on 12 July, without more reliable troops. As a result, in apparent compliance with the National Assembly's request, troops were withdrawn from Paris on 13 July. The British embassy thought the actual immediate motive was to reduce bloodshed, but the effect was that 'the populace remained unmolested masters of everything: much to their credit, however, uncontrolled as they now were, no material mischief was done (except for attacks on customs barmen)'.[11]

(Note: The 'populace' in this context has to be taken to include the bourgeois militia, which had been organized from scratch under the aegis of the Parisian Third electoral colleges (in turn based on the old parishes) on 13 July and was a credible police force by the end of the same day.)

On Monday, 13 July, the crowds seized the corn stockpiled at the Arsénal, and on the morning of Tuesday, 14 July, they seized the weapons which had been made ready for use against them at the Arsénal and Invalides. The British embassy had no hesitation in pointing out where the blame for all this lay: 'the general revolt, with the extraordinary circumstances attending it, . . . has been the immediate consequence of [Necker's dismissal]'.[12]

The British embassy was in a unique position to report on the storming of the Bastille itself as two of their servants had taken part in it, and the account set out below is probably theirs, at second hand (smuggled out of Paris on foot on 16 July): 'two of my servants . . . were compelled to go to [the Invalides] where they received two very good muskets'. The servants recounted going with the crowd to the Bastille, where it seemed all might pass off peacefully until

> the Marquis de Launey contrary to all precedent fired upon the people and killed several: this proceeding so enraged the populace that they rushed to the very gates with a determination to force their way through if possible: upon this the governor agreed to let in a certain number of them on condition that they should not commit any violence: these terms being acceded to, a detachment of about 40 in number advanced and were admitted, but the draw-bridge was immediately drawn up again and the whole party instantly massacred: this breach of honour aggravated by so glaring an act of inhumanity excited a spirit of revenge and tumult such as might naturally be expected.[13]

The servants then described the seizure of the fortress, the liberation of its prisoners, and the wild rejoicings in the capital. The real significance of this account, from the crowd's perspective, is that it places the blame squarely on the shoulders of de Launey and exonerates the conduct of the crowd. The ambassador's immediate reaction to the event confirms this generous and anti-government account and, coming from a British aristocrat holding a position in government, is one of the most extraordinary testimonials to come out of the Revolution. Speaking of events during 14–16 July, subsequent to the fall of the Bastille, he wrote:

Nothing could exceed the regularity and good order with which all this extraordinary business has been conducted: of this I have myself [had experience] upon several occasions during the last three days as I have passed through the streets, nor had I at any moment reason to be alarmed for my personal safety.

The regularity and determined conduct of the population ... exceeds all belief.

The greatest Revolution that we know anything of ... the king a very limited monarch, and the nobility ... reduced to a level with the rest of the nation.[14]

Huber took a very similar view. The villains of the piece were the Comte d'Artois and the Duke and Duchess de Polignac: 'the whole infernal set which has been working at the ruin of the kingdom', and because of whom, 'Paris positively expected to be stormed [by foreign troops]'. The crowd on 14 July, by contrast, 'marched in the greatest order, [and] committed no fault' and, 'that frivolous people of Paris turned at once into a people of heroes, achieving in twenty-four hours what imagination itself cannot encompass'.[15]

Quickly, though, the generosity of the euphoric Revolutionaries was tempered by the realization that their old enemies were still potent:

The disposition of the people at this moment is so unfavourable to the court that I should not be surprised if the States General, by appearing to give too much credit to the king's professions, should lose the consideration in which they have hitherto been held by the nation.

... the execration of the nobility is universal amongst the lower order of people.[16]

The Transfer of Power and Confirmation of the Revolution

To set the seal on the transfer of power from the monarchy to the people Louis XVI had to come to Paris – a 'surrender' as Jefferson termed it. Louis XVI duly travelled to Paris on 17 July 1789, and Jefferson reported the event from the time the government lost control of Paris:

[On 13 July] the people of Paris forced the prisons of St Lazare, where they got some arms. On the 14th they took the Invalides, and Bastille, and beheaded the governor and lieutenant governor of the latter and the *Prévost des Marchands*. The city committee is determined to embody 48,000 bourgeois and named the Marquis de Lafayette commander-in-chief. The king hereupon went to the States General, and surrendered as it were at discretion and this day he and they came in solemn procession to satisfy the city.

The king came to Paris, leaving the queen in consternation for his return.... Crowds of people in the streets, doors, and windows, saluted [the procession] everywhere with cries of *'vive la nation'*. But not a single *'vive le roy'* was heard.... Bailly presented and put into [Louis XVI's] hat the popular cockade, and addressed him. The king being unprepared [was] unable to answer.[17]

The British embassy suggested why no reply had been given – Louis XVI was in a state of shock and depression, probably not helped by Huber's observation that Orléans had insisted on making sure personally that the king understood the true meaning and enormity of the events which had taken place.[18] The embassy reported that there had been cries of: *'Vive la Nation! Vive Necker! Vive les Gardes Françaises!* ... The king appeared much depressed at entering the Town'.

It was a: 'submission to the wishes of the nation'.

'The entrance of the king into Paris was certainly one of the most humiliating steps that he could possibly take.'[19]

For Morris, the king's entry into Paris was soured by two incidents. The first was when his coachman reported that all traffic had been ordered off the streets, so he would have to walk and the second was when his pocket was picked while he watched the king. He was not optimistic about Louis XVI's future. It was not until Louis had,

put in his hat a large cockade of the red and blue ribbons, and then, and not until then, received the general shouts of *'Vive le Roy!'* This day will, I think, prove a useful lesson to him for the rest of his life, but he is so weak that unless he is kept out of bad company it is impossible that he should not act wrongly.[20]

Emigrations

The king's submission to Paris (which included recognition and confirmation of the municipality's powers) provoked the first wave of emigrations led by the Comte d'Artois.

Without exception the early *émigrés* were unregretted and their departure did not make much impression on the commentators, who were far more interested in those who remained. Huber's comment about Artois and his coterie has been noted. The British embassy added that they had left 'with great secrecy' and that, in Artois' case: 'none of his servants dare to appear in his livery'. Even Morris described them as 'the whole conspiracy against freedom' and welcomed that their opposition to constitutional change had been 'blown up to the moon'.[21]

Aftermath

As after the crisis at the setting up of the National Assembly, the commentators tried to convince themselves that the upheavals were over: 'Tranquillity is now restored to the capital: the shops are again opened; the people resuming their labours.... The demolition of the Bastille is going on, and the *milice bourgeoise* organising and training.'[22] The Revolution 'may ... be looked upon as completed'. 'Tranquillity is in a great measure restored to this capital.'[23]

The main attraction in Paris itself was the work of demolishing the Bastille, which Morris inspected in detail. After looking at the masonry he declared, 'The storming of this castle was a bold enterprise.'[24]

Mob Revenge

The first indication that the Revolution might be accompanied by widespread violence was the lynching of two *ancien régime* functionaries, Foulon (or Foullon) and Bertier de Sauvigny. Jefferson reported the news of the killings as they came in:

> P.S.: I just learn that Bertier de Sauvigny was brought to town in the night last night and massacred immediately.

> M. Foulon, one of the obnoxious ministry who ... had absconded, was taken in the country, and as is said by his own tenants, was brought to Paris ... he was hung ... immediately, his head cut off, and his body drawn through the principal streets of the city.[25]

Morris added that the body had been stripped naked and the head stuck on a pike and then: 'This mutilated form of an old man of seventy is shown to Bertier, his son-in-law, the intendant of Paris, and afterwards *he* is also put to death and cut to pieces, the populace carrying about the mangled fragments with a savage joy. Gracious God! what a people!'[26]

Huber added further details which help to put the lynching into its contemporary context: 'They had his mouth stuffed with hay, remembering that twenty years ago he said, when bread was dear, and the Parisians complained, "Let those dogs eat hay".' There was also a report that 'Maréchal de Broglie is besieged in Verdun; ... the peasants surround the place, and refuse to let any provisions in until he is delivered up to them.'[27]

The point of these accounts is that each of the men concerned had held some hated position under the *ancien régime* and had then tried to emigrate. It was the latter action which provoked the mobs – whether of *sans-culottes* or of peasants – into exercising summary justice. On a serious note, Jefferson said that he hoped these lynchings would teach those who had emigrated not to return. In somewhat poor taste he quipped, 'The cutting off of heads is become so much *à la mode*, that one is apt to feel of a morning whether their own is on their shoulders.'[28]

Young's Account of the Revolution in the Eastern Provinces and the Burning of the Châteaux
The news of the fall of the Bastille finally caught up with Arthur Young in Strasbourg:

> On arriving at the inn, hear the interesting news of the revolt of Paris ... in a word, of the overthrow of the old government. Everything now being decided, and the kingdom absolutely in the hands of the Assembly, they have the power to make a new constitution, such as they think proper; and it will be a great spectacle for the world to view, in this enlightened age, the representatives of twenty-five millions of people sitting on the constitution of a new and better order and fabric of liberty, than Europe has yet offered. It will now be seen, whether they will copy the constitution of England, freed from its faults, or attempt, from theory, to frame something absolutely speculative: in the former case, they will prove a blessing to their country; in the latter they will probably involve it in inextricable confusions and civil wars ... I hear nothing of their removing from Versailles; if they stay there under the control of an armed mob they must make a government that will please the mob; but they will, I suppose, be wise enough to move to some central town, Tours, Blois, or Orléans, where their deliberations may be free. But the Parisian spirit of commotion spreads quickly; it is here; ... troops ... are employed to keep an eye on the people who show signs of an intended revolt. They have broken the windows of some magistrates that are no favourites; and a great mob of them is at this moment assembled demanding clamorously to have meat at 5 *sous* a pound. They have a cry among them that will conduct them to good lengths: *Point d'impôt et vivent les états.*[29]

On 21 July Young read as many newspapers as he could find and,

> I have had some conversation with several sensible and intelligent men on the present revolution. The spirit of revolt is gone forth into various parts of the kingdom; the price of bread has prepared the populace everywhere for all sorts of violence. At Lyons there have been commotions as furious as at Paris, and the same at a great many other places. Dauphiné is in arms; and Bretagne in absolute rebellion. The idea

is that, the people will, from hunger, be driven to revolt; and when once they find any other means of subsistence than that of honest labour, everything will be to be feared. *Night* – Passing through the square of the Hôtel de Ville, the mob were breaking the windows with stones, notwithstanding an officer and a detachment of horse was in the square. I ... clambered on to the roof of a row of low stalls opposite the building against which their malice was directed. Here I beheld the whole commodiously. Perceiving that the troops would not attack them, except in words and menaces, they grew more violent, and furiously attempted to beat the doors in pieces with iron crows; placing ladders to the windows. In about a quarter of an hour, which gave time for the assembled magistrates to escape by a back door, they burst all open, and entered like a torrent with a universal shout of the spectators. From that minute a shower of casements, sashes, shutters, chairs, tables, sofas, books, papers, pictures, etc., rained incessantly from all the windows of the house. The troops, both horse and foot, were quiet spectators. They were at first too few to interpose, and, when they became more numerous, the mischief was too far advanced to admit of any other conduct than guarding every avenue around, permitting none to go to the scene of action, but letting everyone that pleased retire with his plunder; guards being at the same time placed at the doors of the churches, and all public buildings. I was for two hours spectator at different places of the scene, secure myself from the falling furniture, but near enough to see a fine lad of about fourteen crushed to death by something as he was handing plunder to a woman, I suppose his mother, from the horror that was pictured in her countenance. I remarked several common soldiers, with their white cockades, among the plunderers, and, instigating the mob even in sight of the officers of the detachment. There were amongst them people so decently dressed, that I regarded them with no small surprise; they destroyed all the public archives; the streets for some way around strewed with papers.[30]

On 25 July Young talked with some travellers from Paris. He was especially struck by the inactivity of so many troops in the Ile de France: 'Here is, therefore, a revolution effected by a sort of magic; all powers in the realm are destroyed but that of the Commons.'[31]

On 26 July Young first felt the direct impact of the Revolution,

The whole country is in the greatest agitation; at one of the little towns I passed, I was questioned for not having a cockade of the *Tiers Etat*. They said it was ordained by the *Tiers*, and, if I was not a *seigneur*, I ought to obey. I immediately bought a cockade, but the hussey pinned it into my hat so loosely, that before I got to L'Isle it blew into the river, and I was again in the same danger.

It seems almost beyond belief, but Young rescued himself by delivering to the assembled crowd a dissertation on the English tax system.[32]
Young first reported the burning of the *châteaux* on 27 July:

The mischiefs which have been perpetrated in the country, towards the mountains and Vesoul, are numerous and shocking. Many *châteaux* have been burnt, others plundered, the *seigneurs* hunted down like wild beasts, their wives and daughters ravished, their papers and titles burnt, and all their property destroyed; and these abominations not inflicted on marked persons, who were odious for their former conduct or principles, but an indiscriminating blind rage for love of plunder. Robbers, galley-slaves, and villains of all denominations, have collected and instigated the peasants to commit all sorts of outrages.[33]

On 30 July Young reached Dijon after a difficult journey, avoiding towns because he could not obtain a passport. At Dijon he was arrested for lack of proper papers, but released when vouched for by a local scientist. The *ancien régime* authorities had fled the province of Burgundy, and the *ad hoc* arrangements made by the bourgeois militia were 'too weak, however, to keep the peace'. At his inn, 'there is at present a gentleman, unfortunately a *seigneur*, his wife, family, three servants, an infant but a few months old, who escaped from their flaming *château* half-naked in the night'.[34]

On 31 July Young spent a frustrating day trying to obtain newspapers and concluded that the lack of political information and news in France would, in itself, be a serious problem for the new regime. At least the company at meal times had improved: 'At the *table d'hôte* only three, myself, and two noblemen, driven from their estates, as I conjecture by their conversation, but they did not hint at anything like their houses being burnt.' Young had a long, but unsatisfying, discussion with one of them trying to argue that the Revolution was not the complete ruin of France, but failing.[35]

Young does not report any further direct experience of urban or rural disorder as August progressed. He was, though, forced to focus his mind on the implications of the Revolution when offered a very attractive property at a price he could hardly refuse. He finally declined: 'But the state of government; the possibility that the leaders of the Paris democracy might in their wisdom abolish property as well as rank; and that in buying an estate I might be purchasing my share in a civil war; deterred me from engaging at present.'[36]

On 19 August Young had the rudest shock of his several visits to France. During the day he had spent many happy hours discussing volcanoes with the local *seigneur* – an acknowledged expert on the subject.

What I had done had more witnesses than I dreamt of; for at eleven o'clock at night, a full hour after I had been asleep, the commander of a file of twenty *milice bourgeoise*, with their muskets, or swords, or sabres, or pikes, entered my chamber, surrounded my bed, and demanded my passport. A dialogue ensued, too long to minute; I was forced first to give them my passport, and, that not satisfying them, my papers. They told me that I was undoubtedly a conspirator with the queen, the Comte d'Artois, and the Comte d'Entraigues (who has property here) ... My papers being in English saved me.[37]

Young noted a lighter side of the Revolution on 30 August:

For a few days past, I have been pestered with all the mob of the country shooting; one would think that every rusty gun in Provence is at work, killing all sorts of birds; the shot has fallen five or six times in my chaise and about my ears. The National Assembly has declared that every man has a right to kill game on his own land.[38]

Young met many aristocrats who had suffered from the Revolution. In Provence in September,

The people are in arms, and at this moment very unquiet. The situation of the nobility in this country is pitiable; they are under apprehensions that nothing will be left to them, but simply such houses as the mob allows to stand unburnt; that the *métayers* will retain their farms without paying the landlord his half of the produce.[39]

Young's account ends in mid-September when he crossed the border into Italy to observe its rural economy. He is the only Anglo-Saxon witness to the Revolution outside Paris; the other commentators were aware of the burning of the *châteaux* but attached little importance to it, keeping their attention fixed firmly on Paris and Versailles.

CHAPTER 6

From the Fall of the Bastille to the March of the Women on Versailles (July to October 1789)

'The summit of impudence'

WHILE the Bastille was being demolished and the *châteaux* looted and burned, the National Assembly was still in session in Versailles. The Revolution, as insurrection in Paris, did not make a direct impact on the Assembly's agenda. Its effect was more to create an environment in which its proposals could realistically be implemented.

To follow their business it is necessary to return to early July when a committee presented an agenda for constitutional reform, which deserves being reprinted in full both in its own right, and for Jefferson's contemporary translation of it:

(1) Every government should have for its only end the preservation of the rights of man: whence it follows that to recall constantly the government to the end proposed, the constitution should begin by a Declaration of the natural and imprescriptible rights of man.

(2) Monarchical government being proper to maintain these rights, it has been chosen by the French nation. It suits especially a great society; it is necessary for the happiness of France. The Declaration of the principles of this government then should follow immediately the declaration of the rights of man.

(3) It results from the principles of monarchy that the nation, to assure its own rights, has yielded particular rights to the monarch: the constitution then should declare in a precise manner the rights of both. It should begin by declaring the rights of the French nation, and then it should declare the rights of the king.

(4) The rights of the king and nation not existing but for the happiness of the individuals who compose it, they lead to an examination of the rights of citizens.

(5) The French nation not being capable of assembling individually to exercise all its rights, it ought to be represented. It is necessary then to declare the form of its representation, and the rights of its representatives.

(6) From the union of the powers of the nation and king should result the enacting and execution of the laws: thus then it should first be determined how the laws shall be established, afterwards should be considered how they shall be executed.

(7) Laws have for their object the general administration of the kingdom, the property and the actions of the citizens. The execution of the laws which concern the general administration requires provincial and municipal assemblies. It is necessary to examine then, what should be the organisation of the provincial assemblies, and what of the municipal.

(8) The execution of the laws which concern the property and actions of the citizens call for a Judiciary power. It should be determined how that should be confided, and then its duties and limits.

(9) For the execution of the laws and the defence of the kingdom, there exists a public force. It is necessary then to determine the principles which should direct it and how it should be employed.

You see that these are the materials of a superb edifice, and the hands which have prepared them, are perfectly capable of putting them together, and of filling up the work of which these are only the outlines.[1]

Jefferson had very high hopes of the Assembly's ability to draft and implement a new constitution, and he followed their debates closely. When the Declaration of Rights came before the chamber, he wrote: 'This will stop the burning of *châteaux*, and tranquilize the country more than all the addresses they could send them.'[2]

He was also confident that men of determination with bold but sound ideas could see off all opposition: 'There has been a faction in the Assembly with very dangerous views. But they have found the mass of the nation is so solidly united, that they seem to have abandoned all expectations of confusing the game.'[3]

The high point of Jefferson's approbation of the Assembly's work came in a report on 28 August:

The leading members [of the National Assembly] have in contemplation the following. The executive power in a hereditary king, with a negative on laws and power to dissolve the legislature, to be considerably restrained in the making of treaties, and limited in his expences. The legislative as a house of representatives. They propose a senate also, chosen on the plan of our federal senate by the provincial assemblies, but to be for life, of a certain age (they talk of 40 years), and certain wealth (4 or 500 guineas a year) but to have not other power as to laws but to remonstrate against them to the representatives, who will then determine their fate by a simple majority.... The representatives to be chosen every two or three years. The judiciary system is less prepared than any other part of their plan. However they will abolish the *parlements*, and establish an order of judges and justices, general and provincial ... with trial by jury in criminal cases certainly, perhaps also in civil. The provinces will have assemblies for their provincial government, and the cities a municipal body for municipal government, all founded on the basis of popular election. These subordinate governments, tho' completely dependant on the general one, will ... have their own judiciary, final in all but great cases, the executive business will principally pass through their hands, and a certain local legislation will be allowed them. In short ours has been professedly their model.[4]

After this time Jefferson began to fear, not that the Revolution would fail, but that the delay in making real progress would allow its momentum to be lost, and that Counter-Revolutionary forces would gather strength and put up more effective opposition. He gave a very full account of the state of the Assembly and of the nation on 19 September. This account was also to be one of his last as he was shortly afterwards recalled to America:

The sloth of the Assembly (unavoidable from their numbers) has done the most sensible injury to the public cause. The patience of a people, who have less of that quality than any other nation in the world, is worn threadbare. Time has been given to the aristocrats to recover from their panic, to cabal, to sow dissensions in the Assembly and distrust out of it. It has been a misfortune that the king and aristocracy together have not been able to make a sufficient resistance to keep the patriots in a compact body. Having no common enemy of such force as to render their union necessary, they have suffered themselves to divide. The Assembly now consists of four distinct parties. (1) The aristocrats, comprehending the higher members of the clergy, military, and nobility, and the *parlements* of the whole kingdom. This forms a head without a body. (2) The moderate royalists, who wish for a constitution early similar to that of England. (3) The republicans, who are willing to let their first magistracy be hereditary, but to make it very subordinate to the legislature, and to have that legislature consist of a single chamber. (4) The faction of Orléans. The 2nd and 3rd descriptions are composed of honest, well meaning men, differing in opinion only, but both wishing the establishment of as great a degree of liberty as can be preserved. They are considered together as constituting the Patriotic part of the Assembly, and they are supported by the soldiery of the army, the soldiery of the church, that is to say the *curés* and monks, the disinterested part of the nobility, which is small, and the substantial bourgeoisie of the whole nation.

The part of these collected in the cities, have formed themselves into municipal bodies, have chosen municipal representatives, and have organised an armed corps, considerably more numerous in the whole than the regular army. They have also the ministry, such as it is, and as yet the king. Were these 2d. and 3d. parties, or rather these sections of the same party to separate entirely, this great mass of power and wealth would be split nobody knows how. But I do not think they will separate. Because they have the same honest views; because, each being conscious of the rectitude of the other, there is no rancour between them: because they retain the desire of coalescing. In order to effect this, they, not long ago, proposed a conference, and desired it might be at my house, which gave me an opportunity of judging of their views. They discussed together their points of difference for six hours, and in the course of discussion agreed on mutual sacrifices. The effect of this agreement has been considerably deflated by the subsequent proceedings of the Assembly, but I do not know that it has been thro' any infidelity of the leaders of the compromise they had agreed on. Another powerful band of union between these two parties is our friend the Marquis de Lafayette. He left the Assembly while they as yet formed but one party. His attachment to both is equal, and he labours incessantly to keep them together. Should he be obliged to take part against either, it will be against that which shall first pass the Rubicon of reconciliation with the other. I should hope in this event that his weight will be sufficient to turn the scales decidedly in favour of the other. His command of the armed militia of Paris (30,000 in number and comprehending the French Guards who are 5,000 regulars) and his influence with the municipality, would secure this city; and tho' the armed militia and the municipalities of the other cities are in no wise subordinate to those of Paris, yet they look up to them with respect, and look particularly to the Marquis de Lafayette as leading always to the rights of the people. This turn of things is so probable that I do not think either section of the patriots will venture on any act which will place themselves in opposition to him. This being the face of things, troubled as you will perceive, civil war is much talked of and expected: and this talk and expectation has a tendency to beget it. What are the events which may produce it? (1) The want of bread, were it to produce a commencement of disorder, might ally itself to more permanent causes of discontent, and thus continue the effect beyond its first cause. (2) A public bankruptcy. Great numbers of the lower as well as higher classes of citizens depend for subsistence on their property in the public funds. (3) The absconding of the king from Versailles.[5]

In this passage Jefferson has drawn up an agenda for politics of the immediate future for the Revolution. The issues were, the conduct and credibility of the National Assembly; the financial stability of the new regime; the pivotal position of Lafayette; the growth of a Counter-Revolutionary opposition (though Jefferson's phrase about it being a head without a body is most instructive); attempts to seize control of the Revolution from within (with Mirabeau and Orléans as the initial candidates here); the need to secure food supplies especially for Paris; the position of the royal family and – related to the last point – the threat of civil war.

A footnote can be added to this, with Jefferson's prediction, made at the end of August, for the immediate course of the Revolution's relations with the rest of Europe: 'their probable event is a peaceable settlement.... They fear a war from England Holland and Prussia. I think England will give money, but not make war.'[6]

Jefferson completely failed to recognize the Austrian dynastic dimension to the Revolution's foreign relations, although his assessment of Britain's position was as accurate as many of his predictions on internal French developments.

Conduct within the National Assembly

By contrast to Jefferson's benevolent optimism, Morris took a much more jaundiced view of the Revolution. Taking stock at the end of July, on the eve of taking ship to England, he wrote:

> There are some able men in the National Assembly, yet the best heads among them would not be injured by experience, and unfortunately there are a good number who, with much imagination, have little knowledge, judgment, or reflection. You may consider the revolution as complete; that is to say, the authority of the king and of the nobility is completely subdued, but yet I tremble for the constitution. They have all that romantic spirit, and all those romantic ideas of government which, happily for America, we were cured of before it was too late. They are advancing rapidly ... the whole army of France have declared for liberty, and ... His Majesty ... does not know a single regiment that would obey him.[7]

The other accounts of the National Assembly and its proceedings were also of a pessimistic nature. Huber told Eden: 'I believe, that the National Assembly seemed to me to go too fast ... I am even apt to think that the night of the 4th of August, which produced so many unexpected sacrifices, has laid a bed of regrets in many of the members.'[8]

The night of 4 August 1789 had seen the voluntary surrendering of all feudal rights – which in turn led to Arthur Young being peppered by shot in Provence – and every French landowner now enjoyed absolute rights over his own property, where before the nobility (or any owner of the 'feudal' interests in a property) might have owned the shooting rights as a quite separate arrangement to the law covering 'real' estate.

The British embassy made a more sinister comment, that the men of good will in the Assembly

> are under intimidation from the lower people of Paris and of the chief provincial towns ... in effect the kingdom of France is at this hour governed by some nameless individuals who assemble every morning and evening at the Hôtel de Ville. The court of Versailles is not in appearance but in fact in a state of imprisonment.[9]

One debate in particular caused deep fear for the future of the Revolution. This was the debate on the ratification of the Assembly as a single-chamber legislature albeit with a suspensive veto for the king. Mirabeau's bully-boy tactics came in for particular opprobrium:

> I was yesterday at Versailles and present at the most extraordinary scene I have yet witnessed, the decisions of the three great constitutional questions ... [The decision on the future constitution of the Assembly] was carried in the affirmative without much trouble. When the [question of whether to have one or two chambers] was proposed, a most violent disturbance arose. . . . The party of M. de Mirabeau would not let anybody speak, but insisted on interrupting everyone who rose, by crying *au voix! au voix!* ... The greatest insults were offered to the president [who then resigned].[10]

Huber said that Mirabeau's conduct could partly be explained by the fact that 'he saw the *lanterne* over his head'. He ascribed it more, though, to Mirabeau's malice and desire to show that he did indeed have the power to disrupt and control the Assembly. The debate had an overpowering effect on Huber: 'I was for two hours in a high fever; and Mirabeau saw at last that he had done more mischief than he had meant to, and that it was now time to avert the explosion.' By the end of the debate the president for that fortnight (Clermont-Tonnerre, who resigned) was 'perfectly knocked up'.[11]

Morris did not hear the debate, but was terse in his condemnation: 'This is travelling in the high road to anarchy, and that worst of all tyrannies, the despotism of a faction in a popular assembly.'[12]

Financial Situation
The original cause of the constitutional crisis which had led to the summoning of the States-General had been financial, and it would still not go away. The nation still faced bankruptcy, but now it was seen as a distracting irrelevance to the real political issues of the day.

Jefferson summed up the situation:

Their declaration of rights is finished.... It is doubtful whether they will now take up the finance or the constitution first. The distress for money endangers every thing. No taxes are paid, and no money can be borrowed. M. Necker was yesterday to give in a memoir to the Assembly on this subject. I think they will give him leave to put into execution any plan he pleases, so as to debarrass themselves of this and take up that of the constitution.[13]

Morris gave a full report, emphasizing Mirabeau's role in the debate:

At ten the session is opened; ... after ... a tedious verbal controversy on the redaction of yesterday's minutes, much heat and noise and impatience, by which means half an hour is employed in what ought to have been settled in half a minute. The Marquis de Montesquiou makes his report; vast respect for the *Premier Ministre des Finances*, and then sundry details and combinations, which show that the committee understand the business much better than the ministers.... After the report is read the Comte de Mirabeau objects to the consideration of it, and insists that they should immediately take up M. Necker's proposition, in which he has a motion to make. He is called to the tribune, and in a tone of fine irony urges the adoption of the plan proposed by the *Premier Ministre* from the blind confidence which the Assembly have in him, and from that unbounded popularity which he enjoys.'These', says he, 'in that dreadful situation which he has exposed, and in the imminency of danger which produces debate, urge, nay, command us to adopt without examination what the minister has devised for our relief. Let us agree to it literally (*textuéllement*), and if it succeeds let him, as he ought, enjoy the glory of it; if he fails, which heaven forefnd, we will then exercise our talents in trying to discover if yet there remains any means to save our country.' To my great astonishment the representatives of this nation, who pique themselves on being the modern Athenians, are ready to swallow this proposition by acclamation.[14]

One of the most attractive ways of solving the Revolution's financial difficulties made its first serious appearance at this time. This was the nationalization (or sequestration) of the church's assets. It was a proposal which had had a long currency under the *ancien régime*, but had always been unacceptable to the monarchy because of its obvious detriment to the temporal power of the Catholic Church and because of its historical precedent in the English king Henry VIII's dissolution of the monasteries.[15] In its context, however, the proposal was not so extreme or unreasonable as it might appear at first sight. The *ancien régime* church, despite its vast assets, was financially a microcosm of the regime as a whole, unable to balance its books and unable to countenance the sort of reforms which could restore solvency. Above all, the church was debarred from disposing of any of its assets, and thus unable to realize capital or rationalize its portfolios. Coming to some arrangement with the state was an attractive proposition for all concerned, except the most conservative of the upper clergy and, of course, appealed greatly to the radically minded *curés* who had done so much to create the National Assembly.

Morris had a long discussion with Talleyrand on 4 October about the financial condition of the nation, and they inevitably moved on to the subject of the church's property.

> He says the present ministry will last for ever; that is, longer than he wishes; but Necker's health and the difficulties he is already plunged in seem to me to augur differently. We cannot even sketch the outlines of a future plan distinctly, but in general we agree as to what ought to be done. On the subject of church property, I urge that it should be obtained by consent of the clergy, and only mortgaged at first, but sold afterwards by degrees so as to obtain the full value.

Morris went on to propound a system whereby loans could be raised against the security of church property and income still obtained from it in the meantime: 'This scheme is not only practicable but easy', he concluded.[16]

Threats to the Revolution

Jefferson had warned both of the coalescing of aristocratic and clerical opposition to the Revolution and of the threat the king posed as a rallying point for Counter-Revolution, if he escaped from Versailles. The king's position will be considered in detail below, but there was now a more immediate threat to the Revolution from within. This was the Duc d'Orléans, who was a leading force in the National Assembly, but whose motives were highly suspect. Jefferson was very suspicious of him, and had nothing but ill to say of him:

> The lees too of the patriotic party, of wicked principles and desperate fortunes, hoping to pillage something in the wreck of their country, are attaching themselves to the faction of the Duke of Orléans, that faction is caballing with the populace, and intriguing at London, the Hague and Berlin and have evidently in view the transfer of the crown to the D. of Orléans. He is a man of moderate understanding, of no principle, absorbed in low vice, and incapable of abstracting himself from the filth of that to direct any thing else. His name and his money therefore are mere tools in the hands of those who are duping him. *Mirabeau is their chief.* They may produce a temporary confusion, and even a temporary civil war,

supported as they will be by the money of England; but cannot have success ultimately.[17]

Subsequently both Huber and the British embassy were to be equally condemnatory. The embassy described his conduct in the aftermath of the March of Women on Versailles as 'the summit of impudence' and talked of 'numerous accusations against him as the chief promoter of all the troubles and misfortunes of this country'.[18]

Position of the King

After his enforced visit to Paris, Louis XVI had returned to Versailles, where he took no political initiative of any sort. At Versailles he was effectively constrained but still at least in the residence of his own choosing and surrounded by friends and servants. As Jefferson has observed, he could not count on the army for any support – and certainly not the regular or militia units stationed in the Ile de France – with the possible exception still of the Swiss. There was armed hostility between the Swiss and the French troops, which at times erupted into fighting.[19]

This conflict served to remind the Revolutionaries that the army was still an unknown force in the country as a whole, that some elements would probably be prepared to take up arms on behalf of the king and that the king would be a potent figurehead of Counter-Revolution, if the National Assembly lost their hold over him. The real fear was that the king would flee from Versailles. Jefferson analysed the consequences:

> This has for some time been apprehended as possible. In consequence of this apprehension, a person whose information would have weight, wrote to the Count de Montmorin [the Foreign Minister] adjuring him to prevent it by every possible means, and assuring him that the flight of the king would be the signal of a St Bartholemew against the aristocrats in Paris and perhaps thro' the kingdom. M. de Montmorin showed the letter to the queen who assured him solemnly that no such thing was in contemplation. His shewing it to the queen proves that he entertained the same distress with the public. It may be asked what is the queen disposed to do in the present situation of things? Whatever rage, pride and fear can dictate in a breast which never knew the presence of one moral restraint.[20]

Basing his report on documents which Louis, very ill-advisedly, had sent to Spain abjuring all he had had to agree to since 23 June, Morris relayed back to America one of the host of rumours about the king's plans and their consequences:

It is known to very few in this country, and may perhaps (as it ought) be buried in oblivion. The king has actually formed the design of going off to Spain. Whether the measures set on foot to dissuade him will have, as I hope, the desired effect, time only can discover. His fears govern him absolutely, and they have of late been most strongly excited. He is a well-meaning man, but extremely weak, and probably these circumstances will in every event secure him from personal injury. An able man would not have fallen into his situation, but I think that no ability can now extricate him. He must float along the current of events, being absolutely a cypher. If, however, he should fly, it will not be easy to predict the consequences for this country is at present as near to anarchy as society can approach without dissolution.

... if a civil war does not take place it must be from some circumstance which escapes my conjecture ... if [Louis XVI] escapes from Versailles and falls into different hands from those now about him there must be a struggle.[21]

The Abuse of the Cockade at Versailles

The pace of events with relation to the royal family suddenly quickened with an incident at Versailles where the Flanders regiment was suspected of deriding and abusing the Revolutionary cockade, and winning the king's approval for it. The precise details and the rights and wrongs of the incident became immaterial. The incident, as perceived by the Revolutionaries, confirmed their worst fears about the king's attitude, the reliability of the army and the dangers of allowing the king to remain master in his own house outside the immediate control of the Revolution. The Flanders regiment, also, was suspected of being more royalist than other troops around Paris and capable of taking effective action against the Revolution.

Morris reported the immediate effect on Paris: 'Much disturbance at Paris. The foolish story of the [trampling] of the cockades at Versailles and serious suffering for the want of bread have collected from eight to ten thousand wretches, who go to the Hôtel de Ville.'[22]

Recounting the events later, William Short (now replacing Jefferson) thought the whole episode was an Orléanist plot to frighten Louis XVI into fleeing the kingdom. His account of the trampling of the cockades was brief: 'The people of Paris then were stirred up by the scarcity of bread and by a report of the national cockade having been trampled on in a feast given at Versailles by the *Gardes du Corps* to the regiment of Flanders.'[23]

The March of the Women on Versailles

The British embassy staff witnessed the whole proceedings leading to the invasion of Versailles: 'On [5 October in the] morning ... we were much surprised and at first much entertained with the ludicrous sight of a female army proceeding very clamourously, but in good order and determined step towards Versailles.'[24]

Morris and Lord Auckland's private secretary (Mr Garlicke), who was on a brief visit to Paris, also watched the women depart. Mr Garlicke specifically described them as *poissardes* (fishwives). He also noticed that Lafayette had had to go with them, 'mentioning the *lanterne* as an alternative'.[25]

Morris exclaimed: 'A host of women are gone to Versailles with some cannon. A strange manoeuvre!'[26]

All the non-journalistic Anglo-Saxon accounts of the march share two features. The first is that they accepted that the march was a *bona fide* demonstration by the women of Paris, which was then joined by men without any subterfuge. This is in contrast to some later accounts, which may originate from the report in the (London) *Times* on 12 October 1789, that a proportion of the *poissardes* were actually men (National Guardsmen according to *The Times*) in transvestite Revolutionary dress. The second is that none of these accounts – written at the time – mention Marie-Antoinette's famous supposed utterance 'Let them eat cake.'

A crowd of both sexes and the Bourgeois Militia joined the march, and on the road to Versailles they met some of the troops who had been accused of trampling the cockades. The brief fighting which broke out was the only serious military opposition the early Revolution was to face, and it bore out all the predictions about the lower ranks' attitude to the Revolution:

> The *Gardes du Corps* were the first who fired on the Parisians and five or six people, chiefly women, were killed: the regiment de Flanders was also drawn up to oppose this torrent, but the word to fire was no sooner given than they, to a man, clubbed their arms and with a shout of *Vive la Nation* went over to the Parisians.... The *Gardes du Corps* being thus abandoned and overpowered by numbers fled precipitately into the gardens and woods, where they were pursued and vast numbers were killed.... The Parisians ... carried some of the heads of their unhappy victims to Paris, and paraded them through the streets on spikes.[27]

After the skirmish in the palace gardens, the *poissardes* broke into the buildings of Versailles and the next day forced the royal family to go back with them to Paris: 'Many circumstances of insult to the royal personages. The queen obliged to fly from her bed in a shift and petticoat, with her stockings in her hand ... pursued by the *poissardes* ... The troubles of this country are begun, but as to the end it is not easy to foresee it.'[28]

Short devoted some attention to the fighting and its implications:

The *Gardes Françaises* were put in motion by a desire to recover the honor of guarding the king's person. These passions fermented a day or two and at length forced Lafayette to march to Versailles. . . . The game now seemed the most favorable possible to the faction of Orléans. Had the detachment of women, which had been sent off in the morning, been attacked, the *Gardes Françaises* and the mob of Paris would have forced the Marquis to engage the *Gardes du Corps* and the regiment of Flanders. In this conflict he would certainly have fallen, and thus one of their principal obstacles would have been removed. If these women were not attacked, and repulsed, the retreat of the king queen and dauphin seemed inevitable, and thus an open field was left to the ambition of the Duke of Orléans. A Council was held at Versailles. Most of the counsellors were for the retreat, but the king's firmness, or if you please his confidence in Lafayette, turned the balance and saved his kingdom from an immediate civil war.[29]

Morris and the British embassy differed greatly on how Louis xvi had borne up under the ordeal. In Morris's account he remains the bluff and hearty monarch: 'The king ate a very hearty supper last night. Who will say that he wants fortitude?' and 'This morning the king's dentist fell dead at his feet. The poor king exclaimed that he was devoted to experience every kind of misfortune!'[30] (It is a notable feature of the person of Louis xvi as king that he failed almost completely to inspire personal loyalty. This incident, where he regards the dentist's death as a misfortune to his royal person, illustrates a quite inadvertent inhumanity he displayed to people in direct contact with him. He was not a man people warmed – or rallied – to.)

The British embassy reported a very different picture. After Louis xvi had been forced to show himself all day (on 8 October) to the crowds outside the Tuileries: 'The king was much dejected and said little. Her Majesty's voice falters and the tears run fast down her cheeks as she spoke.'[31] It is likely that the embassy's account is based on first-hand evidence, while Morris's was a mixture of second-hand account and wishful thinking.

With the king captive in Paris, friendless, fearful and depressed, the Revolution had entered a new phase. The two leading figures seemed to be Orléans and Lafayette, and a struggle between them – with the king's life depending on Lafayette's victory – seemed to be the next item on the political agenda. Both Morris and the British embassy were profoundly pessimistic about the course of the Revolution by this stage. Earlier, at the end of July, Morris had written (as earlier quoted) that 'this country is at present as near to anarchy as society can approach without dissolution'.

The British embassy in more sombre mood still wrote after the abduction of the king: 'the blind and headlong will of the populace directs all and all submit with fear and trembling to their government as the dangerous maxims that all men are equal, and that numbers can overcome a few, are in the mouths of every vagabond'.[32]

CHAPTER 7

From the King's Arrival in Paris to the End of 1789
(October to December 1789)

'Everything is now out of joint'

AFTER the king's abduction to Paris, the nature of the reportage on the Revolution began to change. The generous judgements grew fewer and predictions of anarchy and civil war increased. The agenda for most of the great constitutional issues had already been drawn up and judgements passed on them and thus the correspondents from now on were forced to react to day-to-day events rather than having the leisure to analyse and predict. Increasingly, they lost their status of privileged witnesses, and the Revolution started to impinge directly on them in their capacities as residents of Paris and foreigners in France. For all this, the diplomats were able to stay in daily contact with ministers and with the royal family, and they and Gouverneur Morris were able to move freely in Parisian society and to debate any topic of their choice with whoever they pleased; the days when this might be a death sentence for the Parisians with whom they conversed were still a long way off.

Orléans, Lafayette and Mirabeau

With the monarchy now firmly under the control of the Revolution in Paris, the most immediate threat to the Revolution itself seemed to come from the ambitions of the House of Orléans.

It fell to Lafayette to grasp this nettle, and he confronted the duke and forced him into exile in England. Huber and Short gave very similar accounts of the struggle between them. Huber's is broader, more succinct and more immediate:

The duke was at the head of a formidable party, the purpose of which was to send the king away, if not worse, and to make himself be named regent etc. M. de Lafayette has worked out this plot in wonderful silence, and once master of every proof, he waited on the duke last Saturday ... and told him ... *'Monseigneur, je crains qu'il y ait bientôt sur l'échafaud la tête d'une personne de votre nom.'* [Orléans] has been so much frightened by the king and [Lafayette] that he at last determined on becoming your guest.[1]

Orléans might have been out of France, but he was not out of French politics. Some friends of Lafayette told Morris that 'the friends of the Duke of Orléans will ... denounce him [i.e. Lafayette] to the National Assembly, so as to oblige him [i.e. Orléans] to return, they expecting that his popularity in Paris will make him triumph over his enemies'.[2]

Short described a scenario whereby Orléans would be recalled to Paris even as he was about to take ship for England. He and his fellow conspirators in Paris would set in motion the following attack on Lafayette:

> The conduct of the M. [i.e. the Marquis de Lafayette] was then to have been passed in review. He was to have been represented as an ambitious man taking advantage of the present situation of affairs, whilst he had the king and queen and dauphin prisoners, to force away the only obstacle to his views [i.e. Orléans'], that his plan was to have himself made a Maire du Palais etc.[3]

It is interesting to set Orléans' accusations alongside Morris's account (below) of his conversation with Lafayette about his role in the Revolution.

What of Lafayette's own position? Morris had dinner with him on 18 November, ostensibly to discuss the financial opportunities opened up by the nationalization of church property. The conversation moved on to Lafayette's perception of his own future role in the Revolution: 'Lafayette ... says that Mirabeau has well described the Assembly, which he calls the *Wild Assembly*; that in a fortnight they will be obliged to give him [i.e. Lafayette] authority which he has hitherto declined ... a kind of dictatorship, such as generalissimo.'

Morris was not optimistic that Lafayette would indeed emerge as some sort of populist military saviour: 'This man's mind is so elevated by power, already too great for the measure of his abilities, that he looks into the clouds and grasps at the supreme. From this moment every step in his ascent will, I think, accelerate his fall.'[4]

Meanwhile, a rival to both Orléans and Lafayette was strengthening his position. Mirabeau's star was rising. Short described his position thus on 3 November, illustrating his opportunist and cynical political style:

> it is believed and feared he will force his way into the ministry notwithstanding the execration in which he is held. He has lately shewed more than ever as a man of talents, and even the aristocrats, or some of them wish him in the ministry as the only means of restoring energy to the regal power. – One of the means he is using is to render the place of a minister as dangerous as possible. He some time ago denounced M. de St-Priest as having told the women who arrived at Versailles on the 5th

crying out *du pain*, that when they had one king, they had bread, now
that they had 1,200 kings, they must apply to them for it.[5]

Short reported that relations between Lafayette and Mirabeau were so bad
that they had duelled – one incident among many of National Assembly
members settling their political differences as matters of honour outside the
chamber.[6]

Work of the National Assembly and Outlook for the Nation

Morris had no faith in the Revolution's ability to maintain internal order or
to pursue constructive reform. He wrote to Lafayette on 16 October: 'I am
convinced that the proposed constitution cannot serve for the government of
this country; that the National Assembly, late the object of enthusiastic
attachment, will soon be treated with disrespect, that the extreme licentious-
ness of your people will render it indispensable to increase the royal authority.'
Two days later he wrote back to America:

> Everything is now as it were out of joint. The army without discipline
> or obedience. The civil magistracy annihilated. The finances deplorable.
> They have no fixed system to get through the difficulties, but live upon
> expedients.... [In the National Assembly] they neither reason, examine,
> nor discuss. They clap those whom they approve and hiss those whom
> they disapprove.... I dined in company with the president, and told him
> frankly that it was impossible for such a mob to govern this country.[7]

Unfortunately Morris does not record whether the president thanked him for
this observation.

Against this background, Morris – and to a lesser extent the British
embassy – were amazed when the National Assembly seemed to be acting
with resolution, forethought and popularity. The two most important issues
of the autumn were the nationalization of church property and the suspension – with a view to eventual abolition (finally taking place on 14 October
1790) – of the *parlements*. This latter act Morris applauded: 'This is a better
blow at tyranny than any they have yet struck',[8] and the British embassy
reported public 'joy and triumph' at the nationalization of church property.[9]

The embassy feared, however, that the next logical step would be the
abolition of nobility: 'birth, fortune, and favour are to lose all influence and
every man from the meanest station in life is to rise to the highest honours
in the state if he has the merit.... Such ... is the total subversion of all things
in this country.'[10]

In contrast to this gloomy outlook is Short's more optimistic view, written
in the context of debates on civil rights, citizenship under the new regime
and freedom of the press: 'The truth is that the present calm and security of

the members [of the National Assembly] enables many of them to shew an adhesion to former principles which they did not venture to in times of trouble.'[11]

The Revolution in Paris

The character of Paris as a city was changing. Its importance – both objectively and in its own eyes – had increased. It possessed an ostensibly powerful municipal authority (something explicitly denied to it by the *ancien régime*) and had evolved rapidly a vigorous democratic infrastructure at the grassroots in the 'Sections'. It had been the scene of the storming of the Bastille – the event which symbolized the Revolution as a whole. It had become the permanent residence of the royal family who, after the *Frondes*, had never lived in the capital, as a punishment for the city. With the residence of the royal family, the National Assembly had moved to Paris as well, and was in permanent (and constant) session there.

At the same time the population had become highly politicized. The city also acted as host to a large number of people who had no other constructive activity but politics. The grassroots politicization of the population is attested to by the spontaneous decision of the *poissardes* to take direct action against the royal family in October. A particular group Jefferson had identified in this context was the 'prodigious' number of now out-of-work servants.[12]

Short, as we have seen, was undismayed by the political scene, but the other correspondents were all disparaging. The British embassy staff felt they were living in times 'too fruitful in mischief and depravity'. And, 'many people have been lately taken up and imprisoned on suspicion [of forming conspiracies]'. A particular feature of these arrests was that the suspects' houses were marked by chalk, which 'spread much terror and alarm'. The embassy's verdict on the Parisians was that they had become 'familiarized with blood'.[13]

The motive for these actions was the fear of Counter-Revolution. There was a mood of pessimism and desperation: 'people seem now as if prepared for the worst. They are generally extremely dejected.' A *Comité des Recherches* was set up at the Hôtel de Ville to investigate conspiracies, and was empowered to offer rewards for information.[14]

There was certainly a breakdown in law and order in the streets, which dated back to the crown's loss of control over the army in June. One symptom had been a rash of burglaries – including three against the American embassy – but another was the lynch law whereby *ancien régime* functionaries and grain speculators were strung up on lamp posts at the whim of the crowd.[15]

The hanging of the baker François by a mob made a particular impression on the correspondents. All seemed taken aback by the quick-tempered and drastic action of the mob. The episode as a whole led to (or coincided with) the introduction of martial law (or a Riot Act as Morris called it), and was yet further proof of the military forces' unwillingness to take action against civilians. The fullest account was given by Short:

> On the 21st inst. a mob rose and went to the house of a baker, carried him to the Hôtel de Ville to be judged under pretence of his having concealed bread in his cellar in order to augment the scarcity. Their impatience soon wrested him from the hands of the members of the Hôtel de Ville and the guard who refused to fire on them. They carried him to the lantern, hung him, cut off his head, and carried it in triumph through the streets and under the windows of the Palace on the Pont-Royal. An account of this horrid incident being carried to the National Assembly, a martial law against *attroupements* was immediately passed.... Two of the chiefs were arrested in the evening and condemned by the Châtelet. They were executed the next day without any disorder.[16]

Anti-clericalism also made its first appearance on the streets: 'The person of a clergyman is not secure from violence, and they cannot appear in the street but in disguise.'[17] The Revolutionary organization of Paris was beginning to take shape. In the future the quasi-autonomous Section administrations were to cause the diplomats much trouble as they did not have the central government's regard for the niceties of international protocol or diplomatic immunity. The British embassy described them as 'the sixty districts, which are absolutely so many little sovereignties within the metropolis, [which] exercise the most despotic rule over all'. In December they reported that it was feared the *faubourgs* of St-Antoine and St-Marceau would rise because of the high price of bread.[18]

Short, in similar vein, commented: 'The districts of Paris still continue to assemble and sometimes exercise acts of sovereignty very incompatible with good order. It will be difficult to put an end to them. One protested against the martial law as being contrary to the liberty of the citizens.'[19]

Looking ahead, Arthur Young addressed the issue of Paris's self-assumed leadership of the Revolution in the context of the Jacobin Club. Young asked the Jacobins a straight question, and received a straight answer!

> The violent democrats, who have the reputation of being so much republican in principle, that they do not admit any political necessity for having even the name of a king, are called the *enragés*. They have a meeting at the Jacobins, called the Revolution Club, which assembles every night ... they are so numerous, that all material business is there decided, before it is discussed by the National Assembly. I called this morning on several persons, all of whom are great democrats; and

mentioning this circumstance to them, as one which savoured too much of a Paris *junta* governing the kingdom, an idea, which must in the long run, be unpopular and hazardous; I was answered, that the predominancy which Paris assumed, at present, was absolutely necessary, for the safety of the whole nation; for if nothing were done, but by procuring a previous common consent, all great opportunities would be lost, and the National Assembly left constantly exposed to the danger of a counter-revolution.[20]

The Threat of Counter-Revolution

The fear of Counter-Revolution had become one of the principal engines of the Revolution, but how real was the menace in late 1789? There were, in fact, few overt threats as yet to the Revolution, little organized opposition, and no credible alternative to the new regime from the *émigrés*. What the Revolutionaries could not judge, and dared not experiment with, was whether the lack of a Counter-Revolution to date was caused by the incompetence and weakness of their enemies or whether it was due to their own vigilance and resolute action. The National Assembly was taking forthright action to nip in the bud any potential hostility by removing any institutions which could act as rallying points.

The king was an obvious focus for any plots, and, looking forward to January 1790, Arthur Young set the whole issue of plots to rescue the king, oppose the Revolutionary regime, or make a serious attempt at Counter-Revolution into its context. He linked them on the one hand to the popular unrest around Paris about food prices and, on the other, to the aristocrats still trying to form an effective opposition in the National Assembly:

> The report of plots to carry off the king, is in the mouth of everyone; and it is said these movements of people, as well as those at Versailles, are not what they appear to be, mere mobs, but instigated by the aristocrats, and if permitted to rise to such a height as to entangle the Paris militia, will prove the part only of a conspiracy against the new government. That they have reason to be alert is undoubted; for though there should actually be no plots in existence, yet there is so great a temptation to them, and such a probability of their being formed, that supineness would probably create them.[21]

The first, and only, real provincial challenge to the Revolution perceived by the commentators in 1789 came from Toulouse, the capital of Languedoc. Both the provincial States and the *parlement* of Toulouse were apparently involved. The British embassy talked of the *parlement* and nobility of Toulouse declaring for the 'power' and 'liberty' of the king. Short gave a fuller and more ironic account of the episode as it related to the States or nobility. He both set the incident in its local context and related it to other provinces:

> It was apprehended that the discontented in the provinces would take
> advantage of the translation of the king and National Assembly to Paris,
> in order to foment complaints or anything else that might interrupt the
> present progress of affairs. The States of Languedoc assembled and whilst
> they were forming remonstrances, viz. the clergy and nobility, the people
> were employed in counter remonstrances by pillaging their *châteaux*.
> These movements have since ceased. Some provinces have declared their
> satisfaction at the translation of the king etc. to Paris. But the province
> of Dauphiné gives uneasiness still.

The embassy reported that as a result of this episode the National Assembly
had forbidden any local provincial assemblies from meeting. The embassy
interpreted this as Paris acting against the provinces, and predicted it would
not be tolerated: 'a civil war is talked of as infallible'.[22]

A milder threat from the north of the country was dismissed by Short: 'The
opposition to the decrees of the National Assembly which had begun to shew
itself in some of the *parlements* and the States of Cambrai has ceased and
served only to show the inutility of resistance.'[23]

It should be remembered that at this stage of the Revolution, new and old
institutions existed in parallel. The National Assembly had successfully seen
off the old ones, but Morris reported on 1 November 1789 that there was
already trouble with the new: 'the municipality of Rouen have stopped some
grain intended for Paris. This leads to observation on the many-headed
monster they have created in the executive department.' Morris did not lose
sight of this problem, and on 10 January 1790 he wrote that Lafayette 'asks
me how they are to provide for the case of disobedience in the provincial and
district administrations, which are submitted to the orders of the king, but,
being elected, may not respect those orders'. Morris rather unhelpfully told
him that if the problem did not resolve itself of its own accord then a Counter-
Revolution would in any case sweep away all the new institutions.[24]

Morris also devoted some time and attention to the possibility of effective
opposition from the old Orders and corporations (it is still too early in the
history of the Revolution to talk of modern sociological classes):

> The church, the law, and the nobility, three bodies intermediary, which
> in this kingdom were equally formidable to the king and people, are now
> placed by the Assembly in direct hostility, and they have at the same
> moment, by the influence of ill-grounded apprehension, tied the hands
> and feet of their new natural ally, the king. In a very little time must
> unite the opposition, and when united they will of course place them-

selves under the banners of the royal authority, and then farewell democracy.

This was a long-term prospect, however, as 'The Comte de Luxembourg comes, and detains me a long time for nothing. Tells me, however, that the party of the nobles are determined to be quiet. This is the only wise conduct.'[25]

The commentators themselves were never to use the term 'federalist' in the context of provincial opposition to the Revolution. In this respect they were viewing the Revolution very much on the terms of the Parisian leaders' choosing, and did not gain a proper perspective on the scope of differing provincial responses to what was happening. This said, their specific comments on individual episodes or issues of the Revolution – above all Arthur Young's challenge to the Parisian Jacobins – are of great value in judging some aspects of the provinces' relationship with the metropolis.

Finances

While the Parisians became increasingly obsessed with the fear of Counter-Revolution and intensified their own Revolution, the National Assembly and the ministry (still led by Necker) tried to tackle the perennial financial crisis, which had been the very cause of the constitutional upheavals a year earlier.

The cares of office weighed heavily on Necker. On 13 October Morris found him 'sombre and *triste*, and so engrossed by affairs of subsistence that I cannot speak to him'. The outcome of his 'engrossment' was the plan to nationalize church property. This was agreed by the National Assembly on 20 November in a 'tedious session, from which I [Morris] derive a violent headache'.[26]

On 16 December Morris wrote despairingly of the ministry's inexplicable refusal to take his advice on how to run the fiscal system: 'Montesquiou will propose tomorrow a plan of finance, which consists in issuing a large sum of *billets d'états* bearing interest ... it is good for nothing ... but the character of this country is precipitation, not to mention the vaulting ambition which o'erleaps itself.'

These *'billets'* were not in fact the *Assignats* eventually to be issued against church property, but an initial measure in the nature of government stock backed by the ecclesiastical assets.[27] (Montesquiou was in fact presenting the plan as chairman of the relevant committee. The detail of the plan to alienate church property had been worked out by Talleyrand.)

It is fitting to end this survey of comments about the state of French finances in late 1789 with an observation from Short. Talking of the 'evil' of the still-present threat of bankruptcy, he said: 'Still the resources of this country are so immense as well as from their annual revenue, as the great objects of ecclesiastical property and the royal domains that the evil can only be temporary.'[28]

The King's Position

Short described the king's life and duties in Paris, paying particular attention to his personal popularity with the Parisians now that he was living among them: 'The king went on foot some days ago from the Tuileries to the Champs Elysées to review one of the divisions of the *Garde Nationale*. His familiarity was received with such cries of joy and *vive le Roy* as cannot be described. He returned on foot through the crowd to receive the *corps diplomatique*.'[29]

The British embassy, however, talked in terms of a 'dark face' in the context of the royal family's enforced presence in Paris. They were 'guarded more like prisoners than princes', and Louis XVI was forbidden to go out for exercise. The embassy predicted a third and bloodier revolution to come, implying their executions.[30]

Short's Summary and Arthur Young's Return to France

The events of 1789 were summed up by William Short on 30 November: 'Thus the political revolution may be considered as effected so far as it relates to the transfer of all power into the hands of the representatives of the people.'[31] With the winter relatively mild,[32] the political situation in Paris stable if unpleasing, the Counter-Revolution still an empty threat and the king a prisoner of popular democracy, the commentators in Paris could convince themselves that the great days of the Revolution were over.

Arthur Young re-entered France on 25 December 1789, and his account of the southern provinces also suggests a Revolution which had burnt itself out:

> At Pont-de-Beauvoisin and Bourgoin, our passports were demanded by the *milice bourgeoise*, but nowhere else; they assure us, that the country is perfectly quiet everywhere, and have no guards mounted in the villages, nor any suspicion of fugitives, as in the summer. Not far from La Verpilière, pass the burnt *château* of M. de Veau ... in August ... it had then but lately been laid in ashes; and a peasant was hanging on one of the trees of the avenue by the road, one among many who were seized by the *milice bourgeoise* for this atrocious act.[33]

The picture of the militia stringing up peasants who took direct action against their *seigneurs* shows how different the Revolution in Provence was at this date from the situation in Paris.

Young journeyed on to take up an invitation to inspect the Lyons' silk industry with a Protestant minister, Monsieur de Frossard:

> M. de Frossard is a steady advocate for the new constitution establishing in France. At the same time, all those I have conversed with in the city represent the state of the manufacture as melancholy to the last degree.

Twenty thousand people are fed by charity, and consequently very ill fed; and the mass of distress, in all kinds, among the lower classes, is greater than ever was known, or than anything of which they had an idea. The chief cause of the evil felt here is the stagnation of trade, occasioned by the emigrations of the rich from the kingdom, and the general want of confidence in merchants and manufacturers; whence, of course, bankruptcies are common.

Young hurried on to Paris much faster than he normally liked to travel 'for the sake of observing the extraordinary state of things; of a king, queen, and dauphin of France, actual prisoners'.[34]

CHAPTER 8

1790 to the Fête de la Fédération
(January to July 1790)

'The present devotion to liberty is a sort of rage'

THE main feature of politics in 1790 was the mass of detailed, undramatic legislation needed to put flesh on the bones of the new regime. The commentators followed this work and, in the case of the Americans, were actually involved in it. Their main concern, however, was to chart the process of the Revolution as a series of political events and to assess its chances of establishing a permanent and stable regime. To put their despatches into context, they were writing more, in terms of volume, about the international crises of the day than about internal French politics. Arthur Young stayed in Paris in January 1790 and again brought his journalistic skills to bear on the scene. He attended the National Assembly and private functions hosted by aristocrats. He spoke to royalists and to the men who would shortly be called Jacobins, and he attended and was made an honorary member of the Jacobin Club. His very particular strength was to interview, in a modern sense, the political figures he met and to insist on straight answers to deliberately provocative questions.

Overview

At the start of the year a number of assessments were made of the political scene, which provide a framework for the forthcoming commentaries.

Summing up the despatches he had been receiving from Auckland, Lord Sheffield, the British Foreign Secretary, wrote pessimistically:

At present there seems no symptom of attaining anything worthy the description of a government in France. I cannot conceive it possible that a Revolution, so managed as it is, can proceed smoothly. Progressive distress must produce a crisis, and probably a grand burst. As yet there is no appearance of a great man rising either to restore the monarchy or lead the commonwealth.

He went on to lament the attacks on the crown and aristocracy.[1]

The best general account of the scene was given by Morris:

At present the people are fully determined to support the Assembly, and although there are some discontents, I do not believe that anything very serious exists in the style of opposition. Indeed, it would be wonderful if there should, for hitherto an extension of privileges and a remission of taxes to the lower class has marked every stage of the progress. Besides, the love of novelty is a great sweetener in revolutions. But the time will come when this novelty is over, and all its charms are gone. In lieu of the taxes remitted other taxes must be laid, for the public burden must be borne. The elected administrators must then either indulge their electors, which will be ruinous to the fisc, or, in urging the collection of taxes, displease their constituents. In all probability there will be a little of both; hence must arise bickerings and heart-burnings among the different districts, and a great langour throughout the kingdom, as the revenue must fall short of calculation in point of time, if not in amount (and that is the same thing where the revenue is concerned). It will follow that either the interest of the public debt will not be regularly paid, or that various departments will be starved; probably a little of both. Hence will result a loss of public credit, and then with much injury to commerce and manufactures, operating a further decrease of the means of revenue, and much debility as to the exterior operations of the kingdom. At this moment the discontented spirits will find congenial matter in abundance to work upon, and from that period all the future is involved in the mist of conjecture. If the reigning prince were not the small-beer character he is, there can be but little doubt that, watching events and making tolerable use of them, he would regain his authority. The Assembly may be divided into three parts. One, called the *aristocrats*, consists of the high clergy, the members of the law (not lawyers), and such of the nobility as think they should form a separate Order; another, which has no name, but which consists of all sorts of people, really friends to a free government. The third is composed of what are here called the *enragés*, that is, the *madmen*. These are the most numerous, and are of that class which in America is known by the name of pettifogging lawyers, together with a host of curates, and many of those who, in all revolutions, throng to the standard of change because they are not well. This party, in close alliance with the populace ... have already unhinged everything.... The aristocrats are without a leader, and without any plan or counsels as yet.... The middle party, who mean well, have unfortunately acquired their idea of government from books.[2]

Young took some general soundings of the state of the nation:

I have spoken with several persons today, and have stated objections to the present system, stronger even than they appear to me, in order to learn their sentiments; and it is evident, they are at the present under an apprehension of an attempt towards a counter-revolution. The danger of it very much, if not absolutely, results from the violence which has been used towards the royal family. The National Assembly was, before that period, answerable only for the permanent constitutional laws passed for the future; since that moment, it is equally answerable for the whole conduct of the government of the State, executive as well as legislative.[3]

Short reflected Morris's general outlook in his preview of the year:

Every part of the kingdom discovers a fixed determination to adhere to the decrees of the National Assembly and to obey them alone. It is to be observed however that the Assembly have as yet only been employed in abolishing those things which were onerous and obnoxious to the more numerous classes of the society. Many attribute the adhesion of all parts of the kingdom to this circumstance, and say, that when the Assembly proceed to lay new taxes or exact the collection of the old, the number of the partisans will diminish.

Short was pessimistic in January about the soundness of many of the detailed proposals for reform and feared in March that the attempt to do too much too soon would create a sufficient number of enemies for the Revolution, to increase greatly the risk of successful Counter-Revolution.[4]

Political Opinions and Clubs

Young, as seen above, took general soundings of the political mood of the capital. He also spoke at great length with individual deputies. On 15 January,

Dine at the Duke of Liancourt's. Among the company ... two young legislators, as *enragés* as if their names were only Barnave or Rabaut. In some allusions to the constitution of England, I found they hold it very cheap in regard to political liberty. The ideas of the moment, relative to plots and conspiracies, were discussed, but they seemed very generally to agree, that, however, the constitution might, by such means, be delayed, it was now absolutely impossible to prevent its taking place'.

He also observed: 'In a word, the present devotion to liberty is a sort of rage; it absorbs every other passion, and permits no other object to remain in view, than what promises to confirm it.'[5]

It became not just fashionable, but essential for anyone involved in politics to join a political club. Young described his own visit to the Jacobin Club and two features deserve special attention. The first was how the club functioned as a party caucus, and the second was the Revolutionary generosity of Young's reception there:

At night, M. Decretot and M. Blin carried me to the Revolution Club at the *Jacobins*; ... There were above one hundred deputies present, with a president in the chair; I was handed to him, and announced as the author of the *Arithmétique Politique*; the president standing up, repeated my name to the company, and demanded if there were any objections. None; and this is all the ceremony, not merely of an introduction, but of an election; for I was told, that now I was free to be present when I pleased, being a foreigner. Ten or a dozen other elections were made. In this club, the business that is to be brought into the National Assembly is regularly debated; the motions are read, that are intended to be made there, and rejected or corrected and approved. When these have been fully agreed to, the whole party are engaged to support them. Plans of conduct are there determined; proper persons nominated for being of committees, and presidents of the Assembly named. And I may add, that such is the majority of numbers, that whatever passes in this club is almost sure to pass in the Assembly.[6]

Other clubs also sprang up, as Short commented: 'The system of clubs has become general here.... One however which seems to take the ascendant is just opened under the title of the *Société de Quatre-Vingt-Neuf*', and Lafayette and the Duc de Liancourt were leading members. It is also appropriate here to include William Miles's assessment of this club in 1791. Miles found the club to be composed of 'men, who, although they had an active share in the Revolution, are anxious to invest the sovereign with more power than he possesses, and to destroy the Jacobins'.[7]

Lord Gower reported soon after taking up his post of British ambassador in June, that the Society of 1789 and the Jacobin Club 'are the places where most subjects are debated and determined upon before they are proposed in the National Assembly'.[8]

On the relationship between politics and social customs Young remarked:

At this dinner, according to custom, most of the deputies, especially the younger ones, were dressed *au polisson*, many of them without powder in their hair, and some in boots; not above four or five were neatly dressed. How times are changed! When they had nothing better to attend to, the fashionable Parisians were correctness itself, in all that pertained to the *toilette*, and were, therefore, thought a frivolous people; but now they have something of more importance than dress to occupy them; and the light and airy character that was usually given them will have no foundation in truth. Everything in this world depends on government.[9]

The British embassy paid some sociological attention to the nature of the Revolutionaries themselves. They passed an observation which is informative even if the wrong conclusion was drawn: 'It is remarkable: that ... two thirds of the mayors elected in the newly formed [municipalities] are of noble families, which proves that the nobility, contrary to the intentions of the National Assembly, have not lost all influence with the people.'[10]

The Conduct of the National Assembly

The conduct and effectiveness of the National Assembly was the focal point of the Revolution.

Young had been unimpressed by the proceedings at the States-General in June 1789, and he was still unimpressed by the National Assembly in January 1790:

> No other person [than l'abbé Maury] spoke without notes.... It can hardly be conceived how flat this mode of debate renders the transactions of the Assembly. Who would be in the gallery of the English House of Commons, if Mr Pitt were to bring a written speech, to be delivered on a subject on which Mr Fox was to speak before him? And in proportion to its being uninteresting to the hearer, is another evil, that of length-ening their sittings, since there are ten persons who will read their opinions, to one that is able to deliver an *impromptu*. The want of order, and every kind of confusion, prevails now almost as much as when the Assembly sat at Versailles. The interruptions given are frequent and long; and speakers, who have no right by the rules to speak, will attempt it.[11]

The conduct of the Assembly did not improve. The British embassy reported a session in April which had become a 'bear garden' and where troops had had to be called in to restore order after members started pelting 'each other with apples and oranges'.[12] Part of the problem was the payment after February 1790 of an attendance allowance of eighteen *livres* a day, which swelled the ranks of the deputies.[13]

Short gave the first hint – in March – that the members elected as deputies to the *ancien régime*'s States-General might not be able to see the job through under the Revolution. He wrote, specifically in the context of the failure of the *Assignats* to hold their value and restore confidence, 'Most people begin to lose hopes of the constitution being finished by the present assembly, and desire that a new convention be called.'[14]

The National Assembly and the King

The issue which underlay all others in the early Revolution was how an essentially republican representative assembly could coexist with a monar-chy. The one claimed a mandate for sovereignty from the 'people' or the 'nation' while the other claimed a mandate for absolute power from God and from customs sanctified by practice since time immemorial (to use *ancien régime* phraseology). More immediately there was the obvious problem that the king symbolized the old order and the Assembly the new, and the king's very existence could be a threat to the safety of the Revolution.

The solution to the latter problem had to be a political one, and the initiative could only come from the Assembly. The former issue was a constitutional one, and the French had the benefit of being able to draw on the experience of another country, having recently spent several years debating the relationship between monarchical (in the form of Presidential) and representative power and achieving a *modus vivendi* between them. This country was the United States of America, which had only just finalized its own constitution, and two of the men who had helped draft that constitution (Morris and Paine) were in Paris and happy to offer their services as – in effect – constitutional consultants to the new French government. It cannot be an accident that the eventual relationship between the king and the National Assembly paralleled very closely the relationship between the American President and Congress. (As proof of this, America in the late twentieth century is finding itself bedevilled by the very same conflicts between these two powers, in the context of foreign policy and the right to declare or not declare war, as was the French government in May 1790.)

To take the problem of the king's relationship to the Revolution first, Arthur Young made the following analysis of the situation:

> The idea of plots and conspiracies has come to such a height as greatly to alarm the leaders of the revolution. The disgust that spreads every day at their transactions arises more from the king's situation than from any other circumstance. They cannot, after the scenes that have passed, venture to set him at liberty before the constitution is finished; and they dread, at the same time, a change working in his favour in the minds of the people. In this dilemma, a plan is laid for persuading His Majesty to go suddenly to the National Assembly, and, in a speech, to declare himself perfectly satisfied with their proceedings, and to consider himself as at the head of the revolution, in terms so couched, as to take away all idea or pretence of his being in a state of confinement or coercion. This is at present a favourite plan; the only difficulty will be, to persuade the king to take a step that will apparently preclude him from whatever turn or advantage the general feeling of the provinces may work in his favour; for, after such a measure, he will have reason to expect that his friends will second the views of the democratical party, from an absolute despair of any other principles becoming efficient. It is thought probable, that this scheme will be brought about; and if it is, it will do more to ease their apprehensions of any attempts than any other plan.

Young reported the next day, though, that the king had indeed turned the plan down.[15]

Young was, in fact, wrong about the king not accepting the plan. He did indeed present himself to the Assembly to prove he was not being held a prisoner and that he was, in the British embassy's words, 'the true and constant support of the Revolution'.

The British embassy went on to describe the scene when he, in effect, made his formal submission to the Assembly: 'The applause on this occasion was very great and the exulting joy of triumph was manifested [by the Popular Party]. The aristocratical party remained in sullen silence and seemed deeply hurt by this step on the part of the king which they considered as their final blow, as indeed it is.'

The embassy, however, saw the political benefits and wisdom of the act, which 'may produce a good effect in the generality of the nation, and inspire that confidence which is so much wanting to render the Revolution effective'.[16]

Short also described the event in optimistic terms, stating that Louis xvi

went on foot, announced his coming by a short letter to the president and desired to be received without ceremony. The violent of both parties were displeased with the measure and the speech, but the great majority of all classes were highly satisfied. It is hoped it will put an end to the disorders which are prevailing in several provinces against persons and property to those supposed to be disaffected to the revolution.[17]

Morris reported the king's own reaction to his submission to the National Assembly: 'he was very much out of humour, also, all the morning, and that when he returned from the Assembly he passed some time in tears'.[18]

Having gained the king's obedience to the Revolution to the point where it was safe to allow him to continue to play his role, the Assembly had to regularize that role. The king was still nominally the head of state and head of government, but his ambivalent position meant that this had not been confirmed by the National Assembly. The National Assembly had no executive authority and the judiciary was in a state of flux. This meant that there was no effective direction of civil administration, and no universally recognized authority for it. The result, as Short put it, was that: 'The executive as yet continues in a state of torpor.'[19]

Looking at the issue in prospect, Morris wrote: 'Their *Assemblée Nationale* will be something like the old Congress, and the king will be *called* executive magistrate. As yet they have been busily engaged in pillaging the present occupant of his authority. How much they will leave him will depend upon the chapter of accidents; I believe it will be very little.'[20]

The British embassy felt that there was some deliberate delay on the

Assembly's part in addressing this issue, or at least resolving it, because, "They seem much enamoured with their own importance.'[21] In fact the Assembly did confirm the king as head of the executive in an uneasy compromise in which the king held enough power to embarrass the Revolution, but the Assembly with its popular support would always be the *force majeure*.

Foreign Affairs

Having started down the path of making the king head of executive power, the Revolutionaries realized that this must lead to his being the power responsible for the day to day conduct of foreign relations, commander-in-chief of the armed forces, and the authority responsible for declaring war.

In calmer times this issue might have been deferred or fudged, but the international situation demanded that France conduct an active foreign policy and be in a position to react quickly to outside threats. In four areas the Revolution could not ignore the outside world. First, the idea of the Revolution had seized the imaginations of those seeking change in their own *ancien régimes* and filled their rulers' minds with fear of the Revolution spreading. Second, for some legal purposes the provinces of Alsace and Lorraine still fell within the Holy Roman Empire. Thus any moves to abolish feudalism there infringed the prerogatives of the Imperial (i.e. Habsburg) authorities in Germany. Third, the city of Avignon (and the Comtat of Venaissin or just 'Comtat') was part of the Papal States. When the French people living in Avignon rose in rebellion against the Pope in order to join in their compatriots' revolution, it became an international crisis with the Catholic powers supporting the Papacy. Fourth, as mentioned earlier, there was a series of long-running international crises quite separate from the Revolution, which – especially in the case of the Austrian Netherlands – could not help but impinge on France.

Young noted the hostility of other *ancien régime* powers in January:

Certainly the eyes of all the sovereigns, and of all the great nobility in Europe, are on the French revolution; they look with amazement, and even with terror, upon a situation which may possibly be hereafter their own case; and they must expect, with anxiety, that some attempts will be made to reverse an example, that will not want copies, whenever the period is favourable to make them.[22]

Morris commented in very similar terms: 'All Europe just now is like a mine ready to explode, and if this winter does not produce peace [in the Austrian Netherlands], next summer will behold a wider extension of the war.'[23]

Short painted the reverse side of the picture, that delegations of foreign subjects had been petitioning the National Assembly in the name of 'fraternity' to carry the Revolution to their countries.[24]

In the historiography of the Revolution one of its great events is the renunciation of wars of conquest. This renunciation was, in its context, just the footnote to a much more urgent and immediate debate on the machinery for the Revolution to be able to mobilize for, declare, and fight a war if the need arose – and specifically to defend itself from an Austrian and/or Prussian invasion from the Austrian Netherlands or the Empire. The central feature of this debate was whether to confirm the king as the power with the authority to declare war and act as commander-in-chief.

This debate lasted from 14 to 22 May and was conducted against a background of 'unanimous determination in the Assembly to submit to the expense of a war if necessary'.

The debate was held in the immediate context of the Nootka Sound crisis between Britain and Spain (to whom France was still technically treaty bound by the Bourbon Family Compact) and a rumour that Austria and Prussia were planning to partition Germany. To confuse matters still further though, the war would not have been in alliance with Spain but against her because of her support for Counter-Revolutionary *émigrés*.[25]

Short also reported that these debates generated a stronger popular reaction than any other topic in the National Assembly to date, with Mirabeau's (successful) support for the king a particular cause of discontent: 'There were then greater crowds than had ever been seen in the Tuileries. They shewed in their discourses menacing signs of displeasure, swore that Mirabeau was a traitor and should be hung to a lantern, and sometimes discovered even a desire to enter the Assembly.'[26]

The Abolition of Slavery and Commercial Stagnation

Issues of philosophy and foreign and colonial affairs also interacted with internal politics and the national economy. Unlike the Americans during their Revolution, the French did not shrink from addressing the issue of slavery and the contradiction of declaring all (white) men (if not women) equal while enslaving black people. The French perceived the issue of slavery as primarily a moral one, while the British were more concerned at this date with its economic implications.

The scheme of emancipating the negroes, or at least of putting an end to importing them, which they borrowed from England, has thrown Nantes, Havre, Marseilles, Bordeaux, and all other places connected secondarily with that commerce, into the utmost agitation. The Count de Mirabeau says publicly, that he is sure of carrying the vote to put an end to negro slavery. It is very much the conversation at present, and principally amongst the leaders, who say, that as the revolution was founded on philosophy, and supported by metaphysics, such a plan cannot but be congenial.[27]

The British embassy was more forthright, and stated that the proposal to abolish slavery arose 'from a mistaken zeal for humanity'.[28] The Americans remained silent on the subject.

Young linked the fears of the economic implications of abolition to a more general stagnation of trade and industry:

> Another circumstance, which gives great disquiet at present to the leaders of the revolution, are the accounts daily received from all parts of the kingdom, of the distress, and even starving condition of the manufacturers, artists, and sailors, which grow more and more serious, and must make the idea of an attempt to overturn the revolution so much the more alarming and dangerous.

Young also reported outbreaks of Luddism in Normandy: 'The cotton mills [in Normandy] have stood still nine months; and so many spinning jennies have been destroyed by the people, under the idea that such machines were contrary to their interests, that the [cotton] trade is in a deplorable situation.'[29]

Historians have paid a great deal of attention to the Revolutionary government's responses to the country's economic problems, and particularly to the *Loi Chapelier* in June 1791, which forbade strikes. This subsequent legislation went unobserved, but the British embassy did note a measure in February 1790 to control organized labour. They were also all too well aware of the symptoms of economic stagnation, whatever its causes or cures: 'Each day seems to aggravate the sufferings and multiply the complaints of the people.'[30]

The French West Indies

The opening of the debate in January on the abolition of slavery had a dramatic effect in the French West Indian possessions. The full story of the Revolution there lies outside the scope of this book, but the white planter aristocracy were threatening to make – to use a much later term – a unilateral declaration of independence to preserve their economic and racial position, while the black and mixed race inhabitants of the islands rebelled against the planters to secure their own place in the Revolution. Effective control over the islands was lost.

This Caribbean crisis did not disturb the Revolutionary government as much as might be imagined. First, the *ancien régime* had always undervalued the importance of commerce and, therefore, by extension, the contribution made by the sugar trade to the national economy. Second, there had long been a strong anti-colonial movement in the *ancien régime* based on the

economic philosophy of the Physiocrats, a number of whom had held ministerial office. This anti-colonialism was based on the twin observations that
economic success, based on slave labour in the colonies, undermined the
strength of the domestic commercial and agricultural sectors, and that the
cost of defending the colonies in terms of maintaining a premier navy exceeded
any profit derived from the possessions. And third, of course, the country
never doubted that order would be restored there eventually.

The West Indies were, therefore, very much a sideshow. The disturbances
there had the incidental effect of heightening insecurity at home, of aggra-
vating the government's economic problems, of reminding the Revolutionary
government that it had a navy which it might wish to use if its officers were
reliable enough, and of creating the novelty of a revolution in another
continent by people of another race.

In July the new British ambassador, Lord Gower, commented drily: 'it is
difficult to say in what part of the French dominions there are not commo-
tions'. He went on to report what happened when the government tried to
provision the fleet in case it wished to reassert its authority overseas: 'most
of the municipalities, through whose territories powder and other ammu-
nitions are to pass, have stopped them'.[31] Thus an attempt to intervene abroad
had created, or drawn attention to, yet more internal problems.

The Work of the National Assembly: Administrative, Fiscal and Judicial Reform, and the Abolition of the Nobility

The National Assembly dealt with a mass of detailed business in the first half
of 1790 to the varying approbation and despair of the commentators. One of
the Assembly's first acts in the new year was to put a stop to the *ancien
régime*'s practice of paying pensions on the basis of government (or court)
patronage rather than for need, merit or services rendered. This caused Morris
to fall out with Madame de Staël when the topic was discussed at her salon.
'The National Assembly have stopped the pensions . . . I tell [Madame de Staël]
that when privileges were abolished the road was opened for the destruction
of all property. This gives rise to endless dispute, in which she shows much
genius and little good breeding.'[32]

Morris wrote scathingly of the plan to replace the *ancien régime*'s provinces
by *'Départements'*:

This (late) kingdom will be cast into a congeries of little democracies,
not laid out according to the rivers and mountains, but with the square
and compass, according to latitude and longitude; and as the provinces
had anciently different laws (called *coutumes*), and as the clippings and
parings of several provinces must fall together within some of the new

Thomas Jefferson (1743–1826), US ambassador from 1784 to 1789, from a bust by Houdon sculptured in Paris.

John Frederick Sackville, Duke of Dorset (1745–99), British ambassador in Paris from 1783 to 1790.

William Eden, Baron Auckland (1744–1814), attached to the British embassy from 1785 to 1787 and one of Pitt's advisers on France thereafter.

George Granville Leveson-Gower, Earl of Gower and Duke of Sutherland (1758–1833), British ambassador in Paris from 1790 to 1792.

Arthur Young (1741–1820), agricultural researcher and political journalist.

The opening of the States–
General at Versailles on 5 May
1789, as watched by three of the
commentators (see p. 41).

(see p. 41)

Gouverneur Morris (1752–
1816), special envoy from US
tobacco exporters and from
George Washington between
1789 and 1792, and US
ambassador in Paris from 1792
to 1794.

'Lynch law': the hanging of baker François in October 1789 (see p. 87).

The popular violence of the sacking of the Hôtel de Ville in Strasbourg on 21 July 1789, as witnessed and described by Arthur Young (see p. 68).

William Short (1759–1849), *chargé d'affaires* and acting US ambassador from 1789 to 1792.

A rather idealized portrait of the Marquis de Lafayette as commander of the National Guard (p. 64).

An engraving showing a meeting of a local political club.

David's pen sketch of Marie–
Antoinette on her way to the
guillotine (see p. 181 for a
British spy's account of her at
this time).

The second storming of the
Tuileries on 10 August 1792
(see p. 168).

The last portrait of Louis XVI, drawn by Joseph Ducreux three days before the king's execution on 21 January 1793.

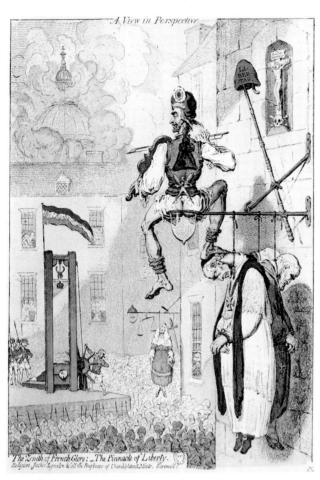

The Zenith of French Glory; _ The Pinnacle of Liberty.
Religion Justice Loyalty & all the Bugbears of Unenlightend Minds, Farewell!

Two views of violent events from opposite political perspectives:

'View in Perspective: the Zenith of French Glory – the Pinnacle of Liberty' (1793); a British caricature by the anti-Jacobin, James Gillray, of the excesses of the *sans-culottes* against the background of Louis XVI's execution.

'Les Journées de septembre' by the actively Jacobin J–L Prieur, showing the massacre in the Abbaye prison (2–3 September 1792) (see p. 175 for a British spy's eye-witness description of this same scene).

divisions, I think such fermenting matter must give them a kind of political colic.

(Morris was, in the event, wrong about the nature of departmental boundaries, as groups of departments fall exactly within the old provincial borders.) Short was also not optimistic that the new structure could be implemented or made to function.[33]

Morris and Short were both invited in late January to help the government with plans to reform the judiciary. Morris wrote that Lafayette: 'tells me that he wishes to have a meeting of Mr Short (*chargé d'affaires*), Mr Paine, and myself, to consider their judiciary, because his place imposes on him the necessity of being right. I tell him Paine can do him no good, for that, although he has an excellent pen to write, he has but an indifferent head to think.'

Short also mentioned the approach, but when Lafayette approached him two days later Paine's name had been dropped. Short also reported the less than satisfactory progress of the reform proposals three months later: 'They are now discussing the judiciary system. The progress, as you may suppose in so numerous an assembly and composed of such exasperated parties, is slow.'[34]

In January Short also reported debates on improving civil liberties for Jews and members of convicted criminals' families. There were several debates about the classification of citizenship as 'active' (i.e. voting) and 'passive' (i.e. non-voting).[35]

In March fiscal reform was on the agenda, with Short's advice again in demand: 'I have had several conversations with some of the members of the committee named for reforming the taxes.' The topics under consideration included abolition of the *Gabelle* (the tax on salt) and the state monopoly of tobacco (on which Short lobbied unsuccessfully on behalf of American importers), and the abolition of the hated tax farms (the system whereby the *ancien régime* had 'privatized' the collection of some taxes).[36] (Short made the suggestion to his Secretary of State that once the *Gabelle* had been abolished, American ships should carry salt as ballast to French ports. Morris was not involved in these discussions as he was on an extended business trip to the Netherlands.)

In April there was great 'heat and tumult' in the debate in the National Assembly on whether the Catholic Church should remain the established church. The strength of reaction on both sides was such that the issue was deferred, leaving the Catholic Church effectively disestablished: 'So that France now approaches more nearly than any other country the example which the United States have given the world on the subject of freedom of conscience and exercise of religion.'[37]

The abolition of nobility, as the British embassy had predicted in December 1789, was a logical step for the Revolution to take. It was in fact heralded

by a move at court where Louis XVI: 'has given orders ... to the herald's office
to receive no longer the genealogical titles which were formerly necessary to
enable a person to be presented at court'.

This was followed, on 19 June, when: 'a kind of enthusiasm took place in
the Assembly and spread from one member to another until they seemed to
be at a loss what sacrifice to make or what prejudices to attack'.

Morris was not amused when he heard of the abolition of nobility, and
predicted dire consequences: 'Advices from France announce the total abolition of the French nobility, down to the very arms and livery; this upon the
motion of some of the Whig nobles. ... Heaven knows how this will all end,
but I fear badly, unless they are saved by a foreign war.'[38]

Assignats

Of all the administrative and fiscal issues facing the Revolution, and one
deserving separate attention, was the *Assignats*. As seen through earlier
comments, the system for realizing credit from church assets had had an
uncertain start. The British embassy watched its progress, and commented
in January and February on the financial climate generally, but giving contradictory assessments: 'the subject of finance seems principally to occupy
the attention of people here at present', and France 'seems to have lost sight
of the foe nearest her door, I mean the disorder which reigns in her finances'.
The embassy was clear, though, that the measures so far taken had not
produced enough cash to meet the state's outgoings.[39]

Short mentioned the *Assignats* themselves in prospect on 10 February.

> The stocks continue falling rapidly and it is apprehended with reason
> that government will ere long be obliged to make use of a kind of paper
> money which is called *Assignats*. This is an emission which is to be
> receivable in preference in the purchase of ecclesiastical lands. The specie
> will then be reserved for the pay of the troops.[40]

As, in effect, credit notes, the *Assignats* were not a success and it was
necessary quickly to turn them into a full-blown paper currency. (One reason
for not having done this straight away was the intense distrust with which
paper currency had been held in France since Law's disastrous experiment
during Louis xv's regency.) Short traced their fortunes:

> The kind of paper money which circulates in Paris depreciates. ... The
> first object of *Assignats* was merely to facilitate the sale of ecclesiastical
> property, but it now seems very certain that the Assembly will be forced
> to go further and convert them into an absolute paper money, to be a
> legal tender in all cases whatsoever. This important question is to be
> brought on in a day or two.[41]

The system still had to reckon with the opposition of some of the clergy to the seizure of the church's assets. They were now in a position to cause economic damage to the regime, as well as more general disorder: 'the clergy are exerting their influence both in the pulpit and confessional to deter purchasers, and to engage their parishioners to petition against the sale of ecclesiastical property.... Thus they have enlisted in their cause the bigoted of every class. Riots and bloodshed already have taken place between the catholics and protestants.'[42]

Mirabeau, Necker, Lafayette and Orléans

While no new figures emerged onto the political scene, the relative fortunes of three of the leading characters (Necker, Lafayette and Mirabeau) varied. Mirabeau attracted very little attention during this period, retaining his reputation as the Revolution's *enfant terrible* and finest orator. As seen earlier, his support for royal power threatened his popularity with the Parisians.

Morris and Short both felt that Necker was losing his grip on power. Morris wrote what could have been his political epitaph in January: 'he understands *man* as a covetous creature, he does not understand *mankind*, a defect which is irremediable.... From the moment of convening the States-General, he has been afloat on the wide ocean of incidents.'[43] In April Short reported that he was increasingly out of sympathy with the National Assembly.[44]

Lafayette was still the leading figure of the Revolution and the idol of the mob.[45] There was, though, a real problem for him in the shape of doubts about his ability to exercise effective control over the National Guard and Paris militia forces, as Young pointed out:

> This critical situation has made a constant spirit of exertion necessary amongst the Paris militia. The great object of M. Lafayette, and the other military leaders, is to improve their discipline, and to bring them into such form as to allow a rational dependence on them, in case of their being wanted in the field; but such is the spirit of freedom, that even in the military there is so little subordination, that a man is an officer today and in the ranks tomorrow; a mode of proceeding, that makes it the more difficult to bring them to the point their leaders see necessary.[46]

Morris was not convinced that Lafayette could remain master of the situation, but could see no one to replace him: 'I sincerely wish I could say that there are able men at hand to take the helm, should the present pilot abandon ship. But I have great apprehensions as to those who may succeed.'[47]

Orléans decided to end his period of exile in July and return for the *Fête de la Fédération*. Short reported on his arrival in Paris: 'He was received coolly by the king, graciously by the queen, and most contemptuously by the courtiers', but he still enjoyed popular support.[48]

By contrast Gower reported that at the *fête* itself he was 'not applauded by the people and treated with insult by the nobility'.[49]

Condition of the Royal Family

When Young returned to Paris he made it his first priority to find out how the royal family were faring.

> After breakfast, walk in the gardens of the Tuileries, where there is the most extraordinary sight that either French or English eyes could ever behold in Paris. The king, walking with six grenadiers of the *milice bourgeoise*, with an officer or two of his household, and a page. The doors of the gardens are kept shut in respect to him, in order to exclude everybody but deputies, or those who have admission-tickets. When he entered the palace, the doors of the gardens were thrown open for all without distinction, though the queen was still walking with a lady of her court. She also was attended so closely by the *gardes bourgeoises*, that she could not speak, but in a low voice, without being heard by them. A mob followed her, talking very loud, and paying no other apparent respect than that of taking off their hats wherever she passed, which was indeed more than I expected. Her Majesty does not appear to be in health; she seems to be much affected, and shows it in her face; but the king is as plump as ease can render him. By his orders, there is a little garden railed off for the dauphin to amuse himself in, and a small room is built in it to retire to in case of rain; here he was at work with his little hoe and rake, but not without a guard of two grenadiers.... All the family being kept thus close prisoners (for such they are in effect) affords, at first view, a shocking spectacle; and is really so, if the act were not absolutely necessary to effect the revolution; this I conceive to be impossible; but if it were necessary, no one can blame the people for taking every measure possible to secure that liberty they had seized in the violence of a revolution. At such a moment, nothing is to be condemned but what endangers the national freedom.[50]

Morris gave a very similar account, but adding some advice on the royal children and criticizing very severely the king himself for the impossible position in which he placed his own supporters:

> the king should send the Comte d'Artois his children, so that the whole of the royal family should not be in the power of their enemies.... The king is in effect a prisoner at Paris and obeys entirely the National Assembly.

... what will you have from a creature who, situated as he is, eats and drinks and sleeps well, and laughs and is as merry a grig as lives? The idea that they will give him some money when he can economize, and that he will have no trouble in governing, contents him entirely. Poor man, he little thinks how unstable is his situation. He is beloved, but it is not with the sort of love which a monarch should inspire; it is that kind of good-natured pity which one feels for a led captive. There is, besides, no possibility of serving him, for at the slightest show of opposition he gives up everything, and every person.[51]

Unrest and Counter-Revolution

The position of the king cannot be separated from the more general problems of public order and the threat of Counter-Revolution. The king himself was trebly at risk. He would always be a legitimate target for Revolutionary zeal by his very existence, but any suspicion of involvement in Counter-Revolutionary activity would sign his death warrant. At the same time – as will be explored later – the Counter-Revolutionaries were seeing him personally as an impediment to effective action being taken against the Revolution. Into this volatile political situation came the added problem of continuing popular disturbances over food prices.

The Revolution was moving to the stage where any opposition, from whatever motive, could only be interpreted as Counter-Revolutionary unless undertaken in the name of the Revolution itself. Young put it thus in the context of riots about bread in Versailles:

such movements are certainly very dangerous, for they cannot exist so near Paris, without the aristocratical party of the old government endeavouring to take advantage of them....

The riots at Versailles are said to be serious; a plot is talked of, for eight hundred men to march, armed, to Paris, at the instigation of somebody, to join somebody; the intention, to murder Lafayette, Bailly, and Necker; and very wild and improbable reports are propagated every moment. They have been sufficient to induce M. Lafayette to issue, yesterday, an order concerning the mode of assembling the militia, in case of any sudden alarm.

Two days later the rioting spread to Paris. Young showed how this bread riot had managed to link itself to the cause of the Revolution.

A great commotion among the populace late last night, which is said to have arisen on two accounts; one, to get at the Baron de Besenval, who is in prison, in order to hang him; the other to demand bread at 2 *sous* the pound. They eat it at present at the rate of twenty-two millions a year cheaper than the rest of the kingdom, and yet they demand a further reduction.[52]

The British embassy reported that on 8 January the workmen at the Tuileries had demonstrated for lower bread prices: 'The spirit of insurrection seemed contagious that day.' Both this, and a demonstration in sympathy in the *Faubourg* Saint-Antoine, were dispersed by troops. Linked to this lawlessness, often in the name of the Revolution, on the streets of Paris were 'endless' tales of violence against the *seigneurs* from the countryside.[53]

Much more serious, however, was what seemed to be a deliberate attempt to subvert the National Guard on 12 January. The British embassy was aware of a mutiny – ostensibly about pay – but Short had the full measure of it:

> Whilst writing this letter I observed a large detachment of troops paraded and marched off from the *corps de garde* opposite to us. Their return here has informed us of an event which may have dangerous consequences. M. de Lafayette had been informed some days past that money was distributed among the troops of the *garde soldée* in order to excite a sedition. This morning a large number assembled in the Champs Elysées, many with arms and all of them with cartouches. Troops were ordered from different quarters of Paris and marched with so good order as to envelop the mutinous and make them prisoners without firing a gun. There were 250. They were immediately stripped of their uniform and carried off to the prisons of St Denis.[54]

Young found himself surrounded by rumours and alarums of Counter-Revolution:

> I remarked in all these conversations, that the belief of plots, among the disgusted [aristocratical] party, for setting the king at liberty, is general; [the republicans] seem almost persuaded, that the revolution will not be absolutely finished before some such attempts are made; and it is curious to observe, that the general voice is, that if an attempt were to be made, in such a manner as to have the least appearance of success, it would undoubtedly cost the king his life.

He greatly regretted the possibility of successful Counter-Revolution, despite the assurances given to him by royalists: 'every honest man must hope no such event would take place; for if a counter-revolution should be effected, it would establish a despotism much heavier than ever France experienced'.[55]

On 26 January Morris reported that he had discussed the problem of Counter-Revolution being instigated by *émigrés* with Lafayette, who told him: 'he has gotten into his possession a *mémoire* written by the refugees of Turin to stir up the princes of Germany against France'.[56]

The reports of Counter-Revolutionary plots and of plans for armies led by *émigrés* to invade France, became one of the staples of news from Paris and their frequency increased as the Revolution progressed. This type of report did not cease until the declaration of war in 1792, when the *émigré* threat was absorbed into the wider external threat. The rumours of royalist plots within France continued with greater or lesser frequency on into the Empire. Two reports can stand as representative of scores. The first, in fact, follows up Morris's with Gower informing Whitehall in July: 'that a camp of 1,500 men is forming in Savoy'. (Savoy was then still part of the kingdom of Piedmont, whose capital was Turin.) Gower also reported that the *émigrés* had tried to subvert the garrison of Grenoble in order to gain an easy invasion route.[57]

The second is an account of what would seem, for the commentators, to have been the most dangerous of the royalist plots in early 1790, that led by the Comte de Maillebois and involving other Bourbon sovereigns. Short gave a summary of it, putting it into the context of the Revolution's own need for external threats to cement internal cohesion and loyalty:

> A discovery has been lately made of a design to counteract the present revolution, formed by the Count de Maillebois an old and experienced general. It is said he was betrayed by his secretary.... Several persons have been already examined relative to this discovery.... It will probably turn out merely the reverie of an intriguing enterprizing mind.... These conspiracies either real or supposed serve to continue the zeal of the armed militia and will probably produce no other effect.[58]

Almost none of these plots and invasion scares had any intrinsic importance, and not knowing the detail of Louis' correspondence with the *émigrés* the commentators could not make proper sense of them, but taken together they created a climate of internal and external insecurity and kept the ambiguous position of the king ever in view.

The British embassy had no faith in the occasional provincial initiative to oppose the Revolution, describing them as: 'the feeble struggles of the friends of the old system of government to recover their lost preponderance'.[59]

Short reported one of these provincial disorders in more detail:

> The members of the *parlement* [of Rennes] and their partisans endeavoured to frighten the Assembly by asserting that they were supported by the people of their province. Accounts have just arrived here that the people are exempting themselves from that calumny by burning *châteaux*, and committing those violences, which had ceased there as in the other parts of France, on supposing that the aristocratic party had given up the contest.[60]

As part of the climate of apprehension and uncertainty there was a continuing break-down in law and order. Short had direct experience of this. On
3 March he was robbed of 1,500 *livres* by a dishonest courier. He commented
glumly: 'the situation of the police is so deranged as leaves me not the most
glimmering hope of recovering any part of it'.[61]

The Civil Oath of Allegiance and the *Fête de la Fédération*
The Revolution clearly needed a fillip. The old order had been cowed, but not
yet destroyed and the new regime had yet to assert real authority. The
problems of food distribution and prices had not been overcome. The loyalty
of the armed forces was doubtful – whether from zeal to be more Revolutionary
than the National Assembly or from lingering loyalties to the monarchy.
There were clearly those, even if they were only common criminals, who
were profiteering from the breakdown in the *ancien régime*'s system of law
and order. The economy was stagnating, there was no confidence in the
Revolution's new financial measures and revenue from taxation was not
flowing into the Control-General. The Revolution still contained at its heart
the damaging contradiction of a populist assembly trying to coexist with a
monarch subdued only by the power of the mob.

The first part of this fillip was the civil oath of allegiance to the new regime.
This was designed to give all French subjects a focus of loyalty and national
unity to replace the now no longer absolute monarchy. After the oath had
been taken in the Assembly, Short wrote glowingly: 'The same flame will
certainly spread through the provinces, where it is to be hoped it will put an
end to all the violences and disorders.'[62]

The second part was to be a massive privately inspired but state-sponsored
celebration of the anniversary of the storming of the Bastille. Short described
its inception:

> In several parts of France different bodies of *gardes nationales* have
> assembled in order to form a federation in support of the present con-
> stitution. They have in general been nothing more than a kind of patriotic
> feast, with a renewal of the civic oath (*d'être fidèles â la loi, à la nation et
> au roi*) and an address of adhesion to the National Assembly and their
> decrees. These assemblies have given rise to an idea in the municipality
> of Paris to invite deputations from all the *gardes nationales* in the kingdom,
> and from the several regiments of regular troops to assemble at Paris on
> the anniversary of the taking of the Bastille ... it is supposed the whole
> will be between ten and twelve thousand. . . . What is to be the object of
> this meeting, and what its event is uncertain.[63]

Joined to this theme of national unity was one of reconciliation and the
hope that some of the leading *émigrés* might return and end their opposition

to the Revolution. Gower reported, for example, that '*Les Dames de la Halles* have sent deputies from their body to Turin, inviting the Comte and Comtesse d'Artois to Paris, in order to be present at the *Fédération*.'[64] Somewhat disingenuously, as seen earlier, Orléans included himself in this general mood of reconciliation.

The Anglo-Saxon commentators were not so much impressed by the Revolutionary credentials of the *fête* as fearful of the opportunity it would offer for public disorder. Short wrote: 'As the 14th of July approaches the apprehensions of disorder seem to increase.'

Gower mentioned disturbances in the *Faubourg* St-Antoine and continued:

These dissentions, my Lord, become alarming in proportion as the 14th approaches.... it is scarcely to be supposed that [the *fête*] can end without some disagreeable event, occasioned by the intoxication of many thousand people assembled together, but I am far from believing that there is any pre-meditated plan to create fresh disturbances.[65]

The commentators did also give their readers some outline of the content of the event. Gower reported that some of those who had actually stormed the Bastille would take pride of place so that 'France may contemplate the first conquerors of liberty.'[66]

Short reported on the amount of effort being put into preparing for the *fête*:

In the meantime preparations are going on with the greatest activity in the Champs de Mars. 13,000 workmen were employed there three days ago, and two thousand more were to be added yesterday.

The deputies are arriving from all parts of France for the 14th. Besides those who are deputed, a great number of others come as spectators. It began to be feared that the works of the Champs de Mars would not be finished in time. Some volunteers went to assist the workmen employed. This spread like a flame through Paris and people of both sexes and of all ranks and descriptions flock there to work ... Many arms and legs have already been broken in the confusion.[67]

For the French the *fête* itself was a climactic event of transcending importance. The British and Americans, however, could not work up the same enthusiasm. They all reported factually on it, and that it had gone well, but Short seemed as interested in the weather as in the politics of the day, saying that it: 'took place ... in the midst of rain and wind which by intervals lasted the whole day ... In general it is observable that the deputies sent from the provinces to this federation are much more royalist than the Parisians or the National Assembly.'[68]

Morris did not himself attend the *fête*, but it caused him to ponder: 'When we reflect on the incidents which have passed within less than two years, we must forcibly be struck with the mutability of human affairs.'[69]

CHAPTER 9

From the Fête de la Fédération
to the Flight to Varennes
(July 1790 to June 1791)

'The government has been disorganized and without force'

THE successful celebration of the *Fête de la Fédération* set the seal on the Revolution's ability to survive as a reforming new regime coexisting with a cowed monarchy. At no time, however, could the revolutionary regime regard itself as stable or secure either internally or externally.

The volatility of the political scene led the commentators to expect dramatic change almost one day to the next. The main work of the Revolution continued to be what historians have termed 'the regeneration of France'. This was punctuated by moments of higher drama or crisis, such as Mirabeau's death or the royal family's escape from the Tuileries. The Jacobins strengthened their power base while the *émigrés* gathered around the Prince de Condé. The threats of war became more tangible. The period of long-term administrative reform combined with day-to-day crises was ended by the Flight to Varennes. The flight destroyed the Revolution's *modus vivendi* with the monarchy which had lasted since the March of the Women on Versailles.

General Situation and Progress of Reform
The detail of the 'regeneration of France' largely failed to capture the attention or imagination of the commentators. There are disappointingly few analyses of it. Short built up a picture over eight months of the situation faced consciously by the National Assembly and (unconsciously) by the commentators themselves:

The Assembly are at present employed in discussing their judiciary system, and the organisation of their army. There is little hope however that they will adopt the best plan. Their attention is so often diverted from constitutional objects by those which are incidental. The different parties are so opposed and so violent that there is nothing like cool and continued discussion.

Reform in December was going very slowly because of

the accumulation of business in the Assembly, and the facility with which they suffer themselves to be diverted from their main object in order to enter into business of detail....

The National Assembly continue as usual moving on slowly in the line of the constitution, and allowing themselves easily to be diverted from it by the circumstances which grow out of the moment.[1]

A robbery in his coachhouse brought on an attack of pessimism about the political scene generally for Short in August 1790: 'The horizon becomes more and more obscure every day. For a long time the government has been disorganised and without force.'[2] Morris was only too ready to support this outlook:

the Assembly have committeed many blunders which are not to be wondered at. They have taken genius instead of reason for their guide, adopting experiment instead of experience, and wander in the dark because they prefer lightning to light.

Their Assembly is losing ground daily in the public opinion. The army, long encouraged in licentious conduct, is now in revolt. All the bands of society are loosened and authority is gone.[3]

To his credit, Morris was not afraid to tell French ministers what he thought. When he met the Keeper of the Seals he told him that 'I consider the Revolution a project that has failed; that the evils of anarchy must restore authority to the sovereign.' The minister did not react favourably to this analysis. Undeterred, Morris tackled Liancourt and Montesquiou a few days later: 'I say that the constitution they have proposed is such that the Almighty himself could not make it succeed without creating a new species of man.'[4]

Resuming the theme of the tedious and unconstructive nature of day-to-day politics as perceived by the commentators, Gower, in June 1791, passed this verdict on what he saw as a typical seven days: 'This week has made little difference in the dismal appearance of public affairs. The Comtat continues to suffer all the calamities of civil war. Money in specie has sunk but little in its price; the taxes are not levied; few *Assignats* remain in the Treasury.'[5]

William Miles's Assessment of the Revolution
At this point it is appropriate to introduce in earnest a new commentator – the British agent William Miles – whose observations will feature largely (but not exclusively) in this and the next chapter.

Miles had travelled to France hoping to find a regime greatly preferable to the 'tyranny' of the *ancien régime*, but was instead disgusted by the Revolution as he found it.[6] His disillusionment permeated his despatches, which have to be read in this light, but on the few occasions when he made observations of depth they contained real insight. Like Arthur Young, he openly joined the Jacobin Club, but, unlike Young, he attended regularly and he used it as the base of his operation to lobby against the Family Compact.

In September and December 1790 he passed general judgements on the Revolution, stating in September that after fourteen months of Revolutionary administration: 'The government is without credit, and its authority is so precarious that its very existence depends upon the zeal and activity of the National Guard.' In December he wrote in similar vein that

> The nation is without revenue and government, its metropolis and provincial towns are without police, its legislature without talents, without probity, and without credit, except with a senseless and sanguinary rabble who would suspend their representatives from a 'lantern' with as little motive, and with as much facility, as they applaud their tumultuous and indecent harangues in the Senate.

He described his overall reaction to the Revolution in Paris: 'I fancy myself in the midst of a great carnival.'[7] By this he meant black comedy.

He focused his disillusionment most sharply on the municipality's and National Guard's wilful – as he saw it – refusal to keep public order (or 'police' to use the contemporary term already cited above): 'The military does not dare fire, nor even assemble to disperse a mob, without orders from the first magistrate [Mayor of Paris], and the magistrate dares not proceed to violence.... The municipality of Paris [is] without power to suppress a riot and submissive to the dictates of the mob.'[8] (When once the municipality and National Guard did take action – albeit inadvertently – to enforce law and order at the Champs de Mars on 17 July 1791 (see below) steps were taken to restrict their powers.)

Miles wrote at great length about the Jacobins and about Robespierre, and these subjects will be explored in their context below. He was the only commentator after Jefferson to make comment on the role of women in the Revolution. He expressed shock and disgust at the very idea and existence of a women's section of the Jacobin Club, which met in the crypt of the former church. He attended one of their meetings, but noted only speeches made by men.[9] In one of his last general commentaries on the Revolution written from Paris he again mentioned women and talked also of the inexorable progress of the Jacobins:

> Clubs abound in every street, and almost in every *hôtel* in Paris. The women assemble and discuss political questions. All is uproar and confusion; and, during the illusory pursuits of the red-hot royalists, and the

interested cabals of the limited monarchy party, the republicans, under the cautious and wily guidance of Robespierre, are silently and rapidly marching to the great object they have in view.[10]

The 'great object' was the capture of the Revolutionary government.

Miles despaired of the Revolution in the short term. He felt it could only lead to civil war.[11] If it did survive, though, he wrote on more than one occasion that the next generation of Frenchmen in twenty-five years' time would have received an education which would make them politically mature.[12]

Sale of Church Assets

In one area, at least, all seemed to be going well for the Revolution. The sale of Church assets was proving a well-managed success (despite Gower's comment above). There were several observations on this, but the most perceptive was Short's on 26 November 1790. He also added a warning for the future:

> The operation of the sale of ecclesiastical lands is going on with a rapidity and success beyond their most sanguine expectations. . . . This is a rich mine and if properly managed might very soon enable them to put their immense debt on a very favourable footing. It is to be feared however that with such a legislature and such administrative bodies as they have at present, the facility that these sales will give them with respect to the paper money system, will have an evil tendency.[13]

One reason for the success was identified by Gower: 'The lands and houses formerly belonging to the clergy continue to be sold much higher than their valuation, but were, for political reasons, evidently rated too low.'[14]

The only flaw in the system was the ease with which the *Assignats* could be forged. The British embassy found itself directly involved with this problem, as many of the forgeries were emanating from London. For Gower's comfort – and amusement – the most serious forging ring turned out to be nearer to home for the French authorities. It was being run by a prisoner already incarcerated in the Châtelet.[15]

Hand in hand with the success of the *Assignats*, Short reported that government credit had improved and that revenues from taxation in general were now reaching Paris (after a hiatus of nearly eighteen months).[16]

The Threat of War

The war scares of the late summer of 1790 were more tightly focused than the generalized alarms of the early summer.

The first fright was occasioned by the Austrians insisting on their treaty rights of moving armed forces across French territory. The Austrian troops were being sent to suppress the rebellion in the Austrian Netherlands, and their presence in France was doubly objectionable for the potential threat they and Austria's German allies posed to a disorganized France and for the actual threat they posed to the co-Revolutionaries north of the border.[17] This incident concentrated the Assembly's mind on its international position, and its need for allies. The Bourbon 'Family Compact' with Spain was renewed, but only on the Revolution's own terms: 'a regard for peace being the basis of the constitution of France, the nation cannot acknowledge any other stipulations made in the treaties [of the *ancien régime*] except such as are merely defensive and commercial'.[18] (This was before Miles began his mission in earnest.)

This tension was heightened by a quarrel with Britain, which led to the Assembly fearing a pre-emptive strike against French ports. The internal politics of the Revolution did nothing to reassure Britain that France herself would not declare a war: 'there is certainly a very large body of men, in this country inclined to war. The aristocratical party has little to hope from peace, and shews evident signs of wishing to profit by the confusion which a war would certainly occasion.'[19]

One ironic outcome of the scare was the need to refit the army with supplies ordered from Britain. The consequence of this in Paris was that 'A very large importation from England of buttons for the national uniform had made it necessary for every possible precaution to be taken in order to prevent tumults in this town: the journeymen manufacturers having threatened to destroy the shops of all those who sell English goods.'[20]

After this particular period of international tension it became impossible to separate France's international relations from the possibility of Counter-Revolutionary intervention inside France by hostile *ancien régime* neighbours.

Lafayette

Lafayette was the only figure resembling a national leader who had emerged from the Revolution and still enjoyed cross-factional respect and support. When Miles had arrived in Paris on his mission to break the Family Compact, he had immediately made contact with Lafayette, who was an old acquaintance from America. Miles found him embroiled in factional politics and fighting against the Orléanists and other radical deputies:

I have dined three days in succession with M. de Lafayette ... he has a powerful rival for popularity, or rather an enemy, in the Duke of Orléans, and, secure as he fancies himself in the affections of the National Guards and of the municipality, he will fall, I fear, a victim to his confidence and to the depravity of those he is endeavouring to serve ... all [the

acclamations he received from the National Guard] were in opposition
to the Orléanist faction, who wish to place one of the Lameths at the
head of the National Guards.[21]

Morris also doubted Lafayette's ability to survive politically and to overcome
his enemies: 'Poor Lafayette! He begins to suffer the consequences which
always attend too great an elevation. *Il s'éclipse au premier.*' Morris spoke his
mind to Lafayette on 25 November 1790:

> and while I speak he turns pale. I tell him that the time approaches when
> all good men must cling to the throne: that the present king is very
> valuable on account of his moderation ... that the thing called a con-
> stitution which the Assembly have framed is good for nothing; that as
> to himself, his personal situation is very delicate.

This 'delicacy' was demonstrated in January 1791 when Lafayette (and
Talleyrand with him) was talked of as the hope of the Counter-
Revolutionaries.[22]

Short had observed in September 1790 that Lafayette had not been as
successful in placing himself above faction as he supposed or hoped. He traced
Lafayette's position *vis-à-vis* the Jacobins, who 'pursued [him] with much
bitterness and hatred', and who were seeking to discredit him over the
administration of food supplies to Paris. Lafayette's grip on power faltered
with a temporary illness. Short commented on his career to date at the start
of May 1791: 'He has committed several errors in the command which he
has had. . . .' Six days later Short detected a campaign being mounted against
Lafayette in the Sections, and as a result he spoke of a 'natural decline in his
popularity which must necessarily come with time'.[23]

On 28 February Lafayette handled an incident at Vincennes very badly.
This related to the possible future use of the *château* of Vincennes as a prison
under his control. Short described what happened: 'The repairing of the
château de Vincennes in order to transport there some of those confined in
the different prisons of Paris, gave rise lately to a mob which threatened
bloodshed between rioters and the garde nationale', while Gower reported
that the rumour had gained ground that Vincennes would become a second
Bastille.[24] Lafayette, apparently, had allowed the National Guard and con-
tingents from the Sections to get out of hand when they had begun protesting.
He admitted to Morris that he had done himself no credit: 'He acknowledges
that the *Garde Nationale* was drunk and himself so angry as to have behaved
indecorously.'[25] Miles believed that Lafayette had nearly lost his life, and then
added an intriguing footnote that the Sections would never have marched to
Vincennes had the court not stopped payments to them to keep them quies-
cent.[26] The incident at Vincennes followed close on Lafayette's failure to

exercise authority over the National Guard units stationed outside the Tuileries at the time of the *Mesdames'* departure for Rome, and then, was followed on the same day by a co-ordinated demonstration in the same place. In April he suffered another loss of face with the National Guards' refusal to allow Louis XVI to go to Saint-Cloud (see below). All these incidents confirm the picture, painted previously by Miles, of the Guard's unwillingness to carry out policing duties in opposition to the Parisian crowds. In this context, Morris summed up the latter incident: 'We have this day much of a riot at the Tuileries. The king intends for St-Cloud, but is stopped, not merely by the populace, but by the national militia, who refuse to obey their general.'[27]

Lafayette decided to take drastic measures to reassert his authority. He ostentatiously resigned his command of the National Guard, and waited for the reaction. It impressed most of the commentators, who were relaxing in each others' company at the time: 'Dine with the British ambassadors. We are *en famille* ... Lafayette's resignation makes much noise.'[28]

Short reported that on hearing of the resignation: 'The municipality in a body went also to entreat his remaining at the head of the guard', but had had to wait until midnight for him to return home. Two days later Lafayette accepted the request for him to reassume command.[29] Gower believed that the stratagem had succeeded as 'The Jacobins, whose plan it was to have one of their party chosen commander, shew evident marks of disappointment.'[30]

In June Short reported that Lafayette's influence was again on the wane, and after the flight to Varennes he wrote of Lafayette's position: 'On the whole his post becomes every day more untenable.'[31] After July 1791 the question was not so much whether Lafayette would go, as when.

Necker, Talleyrand, Orléans and Sieyès

Necker's long and chequered career finally ended in September 1790 with his resignation. He gave as his reasons ill-health and Madame Necker's dislike of living in Paris. He had opposed the *Assignats* and outstayed his welcome in the Revolution; Gower said that his resignation 'pleased all parties'.[32]

Talleyrand continued to be a figure to be reckoned with, but in an increasingly ambiguous position *vis-à-vis* the clergy. At the start of 1791 Talleyrand had been active in public life as a bishop, a leading member of the Assembly, and an official in the municipality of Paris. When the Revolution took steps to end the 'abuse' of one individual being able to hold several offices at the same time Talleyrand had to choose where his real interests lay. He surrendered his bishopric. This was very badly received by the clergy, and Morris reported him 'horribly frightened for his life'. He had written his will and was contemplating suicide to avoid being assassinated by his clerical enemies.[33]

A month later, however, Morris tipped Talleyrand to be Mirabeau's successor:

Mirabeau died this day. I tell [Talleyrand] that he should step into the vacancy he has made, and to that effect should pronounce his funeral oration.... He says his thoughts have run much upon that subject this day. I tell him he has not a moment to lose, and, that such occasions rarely present themselves.[34]

To strengthen his position he joined the Jacobin Club, but by the end of April this had, as yet 'had no apparent good effect'.[35]

One of Talleyrand's fellow clerics, the abbé Sieyès, was also still jockeying for position in the Revolution. Like Talleyrand he joined the Jacobin Club: 'The abbé Sieyès and many members of the club of '89 have joined the Jacobins; whether they hope by their influence in that meeting to moderate their proceedings or whether they intend to go with the current remains to be seen.'[36]

Short reported in early May on an anti-Jacobin 'clique', which included Sieyès, Talleyrand and Condorcet, and which was trying to make Lafayette play a more active role against the Jacobins.[37]

After his return for the *Fête de la Fédération*, Orléans remained active on the political scene (he was still a deputy by his original right to sit in the States-General as a Prince of the Blood). He increasingly allied himself with the Jacobins, so that in September 1790 Gower wrote of '*les enragés*, or they may be now called the Duke of Orléans's friends ...'. Between them Gower felt that the Orléanists and Jacobins dominated the Assembly.[38]

In April Orléans had a public disagreement with the Duchess: 'the Duchesse of Orléans sets off tomorrow, under pretence of her father being indisposed, to visit him, but in fact to bring about a separation with her husband, whose conduct is become too brutal to be borne'. Relations cannot have been improved when Orléans, on the occasion of the abolition of nobility: 'declared publicly that ... since there are no longer Princes in France [the Duchess] must expect a *pied à terre* instead of a palace at Paris'.[39]

Mirabeau

Mirabeau and Lafayette were seen as the two main contenders for the leadership of the Revolution, with Mirabeau wishing to remove Lafayette from his unofficial position of pre-eminence. Morris passed on a report that Mirabeau was plotting with the queen and the Austrian ambassador. He then set out their respective merits in the context of their rivalry: 'I am inclined to think, however, that Lafayette will hold a good tug, being as cunning as anybody. Mirabeau has much greater talents, and his opponent a better character.'[40]

Gower gave a very different assessment of Mirabeau, based on his political talents and work rather than his personality:

During Mirabeau's presidency more essential business will have been dispatched by the Assembly than has been done by that body in the space of months before.

... Mirabeau, whose conduct since his presidency and his election as one of the administrators of the department of Paris has been much and deservedly applauded.

Gower specified legal reform and 'The reduction of the number of munici-palities, a consummation most devoutly to be wished for by all those who are enemies to anarchy and confusion.'[41]

Mirabeau's death in early April 1791 was totally unexpected. It was the Revolution's first great loss, and removed the monarchy's most potent champion. Gower eulogized him as:

A man possessing the greatest talents, which, if accompanied by good principles, might have rendered him not only an ornament of the age but the saver of his country.

The Jacobins will no longer be curbed by Mirabeau and the friends of the Government will feel the loss of his abilities.

Miles added that 'The death of Mirabeau has rendered the National Assembly blind of an eye.'[42]

Short spoke in similar terms:

An event which has produced a very uncommon and unexpected effect here is the death of Mirabeau, after a short and violent illness of a few days. If you except a few of the aristocratical party who really desire the prolongation of disorder and civil war, and the demagogues of the Assembly who saw in him their most formidable rival, he is universally regretted, and what is most extraordinary more at court than any where else.

(This gives credence to Morris's report of his collusion with Marie-Antoinette.) Mirabeau was a man who 'changed his party several times without changing his principles'.[43]

Morris, as seen earlier, was trying to bestow his mantle on Talleyrand before the corpse was cold, but he attended the funeral – along with 100,000 others.[44] Within six days of Mirabeau's death, Gower was writing: 'The want of his advice is conspicuous in the ... Assembly.'[45]

Law and Order in Paris: the Hôtel de Castries

As well as the previously noted breakdown in general law and order, the Sections in Paris were beginning seriously to assert an authority separate from – and sometimes opposed to – that of the king, the Assembly, or the municipality. The incident which seems to have most concentrated the minds of the Anglo-Saxons was the sacking of the *hôtel* of the Maréchal de Castries (a former *ancien régime* minister) in November 1790.

None of the diplomats actually witnessed it, but they agreed that it was simultaneously violent, unexpected, controlled and politically directed. Short, on hearing of it, wrote: 'the mob which arose suddenly on the 13th inst. destroyed the furniture of the hôtel de Castries, and then dispersed without committing any other violence'.[46]

Gower dwelt more on its consequences and implications:

> Two hundred families have applied for passports to the Mayor since the pillage of M. de Castries's house; he obtained one under a feigned name and is now out of the French dominions.

> While the National Guard continues to be unanimous there is little cause to fear the mob of Paris, but, as endeavours are not wanting to foment dissentions in that body, the peace of the capital may, with reason, be supposed to be in danger.[47]

By far the most instructive account, however, comes from one of Auckland's agents, who had spent a month in Paris and reported back in general terms on his impressions and experiences there:

> very little leisure did the bustle of Paris, in its present agitated, distracted state permit me to enjoy....

> I spent nearly a month at Paris, and it was there only I could form an adequate idea of the state of the people's mind, of the violence of party, of the confusion, anarchy, effervescence produced by so sudden and so great a change as has been that of the Revolution.

> I am now neither aristocrat nor democrat.... The violence, injustice, ignorance of both, are equally disgusting.

And specifically on the sacking of the hôtel de Castries:

> I have now been a witness to the violence with which the Revolution is carried on, and the system of injustice which prevails, and must with Mr Burke reprobate the proceedings of the National Assembly. More

violence must yet be committed, however, before the late system can be regretted.[48]

The Paris mob, directed by the Sections, made several attempts to intervene in politics and influence ministers individually or the Assembly as a whole. During the war scare, in September 1790, Short reported:

The mob insisted on the ministers being turned off, and many on their being hanged. Motions were also made for going to bring the king from St-Cloud where he then was. No attempt was made to disperse the mob, but strong guards were placed before the houses of ministers.[49]

(This may have been the incident which turned Madame Necker against staying in Paris.) The harnessing of discontent about food prices or wages to Revolutionary zeal, which Young had noted in January 1790, was now well established. In late September Short described an intervention in these terms at the National Assembly:

The National Assembly are deliberating today on the great question of paper money.... The districts of Paris have shewn an almost unanimous wish for this paper emission, and the mob who surround the Assembly house, and fill the galleries shew almost as much favour of the *Assignats*, as in the destruction of the Bastille. They are made to believe that they will lower the price of bread, and augment the price of labour, and that all those who are opposed to them are aristocrats, and a variety of other such things. This criminal method of carrying a plan in the Assembly by enlisting the mob in favour of it has been used on several occasions. Some of the provinces are already dissatisfied with the influence which this gives the city, and particularly the mob of Paris.[50]

Gower detected in October the alliance of political clubs and the Sections in order to influence politics: 'The two clubs, the Jacobins and of 1789, and the different Sections of Paris have declared themselves highly dissatisfied at the continuance of the ministers.'[51] Short echoed the comment made by Auckland's correspondent, John Stanley, at the looting of the hôtel de Castries: 'The acts of tyranny exercised by the people assembled ... are considered for the most part as legitimate.'[52]

The refusal by a substantial number of clergy to take the civil oath or willingly to surrender their livings (see below) created a new permanent source of (legitimate) agitation. Gower reported a number of incidents, typical of which was the occasion when a non-juring priest attempted to celebrate Mass: 'Some people, for they were too few to be called a mob, meeting with no resistance, overturned the altar and dispersed the congregation.' He reported a more dramatic incident in April 1791, in which nuns had been 'flagellated' by *poissardes*.[53]

In a different context Gower made an observation which sheds light on the people who probably composed these mobs:

> [the] municipality has stated to the Assembly that Paris is no longer able to bear the weight of those taxes which the former abuses of government enabled it to pay.... That they are obliged to maintain twenty-seven thousand adventurers and needy persons (the fact is that, under the name of workmen and labourers those people receive fifteen *sous* a day although they scarcely work at all).[54]

Another development – first noted in April 1791 by Gower, to his own embarrassment and discomfiture – was the right assumed by the Section activists (in this case women) to deal directly with ministers and other officials and to impose their views outside the ordinary workings of political machinery:

> I was surprized at my entrance into [Montmorin's] drawing room, to see it uncommonly full of company, and my surprize was considerably increased when I perceived that the female part of it consisted of ... *dames de la Halles or poissardes* [who insisted on embracing all the members of the diplomatic corps] who had the misfortune of dining there.[55]

Gower also detected some beginnings of what might, in a modern socio-logical sense, be termed class war: 'The attendance at the Constitutional Clubs has occasioned a general disposition among the soldiers to cashier their officers', and 'Want of energy in the civil government encourages seditious language among the journeymen and workmen who demand an increase in wages.'[56]

Rise of the Jacobins and Robespierre

The Jacobins had been a powerful and influential political club for some time, but as 1791 progressed they came to be seen as a coherent and dangerous political party by the commentators. The name 'Robespierre' first appears at this time, but the British embassy took some time to establish the correct spelling and be sure that he was not an Irish renegade by the name of 'Robert Spier'.

Throughout the winter there was much wishful thinking in the reports covering the Jacobins. Each new increase in their strength was heralded as a precursor of their downfall; thus Gower wrote on the occasion of the reform of the royal military household that it had 'given the greatest alarms to the democratic party, and, as they perceive their popularity on the decline they seem determined to take some strong measures'.

Morris wrote in similar terms about the national situation:

The *enragés*, long since known by the name of Jacobins, have lost much in the public opinion, so that they are less powerful in the Assembly than they were; but their Committees of Correspondence (called *sociétés patriotiques*), spread all over the kingdom, have given them a deep and strong hold over the people.[57]

By April, however, Gower was more resigned:

In the present anarchy, in and out of the Assembly, it is impossible for me to give your Grace any certain account of the state of parties: this much however is evident, that there is a set of men whose object is the total annihilation of monarchy however limited. The heads of this party are: Robertspierre ...

(The other names given were nonentities who made no impact on the political scene.)

The constitutional monarchist faction of Barnave and the Lameths was apparently considering throwing in its lot with the Jacobins.[58]

Mirabeau's death, as we have already noted, was thought to have removed the most effective check there had been to the Jacobins. A month later Morris reported that 'Montmorin fears the municipalities will be entirely under the guidance of the Jacobins.'[59] This fear was shared by Short, who reported that the Jacobins had manoeuvred Lafayette out of their club, and he went on to predict: 'the Jacobins will throughout the kingdom influence the ensuing elections'.[60] Miles, too, was very conscious of the powerful national organization which the Jacobins had built up through their corresponding clubs, and which by January 1791 they were using to whip up a nationally co-ordinated fear of Counter-Revolution.[61] In January 1791, again, he wrote: 'The Jacobins ... carry everything before them.' He went on to describe them as 'A strong party in the nation [which] wishes for a republic', in opposition to both the royal family and Lafayette.[62]

He continued in March 1791 with a remarkable prophecy:

The man held of least account in the National Assembly by Mirabeau, by Lafayette, and by the Lameths and all the Orléanist faction, will soon be of the first consideration. He is cool, measured, and resolved. He is *in his heart* republican. ... He is a stern man, rigid in his principles, plain, unaffected in his manners, no foppery in his dress, certainly above corruption, despising wealth, and with nothing of the volatility of a Frenchman in his character ... as to the destruction of the monarchy, he is an honest man ... he is growing every hour into consequence, and, strange to relate, the whole National Assembly hold him cheap, consider him as insignificant, and, when I mentioned to some of them my suspicions and said he would be the man of sway in a short time, and govern the million, I was laughed at.[63]

The man was Robespierre.

Civil Oath of the Clergy
The idea of an oath of loyalty to the Revolution had excited universal acclaim when first mooted (or those who disapproved of it were wise enough not to say so), but its logical extension to the clergy (by a decree on 29 November 1790) provoked one of the Revolution's deepest crises. The combination of the seizure of church assets and treating the clergy as any other group of citizens led Morris to speculate as to whether the church could survive at all: 'I tell [l'abbé Maury] that, from the moment when the church property was seized, I considered the Catholic religion at an end, because nobody would be priest for nothing.'[64] Gower hoped that Catholicism would continue to be 'tolerated' in France.[65]

Short followed the Assembly's growing realization in January 1791 that forcing the oath on the clergy would become one of the single greatest issues to face the new regime. The Assembly feared clerical opposition and a rally to the cause of the church, and was considering 'violent measures ... respecting this resistance'. The flashpoint came when the oath was enforced and non-jurors proscribed. Short embarked on an interesting speculation, bearing in mind that Loménie de Brienne was one of the very few juring bishops: 'Some think it is the intention of the holy see to declare France schismatic. In that case [Loménie de Brienne] would probably be made Patriarch.'[66]

A constitutional crisis threatened when Louis XVI insisted on hearing mass from a non-juring priest, but receded again when the king, as usual, capitulated to the pressure from the Revolutionaries.[67] The running sore of the civil war in Avignon compounded the growing mood of anti-Papism in the Revolution. On 3 May crowds in Paris 'dressed up a figure in straw representing the Pope with his brief in one hand and they say a crucifix in the other, an inscription on back of *guerre civile* ... he was burnt to the great satisfaction of the immense crowds present'.[68]

An added dimension to the regime's religious problems was an outbreak of sectarian strife in the old Protestant stronghold of Languedoc. The Protestants supported the new order, and Morris was told: 'there is the devil to pay in Languedoc. A kind of religious war is kindling there between the Catholics and Protestants ... the latter, who are rich, have purchased over the national troops, and turned their swords against the Catholics, under the pretence of supporting the new constitution.'

Miles saw a deeper explanation. For him the religious antagonism had been fanned into flames by *émigré* Counter-Revolutionaries hoping to provoke and profit from civil war. He also linked the Languedocian strife to attempts to thwart the annexation of the Comtat.[69]

Counter-Revolution

The most serious military Counter-Revolutionary threat of late 1790 was mutiny in the army. Gower reported the worst incident to date: 'A most alarming insurrection of the garrison of Nancy has obliged the National Assembly to give to the king the full power of the sword.' (To this army mutiny in Nancy should be added a serious and long-running naval mutiny at Brest, also stretching over the autumn of 1790.)[70]

Gower reported that the aristocratic party were optimistic in December:

> The aristocratic party express openly in public their hopes of a speedy counter-revolution. It is certain that the capital is regarded with a jealous eye by the provinces; which jealousy is industriously fomented by all those, a considerable number indeed, who are dissatisfied with the present government.[71]

For all this, the fervent hatred of all aristocrats and *émigrés*, associated with the Revolution in later popular imagination, had still not taken root in March 1791, when Gower could write that the law against the *émigrés* had proved so unpopular that 'unless some fresh popular motive shall occur, it will probably be dropt'.[72]

Condé's assumption of the leadership of the *émigrés*' armed forces did not strike fear into the hearts of the Revolutionaries in the way that he might have hoped; at this stage it had only nuisance value: 'The Prince of Condé's little army, ridiculed in its present state, by men of sense, is still a bugbear to many.'[73]

The idea of foreign intervention was still not taken seriously by any but the most staunchly optimistic royalist. Morris had the misfortune to have to talk to one:

> Sit a while with the Baron de Besenval, who, in the fervour of his zeal in the cause of despotism, tells me that all the princes of Europe are allied to restore the ancient system of French government. This idea is ridiculous enough, but yet there are thousands who believe it and who are not fools either.[74]

It is interesting to compare the phraseology here with the assurances given to Arthur Young by royalists in January 1790 that they did not seek tyranny or despotism (i.e. a return to the Bourbon ideal of an absolute monarchy).

Short noted the disingenuousness of the royalists: 'It is remarkable that for some time past those who are considered as the greatest enemies to liberty have been obliged most often to invoke the declaration of rights and the principles of the constitution.'[75] Miles too had a very low opinion of the 'aristocratic' party, against whom he levelled the accusation that they were actively fomenting war and 'the fears of the people are worked upon by the aristocratic party'. He described them as 'no less cowardly than stupid'. On the general fear of Counter-Revolution he wrote: 'Reports of a counter-Revolution, equally void of humanity and truth, have been in constant circulation since the commencement of the year ... every trifling dispute between even the lowest of vagabonds in the filthiest cabarets has been magnified into a serious attempt to destroy the infant liberties of France.'[76]

Short also noted that it suited the National Assembly to take the threat of Counter-Revolution – and Condé's army – seriously:

> The Assembly ... have the means of making money out of exciting the alarms of the people with respect to what they call the counter-revolutionaries, it is difficult to say when their popularity will cease.

> The alarm in the Assembly with respect to the efforts of the Prince de Condé and the designs of foreign powers increases every day, although it does not appear warranted by authentic information.[77]

Despite this last somewhat dismissive statement, Short had, earlier in March, thought foreign intervention a serious threat, not in the context of other monarchs wishing to crush the Revolution, but in response to France's weakness: 'The disorders of France may in time beget so much internal discontent as to invite foreign interference.'[78]

There were scattered references in a number of contexts to provincial disquiet at the leadership of the Revolution and the nation being assumed by Paris and its citizens. The most serious outbreak of provincial unrest came from Alsace, and it was an unpleasant shock for the authorities in Paris. Short talked of a 'sensation' in Paris when a petition arrived from 2,000 Strasbourgeois asking for the restoration of the clergy and nobility. Morris added that the militia in Alsace had resigned *en masse* as a Counter-Revolutionary gesture: 'This gives uneasiness at Paris. It is the first thing of the kind which has happened and makes many fear that the tide is turning.'[79]

The Continuing Work of the National Assembly and Plans for the Legislative Assembly

The National Assembly continued to debate the many aspects of the 'regeneration of France' in an unspectacular fashion. One not touched on so far is the overall regulation of the economy. The *ancien régime* had been a curious mixture of rigid state control and unexpected areas of privatization. The Revolution set out with a presumption in favour of change for its own sake.

Morris described this succinctly 'Those who rule the roost here seem to think that because the old government was sometimes wrong, everything contrary to what they did must be right.'[80]

In the field of the economy the watchword was – to use a modern term – 'deregulation': 'But as is probably expected in America ... the present revolution [will] remove the shackles of commerce.'[81] The commentators were ambivalent about this policy as, while it might bring general benefits to their countries' economies, it would prejudice the existing favourable positions of individual industries and attract intense lobbying back home. These considerations took up a considerable amount of the correspondents' attention during this period.

One reform which gave the Parisians a break from agitating about more knotty constitutional issues was the final abolition of the internal customs barriers which had been physically restored after the attack on them in July 1789 and the abolition of the tax on foodstuffs entering Paris (*'octroi'*) in February 1791. This was the type of reform which gave the Revolution a good name: 'The inhabitants of the capital are in a state of much joy and contentment occasioned by the abolition of the barriers of Paris.... A procession of the municipality and *Garde Nationale* made the round accompanied by music and numberless crowds of people and had the iron gates taken down.'[82] (The abolition of the *octrois* and barriers should not be confused with measures taken to isolate Paris physically – imposing a curfew for example – which the Revolution pursued rigorously.)

An area where the Assembly had a more difficult nettle to grasp, and where it did not, at least at first, acquit itself so well, was that of racial equality. There was a false start when a deputation of *gens de couleur* was not formally received by the Assembly for fear of further exacerbating the feelings of the white planters. Subsequently, however, the Assembly did grant full political rights in the first instance to free men of mixed race, and this, it was reported, '... has separated the West India colonies from France'.[83]

Beneath all the Assembly's work, however, lay the realization that its very existence as a national legislative assembly was a false pretence. The deputies had been elected under the *ancien régime* as members of the States-General, and not all had in fact even been elected. Talleyrand, for example, was in a very ambiguous position. He had acquired his seat as a bishop, but had subsequently resigned his see. The Assembly as a body and the deputies as individuals needed to renew their mandate. Whether the existing deputies would voluntarily surrender power was reckoned to be one of the first great tests of the Revolution's good faith.

Short first considered the problem in January 1791; he was non-committal but optimistic: 'All that seems to me certain is that the revolution will in one way or another end by giving a free government to France.' By April he had added his voice to a general scepticism about the intentions of the deputies. Despite ostentatious preparations for elections he wrote:

> Still I do not think the present assembly will end soon or of themselves, first because I am persuaded that a large majority wish to remain as long as possible, and secondly because I think that movements abroad or disorders at home, the one arising from the impudence and folly of the refugees and the other from an habitual state of anarchy, will furnish the pretext for their remaining. By this means they will have the appearance of being continued by the force of circumstances and not of themselves, and thus secure their popularity.[84]

Gower, writing five days later, assessed the position in terms of the rivalry between the Jacobins and the constitutional monarchists: 'The present constitution has no friends and cannot last. It remains for the new legislature to new model it into a genuine Republic ... or if [the party to a limited monarchy is elected] new [decrees will have to be] substituted in order to give some energy to the king and the executive power.'[85]

The 'self-denying ordinance', whereby the deputies of the National Assembly undertook not to seek election to the new convention or to hold office for a period of years after the dissolution of the present Assembly, did not excite much attention at the time. Gower commented only that 'There is a visible confusion of parties since the decree', because of uncertainty about its exact implications. He did note straightaway, though, that the new Assembly would not be dependent on royal permission to meet and would have fixed sessions.[86]

But before the new constitution was to be ratified or the new Assembly to meet, there was a drama to be played out between the royal family and the Revolution, as the king and queen made their first – and only – attempt to impose their will on the course of events.

CHAPTER 10

The Royal Family and Revolution: From the Flight to Varennes (and its Prelude) to the Dissolution of the National Assembly (February to September 1791)

'The queen's hair is turned gray'

THIS chapter follows the attempts of different members of the royal family to escape from the confines imposed on them by the Revolution. The events which acted as the prelude to the Flight to Varennes run in parallel with many of those described in the previous chapter, but the flight itself carries the story of the Revolution forward a further month – to the king's last significant acts in ratifying the constitution and dissolving the National Assembly.

Up until February 1791 only one of the immediate royal family – the king's youngest brother, the Comte d'Artois – had emigrated or openly opposed the Revolution. Between February and June 1791 all would attempt to escape, plunging the Revolution into confusion and crisis and provoking permanent unrest outside the royal residences. This did much to discredit the municipality and National Guard, to destroy Lafayette's position, and to radicalize the Parisian crowd and turn it into the enemy of the administration of the day.

The commentators always had their gaze fixed firmly on the royal family, and devoted a great deal of time and effort to following their fate. This is duly reflected in the balance of topics covered in their despatches. What was hidden from them, though, was the correlation between Louis' secret correspondence with the *émigrés* and foreign sovereigns and his eventual attempt to escape. They were, accordingly, as much taken by surprise by the Flight to Varennes as were the government and the Parisians. The great strength of their reporting is their linking of the unrest engendered by the royal family with the radicalization of the Revolution.

The Royal Family
Constitutionally, the period between the *Fête de la Fédération* and the flight to Varennes had been something of an Indian Summer for Louis XVI. He exercised the powers of commander-in-chief during the mutinies of late summer 1790, and in March 1791 he was given the power to dismiss ministers.[1]

The king and the royal family suffered a great deal of personal hardship as a result of their situation. Louis' health broke down. Gower attributed it to over-eating and lack of exercise, while Short believed the symptoms had been brought on by a mob breaking into the Tuileries on 28 February (see below).[2] Morris painted a pathetic picture from Montmorin's account of the king: 'He tells me that the king is absolutely good for nothing; that at present he always asks, when he is at work with the king, that the queen be present.'[3] This picture of Marie-Antoinette keeping the machinery of the Revolutionary government running is a novel one, but reflects the undramatic workaday reality of political life. In January Miles had virtually written the king off: 'The imbecility of the royal mind renders the king incapable of any wise or vigorous effort to recover what he has lost.'[4]

Four crises destroyed the fragile relationship worked out between the monarchy and the Revolution (leaving aside Louis' own deep-seated antipathy, which he disguised from the Revolutionaries until June 1791). These crises were: (1) the emigration of the king's aunts (Mesdames) in February and the linked invasions by mobs of the Luxembourg (the Comte de Provence's, or 'Monsieur's' residence) and the Tuileries' courtyard; (2) the disturbances around the Tuileries in late February concerted with the riots at Vincennes (see previous chapter); (3) the king's attempt to go to Saint-Cloud to hear mass from a non-juring priest in mid-April; and (4) the royal family's escape from Paris in June, when Provence made good his escape to Brussels, but Louis, Marie-Antoinette and the dauphin only reached Varennes.

The Mesdames set about their project to leave France (for Rome) openly, but in such a way as to excite attention and hostility: 'The king's aunts seem determined to leave this country; they have employed people to buy gold coin for them in Paris to so large an amount that it has considerably increased the price of it.'[5]

This amounted to a public statement of lack of faith in the *Assignats* by the royal family, and showed clearly the Mesdames' own intention to emigrate to, rather than visit, Italy.

Miles recorded that the Mesdames had made more than one move to leave Paris, but had been refused passports until late February. (This in itself put the Revolutionary authorities in a quandary because freedom of movement had been enshrined in the Declaration of Rights. Political expedience made this the first of the Revolution's liberties to be questioned.) Gower described their actual departure, adding that the *poissardes* had separated them from their baggage. Miles's account, however, suggests that the baggage was a decoy. According to him they had foreseen the ambush and had departed already, disguised as servants, in a wicker carriage.[6]

This provocative behaviour on the part of members of the royal family caused the crowds already gathered regularly around the Tuileries (specifically to waylay, according to Miles) to seek another target for their displeasure. It was an explosive situation – and the predictable disorder duly occurred on

28 February 1791 – the *'journée des poignards'*.

Short placed the onus entirely on the Revolutionary mob, 'a number of persons either totally unknown or known as enemies to the present order of things entered in crowds into the king's apartments. It being found that they had arms concealed under their clothes, they were disarmed, and some of them arrested.'

Gower's account featured these same 'persons', but he believed that at least one of them had been discovered outside the palace, and that the mob had rushed into the apartments to prevent a royalist coup to rescue the royal family. He wrote of the royalists: 'many gentlemen, from motives of duty or principle, went to the royal appartments, and . . . had pistols in their pockets, and many had short *conteaux de chasse* or daggers, in so doing they shewed greater marks of zeal than prudence'.[7]

Gower described the effect of this incident: 'The king's person is now completely in the hands of Lafayette.'[8]

He was also present at the subsidiary incident involving the Comte de Provence, which

> gave me an opportunity of being witness to great firmness and presence of mind in [Provence], I happened to dine, on Tuesday, at the Lux-embourg with a company which was honoured by his presence: while we were at coffee, one of his attendants, with signs of the greatest alarm, rushed into the room and informed us that the mob threatened to force their way into the Petit Luxembourg where Monsieur resides, declaring that they were certain that he intended to quit Paris that night: he immediately gave orders for a *députation* to be admitted into the court, where he went and informed them that they were perfectly mistaken.

The mob then followed him, on foot, to the Tuileries, where they broke into the courtyard. Lafayette called out cavalry to disperse them.[9]

Miles had watched the invasion of the Tuileries earlier in the day. He said that it had made him resolve to help the royal family escape from France if he could. He was also in the crowd which moved from the Luxembourg to the Tuileries in the evening. There he spotted several deputies rabble-rousing, and he buttonholed one of them to demand that he account for his actions. Regrettably Miles's own account suggests that he never then allowed the deputy to get a word in edgeways but instead harangued him at great length with much invective on the shortcomings of the Revolution and of deputies who acted in this way.[10]

The second of the crises occurred on 18 April 1791, coinciding with the riots at Vincennes (reported in the previous chapter in the context of Lafayette's position in the Revolution). All the commentators mentioned it, but only Miles gave a full account. It has to be said that the events he described would be more consistent with those following Mesdames' departure from Paris, but Miles's letters as presented make the relationship with the riot at Vincennes quite explicit. Even if misplaced, the account stands as a fine eye-witness account of an important event in the Revolution, and it also introduces the suspicion that the Counter-Revolution would find Louis more useful dead than alive. Morris later developed this theme in the context of Louis' and Marie-Antoinette's executions, but the first hint at this sinister development came from Miles in his account of the action in and around the Tuileries on 18 April, the mainspring of which he claimed was a *royalist* attempt to assassinate the king.

According to Miles the riot took place outside the Tuileries when news of the events at Vincennes reached Paris. He continued: '[a noble from St Domingo] was seized in the apartment of the dauphin with a poignard and pistols concealed.... There was little doubt but the odium of an attempt to assassinate the king would fall on the most violent of the democratic party.' A large armed royalist crowd was still gathered outside the palace, and Miles recognized members both of the National Assembly and the National Guard among them. After the assassination attempt had been thwarted the National Guard dispersed and disarmed the crowd taking eighty-two pistols from the royalists.[11]

The third of the four crises arose at the end of April when Louis insisted on going to Saint-Cloud to hear mass from a non-juring priest. Lafayette sent in the National Guard, which refused to obey his orders to disperse a rioting crowd. The royal family were trapped inside their carriages by a mob for one and three-quarter hours, and 'The queen abused with the most harsh and indecent language.'

The royal family were punished in three further ways. The Tuileries became a place of close confinement and Louis' hunting trips were forbidden. The Paris Sections took it upon themselves to debate and pass resolutions on the terms of their house arrest – for such it was. The royal household was greatly reduced, as Gower recorded: 'the king received us accompanied by a few remaining attendants on his way to a mass celebrated by a solitary priest'. (This priest would have taken the civil oath.)[12]

Short, writing after the Flight to Varennes, commented that Louis' reactions to the riots and to being debarred from seeing a non-juring priest 'were considered as in fact changing his principles with respect to the constitution and a determination to violate the oath he had taken to maintain it'.[13] A final upshot of all three of these episodes, and of Lafayette's bungled handling of the riot at Vincennes, was that over the first half of 1791 it became increasingly clear that Lafayette was not an effectual figure. His inability to control events, crowds, or even his own troops meant that he was becoming a figure of fun rather than the linchpin of the Revolution, although there was never any doubt among his friends or enemies about his personal bravery and integrity.

Morris's Involvement with the Royal Family

At this time Morris became personally involved in the fate of the royal family. He was too circumspect to be explicit on paper, but hinted that he had started to lend his assistance: 'I have a long conversation after dinner with [Montmorin] in the course of which I show him a note I have made on their situation . . . I give it [to him] with the injunction that none but their Majesties shall know from whom it comes.'[14]

Short was openly hostile to Morris taking this action, and wrote to Thomas Jefferson about it in most forthright terms in a subsequent despatch, arguing that Morris was a man unsuitable to be appointed ambassador:

It is now generally believed that he sent to the king the observations as mentioned . . . with a plan of conduct. A foreigner who thus meddles in the affairs of a country with which he has nothing to do, and particularly in opposition to the public opinion does it at his peril and risk and cannot blame those who attach the seal of intrigue and design to such conduct, and particularly when he is a volunteer. Morris says that his plan was received with 'favor' but rejected by 'fear'.

The plan which Morris had proposed was not a blueprint for the king's escape from France, but rather suggested how he could best exploit the proposals in the (draft) constitution to make the most of his own (and the aristocracy's) position in opposition to the democratic tendencies of the Revolution to date. Although rumour did get out that Morris had been giving direct help to the king in potential opposition to the Revolution, Short did not believe it had noticeably damaged Morris's position, as he explained: 'I do not observe that it has made any great impression, because such a variety of matter and particularly calumny appears in the gazettes that it is readily forgotten.'[15] Thus, despite Short's own subsequent efforts, Morris had not destroyed his diplomatic career, and continued to enjoy the confidence of the American political and commercial establishments.

The Context of the Flight to Varennes

The fourth of the crises which broke the relationship between the king and the Revolution was the 'Flight to Varennes', when the whole royal family attempted to escape from France, and Provence succeeded in reaching Brussels, taking a different route but travelling simultaneously with his brother. Louis had always intended to renege on commitments to the National Assembly at some point, and, as seen immediately above, Short identified the Revolution's refusal to allow him to hear mass from priests of his own choosing as the time when Louis took the actual decision to leave. It may have been planned or coincidental that Louis had also chosen a constitutionally important moment for his action.

For the commentators this episode had three aspects. First there was the sheer drama and human interest of the escape. The commentators as individuals felt real sympathy with the predicament of the unhappy royal family, and, putting political considerations aside, hoped they would make good their bid for freedom. Second, there was the question of whether they themselves would still be able to continue their official duties. Louis xvi was the head of state and they were accredited to his court – not to the National Assembly or to ministers collectively or individually. If the authorities had been paralysed by indecision or allowed popular sympathy for the royal family to become manifest it would have placed the diplomatic corps in a very difficult position. For this reason they paid very close attention to how effectively power was wielded in the king's absence. Third, they feared that a successful escape would plunge Europe into general war.

For its part the Revolution had to take the flight seriously because it was such a snub. It also revealed that there must be traitors in the highest and most trusted positions (although they were never identified) in order for the royal coaches to have gone undetected for seven hours after travelling through the heart of Paris. As Gower's account shows, the flight represented a deliberate and calculated attempt to sabotage the machinery of government in the short term (to say nothing of its being an attempt to overthrow the Revolution in the long term).

Under any immediately planned or foreseeable arrangement of the regime the king was needed to give final effect to the new constitution whose publication and ratification were the next two major items on the political agenda. The timing of the flight could be interpreted as an attempt to pre-empt and prevent the implementing of this new constitution.

The Flight

On the night of 20 June 1791 the royal family escaped from the Tuileries. The commentators describe the facts of the flight and recapture in great detail, but offer no real insights into what actually happened. All, however, add some embellishments to the incident, and describe the political reaction in Paris.

Morris immediately speculated on the consequences of the flight:

> We hear that the king and queen of France have effected their escape from the Tuileries and have got six or seven hours the start on their keepers. This will produce some considerable consequences. If they get off safely a war is inevitable, and if retaken, it will probably suspend for some time all monarchical government in France.[16]

Short wrote:

> I have to communicate to you a very unexpected event.... The king with
> the queen and royal family retired from Paris without being observed the
> night before.... What renders this extraordinary circumstance the more
> remarkable is that ... the municipality and Lafayette were all warned of
> the intended flight, and had increased the guard and doubled their
> vigilance that night.
>
> The event has so astonished every body and is so unaccountable in
> itself that no probable conjecture is formed of the manner in which it
> was effected ...
>
> It is probable that the king counts on foreign aid and that in any case
> he will endeavour to get out of the kingdom for the present by the safest
> route ... to the Count d'Artois and the Prince de Condé.[17]

Short commented on how little reaction there was on the streets of Paris:
'It is surprizing that the king's absence should have produced so little effect
here ... There reigns the most perfect tranquillity and business goes on in
almost the ordinary style.' Morris attributed this to the government placing
an embargo on the news itself and on any public debate of the king's conduct:
'The intention of the Assembly is, I find, to cover up the king's flight and
cause it to be forgotten.'[18]

Gower may, even if unconsciously, have had in mind the equivalent
position of the English government when James II precipitately left London
in 1688. He drew attention to Louis XVI's attempt to paralyse government
by forbidding, as his last instruction, the use of the state seal. This did not
deter the government, as Short reported: 'The National Assembly have taken
provisionary measures for the exercise of government during the king's
absence.' Gower described what this meant in practice: 'The National
Assembly sits night and day, and the ministers transact business in an
adjoining apartment.'[19]

Gower added a detail – unnoticed by the other commentators – about the
recapture of the royal family: 'Had the king forced his way through Varennes
he would have found the bridge beyond the town barricaded in such a
manner that it would have been impossible for him to have proceeded on his
journey.'[20]

The return of the royal family to Paris was marked by 'astonishing' 'order
and regularity'. The same cannot be said of the queen's conduct. When she
met Lafayette at Varennes, she greeted him with 'the most unbounded abuse'.
This served only to reinforce the growing popular suspicion that he had
helped or connived at the escape. Morris passed on a report which maintained
that 'the queen's hair is turned gray by her late adventures'. Miles's daughter,
who had stayed in Paris to await her father's return from London, gave a

more lurid description of the queen: 'She has scarce any hair left; in her despair she tore it off.'[21]

For Short at least one good had come out of the episode. It was 'astonishing' how all shades of political opinion had rallied behind the government in the moment of national crisis when the head of state tried to desert his post and undermine government.[22] This unity would be an invaluable asset if retained for the testing time ahead when the regime would have to reappraise its relationship with the monarchy and face a more hostile outside world at the same time as handing over power to a new national legislature.

Return to Paris
With the king, queen and dauphin back in Paris, the Revolution had to decide what arrangements to make for the monarchy in general and the royal family as individuals.

Miles's daughter had given a succinct, analytical account of the royal family's return to Paris and its implications:

> The king, queen, and royal family arrived in town yesterday, escorted by 150,000 men.... The interment of Mirabeau did not produce such a number.... The dauphin is to have a governor named by the nation; the king is no longer regarded as such. The National Assembly is to finish the constitution; and when it is settled a deputation is to be sent to Louis XVI to know whether the mode of government that is adopted suits him: if it does he is to be their sovereign, if it does not a regent is to be chosen until the dauphin is of age to be crowned. The king and queen are to be conducted to the National Assembly to answer the questions that will be asked of them.[23]

Short saw the choice as being a straightforward one, between a figurehead monarchy or an outright republic: 'The Assembly or a majority of them would prefer I think keeping him as a shadow of a monarchy and exercising all functions of government without him. The people of Paris ... declare loudly in favor of a republican government.' This republicanism seemed to be gaining ground with a flood of anti-monarchical petitions from the provinces (pre-dating the Flight to Varennes), and a spate of republican tracts in Paris (in response to it).[24]

Morris saw a third possibility – a regency – which he discussed with Montmorin:

> observing that it appears to me almost impossible to preserve both the monarchy and the monarch. [We] discuss the different characters who may be appointed either regent or to a council of regency; and here I

find insurmountable difficulties. Of course they must go on with the miserable creature which God has given. His wisdom will doubtless produce good ways to us inscrutable, and on that we must repose.[25]

By the first week in July Gower detected that the republicans had overplayed their hand: 'The republican party certainly loses ground and conscious of their weakness some of the heads of that party declare that they will be contented with *une monarchie sans monarque ou une régence sans régent.*' But the republicans were not going to forgive the royal family: 'The proceedings of the National Assembly on Friday last with regard to the king [have] occasioned much fermentation and the next morning a crowd of people assembled round the *Autel de la Patrie* being harangued by deputations from the club of the Jacobins, who not only spoke of the king and the royal family in the most opprobrious terms but reviled the Assembly.'[26]

The royal family as individuals now found that their lives were no longer their own: 'the king, the queen, and dauphin are closely guarded'. The dauphin was to be given a tutor chosen by the government.[27] Morris reported a campaign of character assassination: 'the king is by nature cruel and base ... and used to spit and roast live cats. . . . It is no wonder such a beast should be dethroned.' (To this calumny was subsequently added the slander that he had committed incest with his sister.) He passed on the pathetic picture of the king painted by Montmorin who 'has passed this morning with the king; the recital of the tale brings tears both in his eyes and mine. Poor man, he considers himself as gone, and whatever is now done must be for his son.'[28]

The king was specifically denied access to the diplomatic corps – not surprisingly in view of the Swedish and American help he had received. Short described the situation at the end of August:

> The king remains in the same state of confinement as yet. He receives any of the French nation that he pleases, and as well as the queen, has always a great number who go to pay their court. The *corps diplomatique* are not admitted, they all go to M. de Montmorin's except the Swedish ambassador. The Assembly have decreed that the king's guard shall consist of 1,200 men of his own choice, to be paid out of the civil list – they reserve to themselves however the right of organising the corps. Until that is done he will of course be guarded by those who are not of his choice.[29]

(The Swedish ambassador was the Comte de Staël-Holstein, who was married to Necker's daughter and a figure as much of the French as of the international political scene. It is also worth noting that Axel Fersen, Marie-Antoinette's admirer, was an accredited Swedish diplomat.)

his desertion of the country. There were two main issues: whether the king could constitutionally be put on trial, and whether, if he could be, his conduct warranted such a measure. In the event, the debate in the Assembly never progressed beyond the first legalistic point. The issue of his inviolability was 'a long debated question', which caused a great deal of agitation inside and outside the chamber. The eventual decision was that he could not be tried.[30] This left the Assembly having to take active steps to protect the constitutional institution of monarchy.

Decrees against the *Emigrés*

The republicans (i.e. Jacobins) might be threatening to outflank the government, but the most immediate and obvious enemies were the *émigrés*. The royal family's attempt to join them demanded some public show of strength against this group. The first act was that 'The Assembly have passed a decree prohibiting any person's leaving the kingdom without a passport.' This measure included foreign nationals, and, by implication, violated diplomatic immunity. A few days later the Assembly debated the prohibition in more detail and dealt with some of the issues it raised – notably the first suspension of civil liberties granted by the Revolution itself in the interests of safeguarding the Revolution: 'The Assembly have thought that their present situation authorized them to violate one of the articles of their declaration of rights.' Short went on to report the prohibition's inevitable consequence: 'The natural effect of this decree is operating sensibly – viz. to inspire a desire to leave the country and an aversion to return to it.'[31]

Short went on to describe some of the specific measures being taken against *émigrés*: 'The pensions and salaries of all those who are out of the kingdom are suspended without excepting those of Monsieur and the Count of Artois. The Assembly are about to take other measures also against the absentees. Additional taxes, sequestration of estates during absence, or some such plan will probably be adopted.' The measures having been duly passed, Gower praised the steps taken: 'The decree last Saturday which subjects to a treble taxation those emigrants who do not return within a month is generally considered as the best measure that could be adopted in the present circumstances of the country.'[32]

Monarchists and Counter-Revolutionaries

The Flight to Varennes had done incalculable damage to the interests of the 'aristocratic' party in the National Assembly and those aristocrats who tried to balance loyalty to the new regime with continuing service to the crown. Soon after the royal family's return, Morris reported: 'I learn this day that about sixty of the aristocratic party have resigned.'[38] The standing of the institution of monarchy was irreparably damaged, as Gower commented: 'Though the rage of republicanism may be overcome, it will be difficult to conquer the disgust the king's conduct has inspired.'[34]

Despite all this, the *ancien régime* had one last constitutional gasp. When the new constitution was being debated, a lobby was organized, as Morris described: 'The Archbishop of Aix tells me that he is engaged in drawing up a protest against the constitution on the part of the nobles and clergy, the former of which desire to object against the natural equality of mankind because kings are of divine appointment.'[35]

Short described the *émigrés* under Condé as being 'in considerable numbers ... [but] ... not strong enough to be formidable'. Morris concurred: 'The aristocrats, who are gone and are going in great numbers to join the refugee princes, believe sincerely in a coalition of the powers of Europe to reinstate their sovereign in his ancient authorities, but I believe that they are very much mistaken.'[36]

Once Provence and Artois, however, put themselves at their head they became more dangerous both to the Revolution and to the royal family, as Short observed:

> The conduct of the king's brothers, who are of course believed to act in concert with him, though probably without reason, would of itself destroy all the national confidence in the monarch. They are openly at the head of the emigrants whose avowed plan is to enter the kingdom in arms, as soon as they become sufficiently strong. The Count d'Artois is gone to Vienna, it is generally believed, to excite the emperor to declare himself with respect to the French affairs, or to press him for the succours with which the emigrants have been sometime flattered.[37]

Marie-Antoinette was well aware of the danger her brothers-in-law posed to her and to her family: 'It seems certain that the queen has written to her brother the emperor to desire he will not interfere for the present in the affairs of France. She presents to him the personal dangers which will result to her family.'

She took very active steps to be seen to be supporting the new order in the form of her unexpected personal attendance at the National Assembly:

> The queen also was present in a lodge adjoining the assembly room. This circumstance though apparently indifferent acquires some importance from the manner in which it is considered by the two parties. As she was not expected to be present – as she had never been there before and of course was at liberty to have absented herself, this volunteer step is considered by them as a proof of her decision to unite with the Assembly.[38]

Morris was convinced that the real threat to the Revolution lay in disaffection in the provinces. He painted a broad picture of their state as perceived
from Paris:

> The southern part of the kingdom is [deeply imbued with republican, or
> rather democratical principles]; the northern is ecclesiastical in its
> temper; the eastern is attached to Germany, and would gladly be reunited
> to the empire; Normandy is aristocratical, and so is part of Britanny; the
> interior part of the kingdom is monarchical. This map is (you may rely
> on it) just, for it is the result of great and extensive investigation made
> by government.[39]

The threat of foreign intervention – whether or not provoked by the royal
family – was considered by the Assembly in late July. Despite a (perhaps
absurdly) optimistic report on the relative strengths of France and her potential enemies the Assembly voted 'in addition an army of *garde nationale*
volunteers of 97,000 men'.[40]
The Revolution was moving in the direction of a nation under arms.

Massacre at the Champs de Mars
In the midst of the crisis over the Flight to Varennes, the preparations for a
second *Fête de la Fédération* went almost unnoticed. The *fête* itself went well;
Morris attended it: 'Today there is a great multitude assembled in the Champs
de Mars when I go there, to celebrate by a mass, the anniversary of the
capture of the Bastille.'[41]
The crowds, however, had acquired a taste for assembling and returned to
the Champs de Mars on successive days. On 15 July they rioted on receiving
the news of the Assembly's decision that the king was inviolate. Morris
predicted: 'As I lodge near the Tuileries . . . it is far from impossible that I shall
have a battle under my windows.'[42]
On 17 July far more serious disorder broke out, with troops of the National
Guard opening fire and killing several people. Morris tried, and failed, to
watch the proceedings, but then subsequently passed on a very full account:

> stopping to take up my telescope, go to Chaillot, but the time lost there
> . . . brings us too late on the heights of Passy to see what passed in the
> Champs de Mars. On our return, however, we learn that the militia have
> at length fired on the mob, and killed a few of them. They scampered
> away as fast as they could. . . . This affair will, I think, lay the foundation
> of tranquillity, although perhaps a more serious affair is necessary to
> restrain this abominable populace.

the militia would not, as usual, ground their arms on receiving the word of command from the mob. The last began, according to custom, to pelt them with stones. It was hot weather and it was Sunday afternoon, for which time, according to usage immemorial, the inhabitants of this capital have generally some pleasurable engagement. To be disappointed in their amusement, to be paraded through streets through a scorching sun, and then stand, like holiday turkeys, to be knocked down by brickbats was a little more than they had patience to bear; so that, without waiting for orders, they fired and killed a dozen or two of the ragged regiment . . . Lafayette was very near being killed in the morning, but the pistol snapped at his breast.[43]

Short stated baldly that the decision that the king could not be prosecuted 'became the pretext for the disorders ... in the Champs de Mars ... which induced the municipality to proclaim the law martial'.

Gower described the facts of the event, and then, like any good ambassador, attended to the interests of British subjects: 'Although I am convinced that none of the many English who are here are in the least personally concerned in the politics of this country, I endeavour to persuade them to use all possible caution in words and actions.'[44] (Gower was very much mistaken about there being no Englishmen involved in French politics. In another department of his own embassy, work was going on to infiltrate expatriate English, American and Irish Revolutionary societies. Gower may well have been kept in deliberate ignorance of this work.)

The real upshot of the 'massacre' was that the Sections and the crowds they could field would be consistently more republican than the government until the monarchy was abolished. It was a windfall to the ministry that they could now associate republicanism with public disorder and use this as a stick with which to beat the Jacobins.

Proscription of Republicans

One of the most unexpected outcomes of the Flight to Varennes, and the National Assembly's decision to retain a monarchy, was a repression of republicans. This repression was not – as is clear to historians of the Revolution – undertaken on ideological grounds or any sudden affection for the institution of monarchy on the part of the ministry or National Assembly, but rather as a cynical move by those in power to cement their own position. For the commentators, though, it seemed – however disbelieving they were of it – that a real change of tempo in the Revolution might be in the offing.

Once news of the royal family's escape was broadcast martial law was declared throughout the kingdom, which made any policing operation easier. The Assembly decided that openly republican statements, which had proliferated, could only exacerbate the situation and make the process of ratifying the new constitution more difficult. They accordingly proceeded against republican authors, but in such a half-hearted manner as to alienate all shades of political opinion.[45]

Morris doubted the sincerity of many of the deputies who had voted out of expedience to uphold the monarchy, 'I see ... the declaration signed by a number of members of the Assembly, declaring their adhesion to the cause of royalty. It is diffuse and weak.'[46]

The Assembly took a more overt step in retrospectively sanctioning the action of the municipality in declaring martial law on 17 July and of the National Guard in firing on the crowd. They also 'made a decree for punishing mutinous people and incendiary writers'.[47]

A wave of arrests followed. One of those netted was a supposed royalist secret agent, and Short's account conveys well the atmosphere of fear and intrigue pervading the capital. Among the suspects was 'the Jew Ephraim, long famous in the intrigues of Europe. Among his papers they have found the commencement of a letter in cypher to the king of Prussia. It is said to have been decyphered and shews an intention in the king of Prussia to meddle at a proper time in the affairs of this country. In the light of subsequent events which put it beyond doubt that he was indeed a Prussian agent, Short's account is ambiguous.[48]

Law and order, and a proper respect for the monarchy, seemed to have been restored by the inadvertently harsh repression of the National Guard. Gower described it as 'a wonderful change' and wrote glowingly: 'As long as the red flag continues to be displayed at the Hôtel de Ville we may expect to feel the effects of that energy which military law has given to government.' It was in this strongly anti-Republican and 'law and order' atmosphere that the *Feuillant* Club was set up.

If another of Gower's reports had had any long-term significance, the Revolution might have taken a very different course: 'Danton is fled and Robespierre is about to be *dénoncé*....'[49] In the event, none of the Jacobin leaders were actually proscribed, but several were badly scared, and felt it prudent to leave Paris for a while.

Morris and Talleyrand retrospectively analysed the public order situation in December 1791. Talleyrand (wrote Morris): 'observes to me ... today that the Jacobins have not been able to raise a riot about their address. I tell him that since the frolic at the Champs de Mars there is little danger of riots, because people are not very fond of them when they find that death is a game which two can play at.'[50]

The moves against republicanism heralded the era when the Revolution would devour its own children. As men with good Revolutionary credentials began to suffer persecution, Short commented: 'The acts of irregularity and despotism which the [Assembly] tolerate or authorize are overlooked by a great many as they consider them the only remedy to the greater evil of anarchy.'[51]

Factions and Politicians

The political factions of the Revolution became particularly complex in the late summer of 1791, as deputies who already knew they would become members of the new Assembly coexisted with the old deputies and ministers. These prospective deputies enjoyed various legal immunities which strengthened their position. Names shortly to become very familiar made their appearance; factions coalesced around them and there were moves made to secure ministerial appointments under the new assembly.

Gower noted the creation of the *Feuillant* Club: 'The members of the Jacobins who are deputies, except M. Robertspierre M. Buzot and M. Pétion, have quitted that club and have composed another at the *Feuillants*.'[52]

Short charted the career of another faction within the Assembly, also, apparently, trimming away from republicanism:

By one of those vicissitudes which takes place in the course of revolutions the three members who formerly were the demagogues of the Assembly (A. Lameth, Duport, and Barnave) have now lost all their favor and gained in some measure the confidence of the king and queen – there is no doubt that they have secret communications. This triumvirate resolved to risk everything to attain the ministry, have removed all the obstacles, except the decree of the assembly which excludes its members.

They failed to persuade Louis XVI to seek an alteration to this article.[53] In terms of individuals, Robespierre and Danton – as seen above – seemed temporarily eclipsed by the anti-republican mood. Condorcet, on the other hand, was emerging a leading figure in republican ranks. Brissot also first made a name for himself at this time demanding the most loudly for the king's trial and was making a serious bid to inherit Mirabeau's mantle.[54]

Short wrote of Sieyès, who was to become the Revolution's arch-trimmer, that when his name came up in the National Assembly's debate on whether to prosecute a republican pamphleteer: 'It was supposed the abbé Sieyès was the chief of this republican party, but he has written a letter declaring himself explicitly in favor of monarchical government.'[55] Sieyès did at least have the grace to withdraw from political life for a time after this episode. Lafayette had been deserted by all his erstwhile supporters, and, although he had not resigned his command of the National Guard, 'his sun seems to be set'.[56]

Orléans' position requires some attention. He was caught by the new constitution's provisions for the royal family generally, that he would continue to enjoy all the courtesies and rights of succession due to a Prince of the Blood, but was debarred from taking any direct part in the process of representative parliamentary democracy. Short wrote what he hoped would be his epitaph:

> The Duke of Orléans and his friends opposed the decree with all their force. He declared he was ready to resign all the rights attached to members of the [House of Bourbon] rather than be deprived of those of a French citizen. This like all the other efforts which he has made during the present revolution, only served to expose him to the sarcasms and contempt of his enemies.

Gower added that he was still hoping for a naval command (as he had been for decades), but 'That star is sunk never to rise again.'[57]

Elections to the New Assembly

The regulations for the elections (originally composed by Sieyès) had laid down that only 'active' citizens could exercise the vote. Short was dismissive of the level of wealth set for this qualification: 'Still it is so inconsiderable as not to exclude from that body men who are poor enough to be dependent for their subsistence or that of their families, on those who are rich enough to purchase their votes – this is with reason considered as a great defect in the constitution.'[58]

On the conduct of the elections in the provinces, Gower wrote: 'The primary assemblies are almost finished and no inconsiderate corruption has been used to influence the choice of electors.' As regards their conduct in Paris he wrote, 'although many of the most democratical of [the electors in Paris] are in prison or fled, yet a sufficient number remains to allow one to believe that the members chosen by this department will be for the most part, of the democratical party'.[59]

At first Short took a similar view: 'It is feared ... that the next assembly will be composed of many violent, exaggerated and bad men.' A few days later he modified his view in a way which can usefully be compared to Morris's previously quoted account of the political state of the provinces: 'The elections for the new legislature continue to go on peaceably throughout the kingdom. Such as have already taken place shew more moderation than was expected except in the southern provinces, where those who possess the most exaggerated principles have for the most part been chosen.'[60]

Gower's verdict on the final outcome of the elections was: 'It appears that more than half of the next assembly will be composed of country attorneys; not only the nobility but the commercial interest will be very much excluded.' While Morris predicted: 'The new assembly, as far as can at present be determined, is deeply imbued with republican, or rather democratical principles.'[61]

The New Constitution, Relaxation of the Royal Family's Internment and Dissolution of the National Assembly

The National Assembly's last great act would be to ratify the new constitution which its constitutional committee had so long been preparing. It then had to persuade the king to swear allegiance to it and formally dissolve the Assembly itself. The constitutional need for a monarch to be on hand to discharge these functions was one of the principal reasons for his virtual imprisonment. Morris was dismissive of the constitution. He told Short: 'it is a ridiculous one'. At the end of September he added: 'It is a general and almost universal conviction that this constitution is inexecutable; the makers to a man condemn it.'[62]

Short was sceptical but prepared to give it the benefit of the doubt:

> Out of the Assembly the opinions are various with respect to this con- stitution – great defects are acknowledged to exist in all its parts. But the necessity of having some kind of government established strikes most people here so forcibly that they are impatient to have the experiment made on this such as it is. And indeed that is the only mode by which it can be judged of to the general conviction. Individuals may be con- vinced of its defects by reflection and argument but it would seem that practical proof is indispensable for the nation. To me there appears insurmountable difficulties in the organisation of all its parts, legislative, administrative and judiciary, but I find so many others thinking so differently from me, that I conclude such variety of opinions can be brought to co-incide only by experience.[63]

Gower immediately focused on the problem of the king's role in the rati- fication of the constitution: 'if in his present state of confinement it will be a mere mockery; if he is previously allowed his liberty it is uncertain what use he may make of it'.

Four days later Short enlarged upon this view:

> One great danger and difficulty however which strikes everybody is that which arises from the king. The impossibility of keeping him a prisoner if he is to be charged with the government is manifest, and if at liberty great numbers are convinced and all suspect that he will take the first opportunity of retiring to the frontiers or out of the kingdom. This circumstance renders it impracticable to place the national confidence in the crown, where it is the more necessary for the preservation of order and government, in proportion as the point it was formerly vested with is diminished. It is much to be apprehended that a government thus without either energy or confidence will not secure those advantages to

such a country as France, which were expected from the recovery of liberty.[64]

Short gave a factual but favourable account of the informal discussions between Louis XVI and a deputation of deputies which led to the understanding that he would approve the new constitution and swear an oath of allegiance to it:

> But as it is evident that he is not freer in this acceptance than in the sanction of the laws against which he protested, it is much to be feared that the nation at large will have no confidence in this adhesion. Such a government without confidence, which is its essence, is nothing more than a state of anarchy and will be productive I fear of much misfortune.[65]

(The 'laws' referred to were those against *émigrés*.)

The king's subsequent formal oath of allegiance to the new constitution was carried off smoothly and without controversy. Neither Short nor Gower, however, believed in the king's sincerity. Gower said explicitly: 'The sincerity of his acceptation is doubted by many', and as a result the constitution could not be regarded as a secure or lasting arrangement for the country.[66]

The National Assembly, however, seemed to be prepared to honour their side of the bargain and the king's access to the diplomatic corps was restored and the royal family were allowed greater freedom of movement within Paris. Gower reported back on his first audience since June:

> On Tuesday last the foreign ministers were received by the king and royal family. His Majesty's health does not seem to have been impaired by his confinement: the queen received us with her usual dignity but her deportment and appearance discovered a mind suffering under affliction but not easily subdued.[67]

After an initial comment on the atmosphere in the Tuileries gardens (newly reopened), Short's account of the same audience put the relaxation of the royal family's confinement into its wider context. On 4 September 1791 Short found that the palace gardens had, 'the same appearance of contentment, gaiety, and security which existed before the revolution'.

So far as the constitution was concerned, Short had this to say:

> Since the king's solemn acceptance of the constitution ... he seems to have taken much pains to shew that it was his free choice. The day of the constitution being proclaimed throughout Paris agreeably to the decree of the Assembly, the *château* and gardens of the Tuileries and the Champs Elysées were illuminated at the king's expense. He went in the course of the evening with his family to visit the illuminations and received the loudest applauses from all quarters; two days ago he went

also with the queen and family to the opera. This circumstance seems to have given uncommon pleasure, as it is not only the first time they have been to a theatre since the Revolution, but the first time the king was ever at the opera in Paris.[68]

Gower reported on the following day (and for the rest of the month) that the king was moving freely around Paris and receiving popular acclaim: 'The king upon his passage was very much applauded by the people.... Paris is in a state of perfect tranquillity and a general illuminations and rejoicing have taken place on this occasion.'

Morris reported further celebrations on 18 September: 'This morning is introduced by peals of artillery. It is a high festival on the adoption of the constitution ... no carriages can move.' Morris had learnt from previous experience, and carefully emptied his pockets before leaving home.[69]

Morris had further thoughts on the king's allegiance to the new constitution:

These external marks of adhesion [to the new constitution] have so displeased those who are here of the aristocratical party that they have almost entirely abandoned the court. On the contrary those of the courtiers who had for some time absented themselves on account of the active part they took in the revolution have now returned there. The king and queen are apparently well satisfied with this circumstance and treat them with marked civility. Time alone can shew whether the king will be able by such measures and by his future conduct to obtain the confidence of the nation in his acceptation of the constitution.[70]

The formal dissolution of the National Assembly on 30 September 1791 was performed by Louis XVI with dignity and in an atmosphere of reconciliation. Morris's account is the most analytical:

The king goes this day, in about an hour hence, to close, or rather to bid farewell to the session of the National Assembly ... he has accepted the new constitution, and been in consequence liberated from his arrest. ... The king's present business is to make himself popular, and, indeed, his life and crown depend on it.[71]

Short's Perspective

Although he was not yet to know it, a shadow was falling across Short's career. Jefferson was taking exception to the tone of some of his despatches, and the decision was being taken in Philadelphia not to confirm him as the next ambassador, but to appoint Morris in his stead. There is, therefore, some poignancy in the detailed analyses and predictions he made at the time of the dissolution of the old assembly. On 14 and 22 September 1791 he penned some thoughtful observations on possible future developments:

> You will see by the king's letter that he desired an amnesty for those prosecuted on account of the revolution. Lafayette immediately moved that this should be adopted and it was done in the midst of the applauses of all present. These circumstances give a favorable appearance to the present moment. Much will depend on the conduct of the king and the future legislature. I fear however that events will occur either at home or abroad which they will not be able to control by the force of the constitution as it remains at present.

> For my own part I am well persuaded that at this moment he is fully determined to act up to his professions as he was also at the time of his going to the Assembly in February 1790. – But should future events be different from those he expected and should an opportunity present itself of flying from them it can hardly be supposed that it will not be made use of again.

> At present the king thinks he sees order and tranquillity restored by his acceptance – in his refusal he sees personal danger to himself and family, and even if he should be able to escape, he sees the necessity of reconquering the kingdom under the auspices as it were of his brother. Of course his own power passed into his hands, a circumstance highly displeasing to the queen and which it is supposed decides her to shew so perfect an adhesion to the Assembly. Should the king be deceived in his expectations, should the next legislature be domineered by factions in or out of the Assembly, and following the example of their predecessors attempt to take the exercise of the functions of government into their hands and thus continue the state of anarchy, which is too much to be apprehended from the nature of the constitution and the present disposition of men's minds, he may then prefer the alternative, however disagreeable, of putting himself under the protection of his brother and of foreign aid.[72]

CHAPTER 11

From the Meeting of the Legislative Assembly
to the Storming of the Tuileries
(October 1791 to August 1792)

'We stand on a vast volcano ...'

THE new Legislative Assembly met on 1 October 1791, the day after the dissolution of the National Assembly. The king and the new deputies whose elections had been taking place over the late summer, were an unknown quantity to each other. The next nine months saw a refusal by the Assembly to make any concessions to the monarchy, the outbreak of war with Austria, the strains imposed on the Revolution by failure on the battlefield – with the Jacobins waiting in the wings all the while.

The Legislative Assembly

The opening session of the Legislative Assembly was marked by the deputies' refusal to give the king the proper mark of respect which the old National Assembly had always been prepared to give, even at the moments of greatest confrontation. In what looked, to observers, very much like a deliberate attempt to humiliate Louis XVI, they made an issue of who should have the precedence of first being seated at the opening session. It was the episode with the hats at the opening of the States-General all over again, but this time with the king being wrong-footed.

The commentators saw it as an ill omen. Gower wrote: 'The new Assembly has not yet given any proofs of its wisdom: of its rashness and ignorance it gave a convincing one ... it shewed an absurd disposition to quarrel with the king about trifles ... it seems to augur that the fanaticism of liberty will be prevalent.' And Morris added: 'The members of the late Assembly are all high-toned in their reprehension of this day's work of their successors, which is too little respectful towards the king. Are they indignant that any others should exceed them in marks of indignity?'[1]

Short reviewed the Legislative Assembly's first month's work disdainfully:

The assembly have as yet done nothing. Not a single decree has been passed. Day after day is passed in vain extravagant declamation, and in receiving addresses and petitions by deputations who are admitted at the bar and who flatter the Assembly in the most ridiculous manner. This circumstance joined to the personal want of consideration of almost all the members, exposes the Assembly to popular disrespect and to the assaults of a weapon, ridicule, which in no country is more powerful than in this.[2]

He went on to comment on the difficulty experienced in finding ministers prepared to serve in government:

M. de Montmorin has as yet no successor. M. de Moustier persisted in declining this post and now is in hopes of being appointed ambassador to London. M. de Ségur, after much intreaty, had agreed to accept the place, but the day before he was to take the oath of office the ministers were so indecently treated in the Assembly that he withdrew his word and wrote to the king to be excused. Since then several people have been successively talked of, but it is probable no one is yet decided on, and there will be much difficulty in finding a person to accept a place which has thus been refused.[3]

In mid-December Gower wrote a similarly critical account of the Assembly:

The Legislative Assembly has, as usual, employed the last week in the most frivolous manner; hearing and applauding petitions from the several Sections of Paris against that which the administrators of the department have presented to His Most Christian Majesty;

Last Tuesday [they] consumed the rest of the night, for they did not break up till seven o'clock the next morning, in examining drunken witnesses about a drunken drummer whom the *Comité de Surveillance* supposed of being guilty of enlisting men for the army of the princes.[4]

Emigrés
Short gave a full account of the *émigrés* and the king's and Legislative Assembly's position in relation to them:

Notwithstanding the little hopes of foreign succour emigrants continue in great numbers to go and join the princes. In many provinces not a man of the nobility able to bear arms remains and many of them carry their whole families with them. An idea prevails among them that they are dishonoured if they remain in France, and that only those who go to join the princes will be considered as noble after the counter revolution which they consider as certain. The Assembly are now deliberating on the means of preventing emigrations and punishing the emigrants. If they adopt violent measures the king will probably refuse his sanction.[5]

In this atmosphere Morris passed on the rumour of a Jacobin intrigue: 'that the republican party count with certainty on an attempt of the king to escape; that they mean to facilitate it, and then, laying the blame of all events on the monarch and his nobles, they will stop payment and be ready to meet any attack whatever'.[6]

On 9 November 1791 the Legislative Assembly duly passed the most draconian decree to date against the *émigrés* (including the king's brothers). Gower described the Assembly as 'thundering' and that the decree threatened the death penalty. He predicted that the non-juring clergy would shortly have similar measures applied to them and that the king would find it very difficult to bring himself to ratify these measures.[7]

Louis did indeed veto the decree on 12 November 1791. Short felt that this was 'proof of his liberty'. Gower reported that for his pains Louis XVI had been placed under close confinement again in the Tuileries, and this time allowed access only to certain parts of the palace.[8]

Rebellion and Mutiny

Linked to the fears of *émigrés* and Counter-Revolution were the deteriorating situations in the West Indies and within the armed forces at home. Morris recorded on hearing of the new turn of events in the Caribbean: 'the Minister of the Marine gives us at dinner the account of a dreadful insurrection of the blacks at Santo Domingo. I trust the account ... is exaggerated.'[9]

A fleet was (successfully this time) fitted out at Brest to restore order overseas, but was prevented from sailing, for fear that it would immediately defect to the Counter-Revolutionary white-planter aristocracy.[10] Short passed on a report of the general state of the navy: 'It is favorable as to the number and condition of the vessels but desparate on account of the spirit of insubordination which prevails in the ports among the sailors in general.'[11]

The same fears of unreliability applied to the army. Gower reported, 'it appears that the whole army, regulars as well as National Guard, is in a state of insubordination not very promising at the eve of war.... Such being the state of the French army, the *Comité Diplomatique* and M. de Lessart are intent to avert a war or at least to gain strength by negotiation.'[12]

It has to be added that the British embassy knew it would be pleasing its government with reports of French military incapacity. But the other side of the coin was that the French government was only too ready to propagate such reports, in order to be able to exhort greater loyalty and national unity. The Revolutionaries were not, though, in the last resort prepared to use them as a basis for decision-making, and had to discover for themselves in a succession of humiliating defeats in Flanders that they had been well founded.

Jacobins and *Feuillants*

The group based on the Feuillant Club was effectively the initial controlling group in the new Assembly with the Brissotins gaining ground and controlling the ministry by early 1792. The commentators perceived the Jacobins as the effective opposition, but had not as yet in their own minds separated out the Brissotins from Jacobins as a generic term for any radical Revolutionary. The commentators chronicled how the Jacobins took every opportunity to discomfort the *Feuillants* and to advance their own position.

In Paris the Jacobins and Sections had undermined the authority of the municipality to the point where

> Many of the municipal officers of this town are going to retire; they complain of a want of confidence in the Sections and of the consequent irksomeness of their situation: and in truth to be a *fonctionnaire public* of any sort in the present state of this country requires more than ordinary patience.

Gower wrote of the consequent elections, where Lafayette had stood as mayor against a Jacobin candidate: 'M. Pétion is chosen mayor. A great triumph for the Jacobins! All the principal offices in Paris are now held by members of that society.'[13]

In foreign policy the very complex picture was not wholly clear to the commentators. What they did not grasp was that few of the positions taken up on the issue of war were based on objective assessments of France's best interests or military realities, but were rather extensions of factional manoeuvring, relating only to domestic politics. Thus the Brissotins vied with each other to state the most bellicose policies, and the 'Jacobins' (in both the specific and generic senses) largely followed this lead. There was a small opposition to war around Robespierre. The mainstream Jacobins were all for invading the Austrian Netherlands in the autumn, and, from their side, the Austrians believed that the Legislative Assembly was being pushed towards war largely by the Jacobins: 'it remains to be seen whether the emperor's naming the Jacobins and marking them out as the cause of his continuing to arm will tend to diminish their numbers'.[14]

Gower reported regularly on the struggles within the Jacobin Club. In January 1792 he wrote: 'From the speeches of M. Brissot and M. Verignaud, in the debates of this week, it must appear that the Jacobins are desirous of war; but there is a considerable body of them, the followers of M. Robespierre, who wish to avoid it by negotiation.'[15]

In the war between the clubs the Jacobins scored a success they must have found most gratifying: 'The club of the Jacobins has gained a temporary victory over that of the *Feuillants*, for, by occasioning disturbances at their meetings, they have obliged the Assembly to order them to quit the Church of the *Feuillants* which belongs to and is contiguous to the Assembly.'[16] (The club had to move in fact three times between December 1791 and March 1792.)

Their support for republicanism and war was earning the Jacobins the following they sought: 'The Jacobins are acquiring a popularity in a degree and manner that are truly alarming.'[17]

The State of the Nation

Short, in almost his last major despatch as the senior American diplomat in Paris, reviewed the state of the country on 8 November 1791:

> On the whole it is too true that the horizon here blackens daily. In most of the departments serious and alarming troubles are taking place on account of the expulsion of the curates who refused the oath prescribed last year. Many of the peasantry deluded by them forget the advantages they hoped from the revolution which they now consider can be purchased only at the price of their salvation. These and other disorders contribute to prevent the payment of taxes which from their nature and mode of perception would probably have been illy paid even in times of calm and prosperity. This monthly deficit is supplied of course for the *caisse de l'extraordinaire*, viz., the funds appropriated to the redemption of the *assignats* now go to the support of government – hence a continuance of their depreciation and consequently a nominal and even a real rise in the price of all articles. Bread is that which is the most alarming and gives serious apprehensions for Paris this winter. Government being without force to protect the free circulation of grain gives an additional rise to this article in many places. The emigrants continue to go in great numbers to join the princes, at first they were only nobles and ecclesiastics, at present the discontented of the commons follow the example. They are in great numbers on account of the inhuman suppression without indemnity of the employments by which they and their families were supported. These emigrants suffer cruelly from want of money, but foreign powers will probably furnish them clandestinely merely for their support. Notwithstanding all this, if it were possible for the present government to acquire a sufficient degree of force to protect the persons and property of the citizens and insure the payment of taxes many of the emigrants would return and submit, but the number of those who lose all hopes of such an issue increases daily. It is much to be apprehended that the commercial class of citizens who have been hitherto much in favour of the revolution will become discontented on account of the situation of their affairs in the West Indies and the Mediterranean.[18]

Between November 1791 and February 1792 Gower passed a succession of judgements on the general condition of France. The Home Affairs portfolio, he wrote 'requires the shoulders of an Atlas and the courage of a Hercules, but as this is not an age for such heroes it is plainly to be perceived that the general fermentation throughout the kingdom is at a height and of a kind, which it is impossible for the government, constituted as it is, to repress'.[19]

On 2 and 9 December 1791 he commented:

> An universal expectation of an approaching crisis prevails. Every body acknowledges that France cannot long continue in its present state; but what the *dénouement* of this tragi-comedy will be remains to be known. The moderate party is daily gaining ground, and waits for some event to shew its strength. In the mean time the court exists in a miserable suspense between its jealousy of the emigrants and its fear of the Jacobins.

> The critical situation of this country becomes every day more apparent; the general alarm drives the little money in specie that remains out of the kingdom; the price of it, of course daily increases; and the value of *Assignats* diminishes: a national bankruptcy is more than ever to be expected.[20]

As the war with Austria drew closer, he reported:

> Upon the whole, the rapid increase of anarchy, not only in the metropolis but in every municipality of this disjointed kingdom, renders a war of some sort necessary, and if a bankruptcy should issue it is to be hoped that France will not remain entire.

> With regard to the interior state of the kingdom, disturbances, for which corn is always the pretence, break out in some part of the northern departments of the kingdom as fast as they are quelled in other parts; in the south they are in a state the nearest possible to civil war.[21]

Towards War with Austria

The *émigrés* had long been lobbying Austria to declare war on France to restore full authority to the monarchy. The emperor had not been especially receptive of this idea, but during the winter of 1791–2 a more concrete *casus belli* arose. The Austrians had re-established military control over the Austrian Netherlands provinces, but now feared that they could be destabilized again by agitation from France and Jacobin exhortations for international revolution. Gower recorded the receipt in Paris of a formal Austrian protest on 5 December 1791.[22]

The commentators did not analyse in any depth the process by which the

(Brissotin) government took the decision to fight a war with Austria. They regarded it as a mixture of an inevitable logic in the Revolution and 'hubris'. They were, though, aware of the way a state of war would strengthen the hand of the government and profoundly change the internal scene. One area of foreign policy, on the other hand, seemed eminently logical and susceptible to rational interpretation; this was the policy of peace – at almost any cost – with Britain.

On 4 February 1792 Morris forwarded a report that Brissot had 'proposed in the Diplomatic Committee the cession of Dunkirk and Calais to England as pledges of the fidelity of France'. Two months later Gower confirmed: 'It is evident that the Ministry here have a most earnest desire to be upon the best possible terms with England.' And he went on to report success in various commercial negotiations.[23]

The process of preparing for war with Austria was traced by Gower. On 23 November 1791 more *Assignats* were printed and new loans negotiated if needed.[24] On 27 January 1792 he recorded additional measures to raise troops, and added: 'The probability of war appears so great that this government is buying in specie in Holland and other places at an enormous price.'[25] (The significance of specie is that it would be used to pay troops, with the implied threat that they would be needing it when campaigning deep inside the enemy's territory where *Assignats* would be meaningless.)

In early February various ambassadors were making preparations to leave Paris – a sure sign of hostilities in the offing.[26] In late February there were detailed military preparations.[27] A significant event in the worsening of relations with other countries in Europe was the decision to regularize the situation in the by now annexed Comtat. Morris, now writing as the American ambassador, upbraided the government: 'The French Assembly have pardoned the assassins of Avignon. This is dreadful.'[28]

This move violated the territorial integrity of the Papacy and offered a *casus belli* to any power which chose to regard itself as duty bound to protect the temporal power of the Pope.

On the eve of war, Gower assessed the situation:

if this ministry should continue, and there is every reason to suppose it will, as it is supported by the majority, comprehending the most active and ardent of the people, war will be inevitable, however ill-prepared this country may be for it. It is true that they are not in want of men ... but real soldiers will undoubtedly be scarce.[29]

The Outbreak of War
War with Austria – and Austria alone at this stage – was formally declared

on 20 April 1792. Gower penned an incisive analysis of France's strategy for the conduct of the war:

> I find it to be a very general notion, at least in the Assembly, that if France can preserve a neutrality with England she will be able to cope with all the rest of Europe united. This notion is encouraged by a persuasion that the influence of Jacobinism and an inoculation of their principles will occasion an insurrection, which according to their language is *'le plus saint des devoirs'*, in every country whose government shall dare to oppose them in arms.
>
> [The Generals] seem to place their greatest confidence in the desertion of the enemy's forces. Corruption of every sort and in every manner is employed without reserve, and this mode of making war seems to be the boast of the Assembly as well as of the ministry.[30]

Gower forwarded to London a regular stream of reports from the front. As reports from any war, they were confusing and contradictory on a day-to-day basis, and would do little to further an understanding of either the war or the course of the Revolution. The commentators were, though, well-placed to chart the impact of the news on Paris.

On 3 May Gower forwarded optimistic reports of success in the initial invasion of the Austrian Netherlands, but on 4 May the truth about the state of the French army reached Paris: 'The last two defeats near Tournay and Mons have stunned the Jacobins; ... this blow tends to strengthen Robespierre's party. In one thing, however, they seem all to agree ... that subordination, however disagreeable it may be in civil life, is absolutely necessary in an army that means to be victorious.'

A call for martial law was rejected, but press censorship was imposed. The ministry was fatally undermined by the defeats. Recriminations started immediately between ministers and generals, and between ministers.[31]

Impact of the War in Paris
In the highly-charged atmosphere of Paris, Morris warned his royalist friends that 'they had better be quiet, for the people will certainly oppose the measures which they espouse'. He also predicted: 'France is on the high-road to despotism ... the most ardent advocates for the Revolution begin now to wish and pray, and even cry out, for the establishment of despotic power as the only means of securing the lives and properties of the people.'[32]

The first concrete result of the war itself and of the ensuing defeats was disarray within the Jacobin camp.[33] The Legislative Assembly acted on 28 May 1792 to take the domestic situation in hand: 'In order to impress into the minds of the people an apprehension of imminent danger to the state ...

the Legislative Assembly voted itself permanent last Monday ... and the still more efficient assembly of the Jacobins have followed its example.'[34] (Note: the term 'permanent' meant that the Assembly had put itself in continuous session.)

On 8 June 1792 Gower reported that the Assembly had put aside 'frivolous' and 'absurd' factional in-fighting, and 'Preparations are being made to convey in case of necessity His Most Christian Majesty and the Assembly to the banks of the Loire.'[35] The internal politics of the Revolution, however, militated against full and effective mobilization. The National Guard were opposed to increasing the size and effectiveness of the regular army.[36] The ministry of the day led by Dumouriez duly did fall, partly in response to the defeats – an event which Gower hoped would prove to be the 'destruction' of the Jacobins[37] – a hope which was not to be fulfilled. (The role played in the Revolution as minister, war hero then traitor will be explored in due course.)

The *Marseillais*
While the regime in Paris grappled with the threat of Austrian invasion, the 'democratical' southern provinces made their contribution to the Revolution. Gower traced the progress of the '*Marseillais*'.

On 9 March he reported: 'it is a singular event that a mixt body of two thousand people should arrive from Marseilles at the gates of Aix so unexpectedly that the inhabitants should not be able to make any defence against them'. On 2 April he wrote: 'It is believed that the Volunteers of Marseilles are in possession of Avignon.' And on 20 April he commented on the more general intensification of the Revolution in the south: 'The National Guards in the South are not only permitting, but assisting in the destruction and pillage of those unhappy proprietors whose political sentiments are not *à la hauteur de la constitution.*'[38]

The Revolutionary Situation in Paris
In a despatch on 27 January 1792 Gower gave an impression of the political atmosphere in the capital: 'A notion, which is industriously kept up, that the royal family have an intention of attempting, a second time to leave the kingdom, occasions suspicions and jealousies which, at present, only tend to increase the number of spies and informers about the place and even in private houses.'[39]

The Sections were increasingly becoming an independent force, albeit now able to act in greater concert with the newly Jacobin municipality: 'The inhabitants of the *Faubourg* St-Antoine have already made for themselves about thirty thousand pikes ... they are more calculated for pillage than for the protection of the property of citizens.'[40]

One result of the Jacobin capture of the municipality was that it now faced the hostility of the National Guard – still commanded by Lafayette. On 20 April Gower reported that the National Guard had thwarted an attempt by the municipality to remove busts of Bailly and Lafayette.[41]

That the Jacobins were beginning to acquire a position of immunity was indicated by an incident Gower reported on 18 May 1792. Two agitators were arraigned before a judge, but 'produced their tickets for admission to the Club of the Jacobins, in order to prove their integrity'.[42]

Position of the Royal Family

After the reimposition of their virtual house arrest, the royal family's position could only deteriorate. In December the Legislative Assembly dropped the titles of 'Sire' and 'Majesty' when addressing the king. His status in foreign affairs was formally lowered in January: 'A deputation from the Legislative Assembly has desired the king to declare to the emperor that he cannot treat with any power except in the name of the French nation.'[43]

It is difficult to decide if an incident which took place in February should be classified as harassment or buffoonery, but it indicated the nature of the king's internment. Gower heard that the king had asked to inspect a new writing desk. Having decided it was not to his liking, Louis had it sent back. As it was being carried out of the Tuileries, the National Guard insisted on inspecting it 'lest His Majesty should be concealed in it'.[44]

The crisis with Austria put Marie-Antoinette – and the rest of the royal family – in an impossible position: 'The royal family become every day more unpopular.'[45] Perhaps to placate the revolutionaries, Louis lifted his veto on the confiscation of *émigrés'* estates.[46] It did not cut much ice with the Jacobins, however, whose influence was still paramount in the Assembly. Morris commented on one of Louis XVI's rare public appearances (in the Legislative Assembly in June): 'his tone of voice and his embarrassment mark well the feebleness of his disposition'.[47]

The Position at Dumouriez's Resignation

Dumouriez had formed a 'patriot' (i.e. Brissotin) ministry on 10 March. The significance of this seems largely to have eluded the commentators, although Gower noted that Dumouriez had been applauded for a speech he made at the Jacobin club, and had been embraced by Robespierre on 23 March 1792. The accord within the ministry and between the ministry, the Assembly, and the Jacobins/Brissotins did not last. The ministry exploited the Jacobins' discomfiture over the disastrous progress of the war which they – with the exception of Robespierre's clique – had so fervently urged. For all this, Gower still saw the Jacobins as the group most effectively able to exercise the initiative in politics: 'the prevailing influence of the Jacobins has induced the [Assembly] to decree that the King's Guard should be disbanded'.[48] (The soldiers thus released were to be sent to the front to defend Paris.)

Louis objected to this measure, and to others proposed more specifically by Dumouriez to make more effective the war effort, but Dumouriez did manage to strengthen his position on 13 June 1792, when he persuaded Louis to dismiss some of the more radical Brissotins from the ministry. Gower commented that these changes might prove to be the 'destruction' of the Jacobins. Dumouriez could still not gain Louis' whole-hearted support, and he brought to a head a crisis of confidence on 17 June by proffering his own resignation. This was accepted, and Gower commented with some equanimity: 'Upon the whole it is to be expected that the measures of the new administration will be according to the principles of the *Feuillants*.'[49]

Morris, however, saw Dumouriez's departure as a watershed, and took the opportunity to survey more generally the state of the Revolution:

The king, much to Dumouriez's surprise, accepted his resignation, and, in consequence, all his newly appointed friends go out with him. The Jacobins were busy all last night to excite a tumult in the city, but the precautions taken to prevent it have as yet proved successful, and I am told that M. Luckner and M. de Lafayette still persist in their determination not to risk an action. If so, the present state of uncertainty may continue some time. If they fight and gain a victory, it is not improbable that we may witness some outrages of the most flagitious kind. If, on the contrary, there is any capital defeat, the Jacobin faction will be a little moderated. On the whole, sir, we stand on a vast volcano. We feel it tremble, we hear it roar, but how and when and where it will burst, and who may be destroyed by its eruptions, it is beyond the ken of mortal foresight to discover. This new ministry will be purged (at any rate) of some of its members, but one great doubt exists – whether it will not be driven off by the Jacobin faction. It is in contemplation to make a serious effort against that faction in favor of the constitution, and M. de Lafayette will begin the attack. I own to you that I am not sanguine as to the success. Very much is to be done, and there is very little time to do it, for the foreign army will soon be greatly superior in number, and it seems now to be ascertained that Alsace and Lorraine are disposed to join the invaders. Thus while a great part of the nation is desirous of overturning the present government in order to restore the ancient form, and while another part, still more dangerous from position and numbers, are desirous of introducing the form of a federal republic, the moderate men, attacked on all sides, have to contend alone against an immense force. I cannot go on with the picture, for my heart bleeds when I reflect that the finest opportunity which ever presented itself for establishing the rights of mankind throughout the civilized world is perhaps lost, and forever.[50]

The politics of the Revolution over the summer of 1792, which Morris anticipated so effectively, were of such importance and complexity that the commentators found it hard to keep a proper perspective on them. Following the departure of Dumouriez's ministry there were two parallel threads of political development. The first, conventional, strand was the installation in power of two successive *Feuillant* ministries. Of these, one lasted only three weeks and was replaced by another of lesser talents. These men tried to bolster the position of the monarchy and condoned Lafayette's attempt to close the Jacobin Club (see below). They were, however, ineffectual against the Brissotins and Jacobins.

The second strand of political development was the strategy to achieve a revolution within the Revolution by the elimination of the monarchy and its supporters and of the existing constitution. This Brissotin and Jacobin strategy saw its first manifestation in the invasion of the Tuileries on 20 June 1792. The success of this episode led to deeper-laid plans to create a popular uprising which would culminate in a perceived military victory over the monarchy. After a number of false starts this was successfully carried off on 10 August 1792 with the second invasion of the Tuileries under Danton's self-proclaimed leadership. This act swept away the monarchy, the ministry of the day, and the constitution, and it transformed completely the commentators' own relationship to the Revolution.

The commentators' analysis of the more significant steps towards the second invasion of the Tuileries can now be set into this wider perspective and context.

The First Storming of the Tuileries

For all his wretched position the king still had important powers – notably the right to veto any decree passed by the Legislative Assembly. He was a convenient focus for Revolutionary discontent and scapegoat for the failure of the army. He could be perceived as an enemy of the Revolution nestling at its heart. It would be a climax to the Revolution – rivalling the storming of the Bastille – if the 'people' could seize power from their erstwhile 'tyrant'.

On 19 and 20 June crowds demonstrated against Louis' use of the veto against a decree concerning non-juring priests. On 20 June this crowd unexpectedly (though probably to a plan prearranged by the Brissotins) burst into the Tuileries and physically cornered the royal family, making them fear for their lives. Gower gave a full and factual account of the event, and then analysed its causes and consequences, stating that the attack on the Tuileries by the Jacobins to intimidate His Most Christian Majesty has failed entirely and has served only to impress more strongly on the minds of those who wish for order and good government an abhorrence of their principles and practices. The majesty of the throne was sullied, but it gave the king a happy opportunity of displaying an extraordinary degree of calmness and courage.[51]

Morris concluded his account thus: 'after dinner we learn that the deputation of the Faubourgs has forced the unresisting guard, filled the *Château*, and grossly insulted the king and queen.... The constitution has this day, I think, given its last groan.'[52]

Lafayette

In parallel with these events, Lafayette had seen the resulting revulsion against mob rule and wave of sympathy for the royal family – a particular feature of the Parisian scene noted by Morris[53] – as presenting the opportunity for him to assert his leadership of the Revolution in Paris (he was already the commander-in-chief of the north-east front) after his snub in the municipal elections. He placed himself at the head of the opposition to the Jacobins. Gower described the speech he made as 'totally destitute of that eloquence which excites a popular assembly [but] had that effect which his friends had expected, that of intimidating the Jacobin party'.[54]

Lafayette talked over the constitutional position with Morris, who reported that Lafayette 'says he wishes the American constitution but an hereditary executive [i.e. monarchy]'.[55] Gower then recorded sadly that Lafayette's initiative, which had included an attempt to close the Jacobin Club on 28 June, had failed:

We are at the eve of a great crisis ... M. de Lafayette's conduct during his stay in Paris was not sufficiently bold and energetic to affect the Jacobins with that degree of fear which it was intended to have produced, and it has only served to make them more active in sending for the assistance of their friends from all parts of the kingdom.... Their stay in Paris ... will be long enough to answer any sinister purpose. On the other hand it may be doubted that M. de Lafayette will be able to bring his army to the assistance of the metropolis.[56]

It is appropriate here to complete Lafayette's story. On 29 June, he had returned to the Front. On 1 August Morris confirmed his failure in stark terms: 'I verily believe that if M. de Lafayette were to appear just now in Paris unattended by his army he would be torn to pieces.' The Legislative Assembly initiated impeachment proceedings against him for military incompetence on the grounds of desertion of his post on 28 June, and although he was exculpated on 8 August he defected on 19 August 1792. As news of this spread, Morris penned his epitaph: 'Truly his circle is complete. He has spent all his fortune on a revolution, and is now crushed by the wheel which he had put in motion.' Colonel George Munro, on behalf of the British embassy, wrote of the effect on his faction in the Assembly: 'Lafayette's deputies were sadly alarmed and [some] expressed their fears to me, and their anxiety to get away never to return.'[57]

The *Fête de la Fédération* and the *Fédérés*

The date for the annual *Fête de la Fédération* was approaching and in 1792 the Jacobins determined to exploit the event to the full. According to Morris, Danton also wished to use it to establish his republican credentials: 'Danton has said today publicly, *à propos* of the intrigues of the court, that they would get rid of the whole the 14th.'[58]

Gower reported the approaching event with alarm: 'Although we enjoy perfect tranquillity in this capital at present, we have reason to doubt the continuance of it, for it is certain that the [Jacobins] have sent pressing invitations to the affiliated [clubs], to assist at the *fête* on the fourteenth of July.'

Paris was in 'an awful state of suspense', and the Jacobins were taking care 'to provide accommodation for the [*Fédérés*] ... lest they should be influenced by *Feuillants*'.[59]

The Jacobins kept the *Fédérés*, and especially the *Marseillais*, in Paris after 14 July, as powerful new allies: 'The *Fédérés* begin to insult the Assembly.... The ferocious disposition of the five hundred *Fédérés* from Marseilles was but all too conspicuous on the very day of their arrival' – and several men were killed by them.[60]

Gower wrote of his personal situation: 'For my own part ... I consider myself in as little danger as it is possible to be in the anarchical state of this country.'[61]

The War (*La Patrie en Danger*)

At the front the Austrians were reported to be boasting that they would winter in Paris,[62] but the tumultuous events in the capital completely overshadowed such alarms, despite the best efforts of the Assembly: 'The solemn declaration of the Assembly that the country is in danger has had very little effect at least in the metropolis where the minds of the inhabitants are entirely occupied with providing lodgings for the *Fédérés*.'[63]

The Declaration of Pillnitz (in effect a pledge by the allies to restore the *ancien régime*) was equally ignored: 'The Duke of Brunswick's declaration, which has not been officially noted, has produced very little sensation here.

The aristocrats are dissatisfied with it, and the *démocrates* affect to despise it.'[64]

Moves against the Monarchy

Those whose duty it was to defend the monarchy – and this in effect included the ministry in office on 20 June 1792 – had lost heart. On 7 July there was a ceremony of swearing fraternity in the Legislative Assembly at which it was hoped the king might regain some dignity if not initiative. It was, however, a flop, and led to the resignation of the ministry, as Morris described:

> a farce was acted in the Assembly, in which the principal performers played well their parts, the king was duped according to custom, and things are verging fast to the catastrophe of the play. For some weeks the adverse party, I mean the court and Jacobins, have been labouring each to cast on the other the odium of violating entirely the constitution and commencing the civil war. The party which calls itself independent and which, in fact, is the fearful party, begs hard for peace and seizes eagerly whatever bears the appearance or the name. It was to catch these gudgeons that the scene of Saturday was exhibited. The king and queen, believing that the actors were in earnest, and knowing their lives had been at stake, were overjoyed, and their timid counsellors, trembling under the tyrannous powers of the Assembly, seized with eagerness the bait of reconciliation. . . . This day the king will commence a new career, and if he goes *through* I think he will succeed.

But a day later he wrote: 'The ministers have all resigned . . . their Majesties flashed in the pan.'[65]

Gower described on 20 July Jacobin moves to prepare for a more serious assault on the (now properly defended) Tuileries:

> The situation of His Most Christian Majesty becomes daily more and more perilous.

> The Jacobins finding that the three regiments of regular troops [in Paris], were not sufficiently indisciplined to be relied upon by them, have contrived that they should be sent to the frontiers. There remains one regiment of Swiss which it will be difficult to dispose of in the same manner, owing to the treaty with the cantons, and to the sentiments of the private soldiers, as well as of the officers of that regiment.[66]

Overt constitutional moves, however, against the monarchy failed dramatically:

The committee of twenty-one ... had agreed to report a project of a decree to declare that the crown was forfeited, but [M. de Montesquiou, commander of the troops in the south] assured them, that not only every officer but every soldier would oppose them.... It does not follow that ... His Most Christian Majesty is to be considered in a less dangerous situation than formerly; I rather fear the contrary. I understand that notwithstanding the opinion of his friends ... His Most Christian Majesty is determined to remain in Paris.[67]

Although some Jacobins (Condorcet among them) were reported to be so disheartened by this failure that they were contemplating emigration to America,[68] the Jacobin pressure did not relent. A further part of the softening up of the Tuileries came when part of the gardens was removed from the jurisdiction of the palace.[69] With its defences thus opened up, the royal family were only allowed to retain their liberty within the Tuileries on sufferance: 'it being in the interest of their leaders that they should not at this moment offer violence to the royal family'.[70]

Morris visited the palace on 5 August 1792 and commented: 'Nothing remarkable, only that they were up all night, expecting to be murdered.'[71]

The Second Storming of the Tuileries (10 August 1792)

On 10 August a mixed force of armed civilians and National Guards carried out a methodical and military-style assault on the Tuileries, killing all its defenders. The royal family were (perhaps deliberately) not in the palace at the time, but at the Legislative Assembly. The act symbolized the seizure by the people of the last vestiges of power from the monarchy.

Gower gave a very full but wholly factual account of the storming. Morris's account is terser but more zestful. Shortly after he had finished a regular meeting 'the canon begin, and musketry mingled with them announce a warm day. The *Château*, undefended but by the Swiss, is carried, and the Swiss, wherever found, are murdered. The king and queen are in the Legislative Assembly, who have decreed the suspension of his authority.'[72]

Morris reported in December and January 1792–3 on the role played by Danton and his associate, Westermann:

Shortly after the 10th of August I had information, on which you may rely, that the plan of Danton was to obtain the resignation of the king and get himself appointed Chief of a Council of Regency ...

Those who planned the revolution which took place on the 10th of August sought a person to head the attack, and found a M. Westermann, whose morals were far from exemplary. He has no pretensions to science or to depth of thought, but he is fertile in resources and imbued with the most daring intrepidity.... When the business drew towards a point the conspirators trembled, but Westermann declared they should go on. They obeyed, because they had trusted him too far. On that day his personal conduct decided, in a great measure, his success. Rewards were due, and military rank, with opportunities to enrich himself, granted.[73]

Westermann, a giant Alsatian soldier, became one of Danton's closest associates. He was implicated in Dumouriez's treason, fared poorly against the Vendéean rebels, and was eventually executed with Danton. Morris's account, therefore, hints at Danton's ambiguous reputation of being the hero of the people and instigator of the attack on the Tuileries, while simultaneously being close to men who were prepared to enter into negotiation with foreign countries and seeking the powers vested in monarchy for himself.

Gower reported that aristocratic *hôtels* elsewhere in Paris were sacked at the same time. The British embassy was also visited: 'After the Paris mob had been at Lord Gower's to get hold of his Swiss, for the declared purpose of cutting off his head because he was a Swiss, the ruling powers offered him a guard. He refused this, on the high ground of being protected by his character, etc.'[74]

The constitutional outcome of the storming was that 'The Assembly having first declared itself permanent, decreed ... that the executive power was withdrawn from the king.' The ministry was dissolved and there was an orgy of statue smashing. Morris explicitly stated that the Assembly had fallen under 'the *dictée* of the Tribunes'. He concluded: 'Things are taking on their new order.'[75]

Recall of the British Ambassador

Despite his courage and coolness Gower had to be recalled, as one of Auckland's correspondents explained:

The French business is at length arrived at such a pitch of enormity, that to suffer Lord Gower and Lindsay [his secretary] to remain any longer at Paris was little better than murder. They are both, therefore, directed to come home, and have an instruction to leave behind them a hint that, though we have been, and mean to be, at all points extremely neutral, any personal attempt upon the king and his family will raise strange sensations here.[76]

The actual letter of recall contained the following passage: 'As it appears that the exercise of executive power has been withdrawn from His Most Christian Majesty, the credential under which your Excellency has hitherto acted can be no longer available.'[77]

The British ambassador was not the only one to be recalled. The Venetian ambassador moved too quickly for the authorities' liking and he was stopped from leaving Paris and placed under house arrest.[78] Morris observed, gloomily: 'The different ambassadors are all taking flight, and if I stay I shall be alone.'[79]

POSTSCRIPT

From the Storming of the Tuileries
to the Fall of Robespierre
(August 1792 to July 1794)

'Terror is the order of the day'

THE last two years covered by this book have to take the form of a postscript because of the sharp reduction in the volume of material available for selection.

After the suspension of the king's powers, on 10 August 1792, the diplomats had no recognized authority with which they could treat. The British and other European powers, as described above, withdrew their embassies. Only the Americans elected to recognize the new republic and maintain diplomatic relations with it.

It took Gower a month to negotiate a passport out of France, during which time he continued his political intelligence-gathering as before. After his departure the embassy retained a skeleton staff to keep a watching brief on the Revolution. One of these staff – Colonel George Munro – was a secret agent who had infiltrated expatriate Jacobin societies. He was a known and trusted member of the Parisian Jacobin community able to move freely about Paris. He enjoyed the same sort of contact with Jacobin leaders in the Jacobin Club that ambassadors had previously enjoyed with government ministers. Tragically, for the historian, his cover was blown on 10 January 1793 and he had to make a hasty departure from France. The British government also continued to receive reports from the (increasingly few) travellers to France and to run a secret agent network even after war broke out (on 1 February 1793). Their written reports were, however, very limited in number.

Paris had become a very dangerous city for foreigners – even diplomats – but Morris stayed on and continued reporting events so far as he was able. This, unfortunately, was to a very limited extent because all mail going abroad was opened and censored. Remarks critical of the Revolution were a death warrant to their author and to anyone implicated. Private papers in private or diplomatic premises were subject to search and seizure, so Morris did not dare keep a diary. On several of the few occasions when Morris would seem to have had access to a safe courier he took the opportunity to unburden himself about his personal feelings on the Revolution rather than providing insights into a government with which he was, in any case, having increasingly little contact.

Monro, using secret service channels, was able to write fully and freely about the political scene, confident that his despatches would reach Whitehall. Gower added at the end of one of his last despatches the conditions under which he, and other correspondents not so advantaged, laboured. It is instructive that this was written nearly a year before the 'Terror', properly defined, began: 'I regret much not being able to write to your Lordship in cypher, as the present circumstances afford much curious and interesting matter which prudence forbids me to commit to the common post.'[1]

The sources for the last two years of this study (August 1792–July 1794) are therefore patchy. Up to January 1793 they are as full as for some earlier parts of 1792, but thereafter there is a very sketchy coverage relying almost exclusively on Morris, who often went in fear for his life. His testament to survival during the Terror is a fitting conclusion.

The Situation in Late August 1792 and the Power of the Sections

The second invasion of the Tuileries led to the immediate suspension of the monarchy, and under the impact of this event the *Feuillant* ministry collapsed. Three groups stepped into the resultant power vacuum. The first was a new Brissotin ministry whose leading lights were Danton (Justice) and Roland (Interior). This ministry was to be ably served by its ally at the front line, the (now) General Dumouriez, who would deliver the victory (at Valmy) which was so badly needed. The second group was a committee of twenty-one of the deputies to the Legislative Assembly who still felt they enjoyed some popular confidence (and personal safety). This committee attempted to exercise some executive power, but in the event neither they nor the ministry were able to control events in Paris or run an effective national administration. The only effective power in Paris in the aftermath of the events of 10 August rested with the Sections, the (Jacobin) municipality, and the *fédérés* who had remained in Paris after the *Fête* on 14 July. Collectively, Morris termed these people the 'tribunes'. It was in this environment that the September prison massacres could take place.

The combined effects of the suspension (leading to the abolition) of the monarchy and the collapse of effective executive government were a need to revise the constitution and to dissolve the Legislative Assembly replacing it with a National Convention. This process had the incidental effect of allowing back into the mainstream of politics the men of the original National Assembly who had been debarred from serving in the Legislative Assembly by the 'self-denying' ordinance – chief among these men was Robespierre. At the same time, the fate of the royal family as individuals was decided, and both the Legislative Assembly and the National Convention split into warring factions whose struggles would not be resolved until Robespierre's dominance.

Against this background Gower surveyed the scene in the capital on 27 August 1792:

> The situation of Paris is more quiet than could be expected after the late violent convulsion; and as the people are all armed and the government extremely feeble, the present tranquillity of the town is strong proof of how much Paris must have been taken to instigate the multitude. . . .

Unknowingly predicting the power struggles to come between the Jacobins and the *sans-culottes,* he continued:

> The Jacobins seem to have gone further than they at first intended, and not to have foreseen that the mob, the instrument with which they overturned the old government, was likely soon to become formidable to themselves; the Assembly itself being now a good deal under the influence of the rabble.[2]

On the threat of the approaching Austrians he wrote: 'nothing can exceed the unanimity and confidence which prevails through the country'. Commenting on the state of insurrection in the *faubourgs* and the continued presence of the *Fédérés* he wrote: 'The Assembly may be regarded as in a sort of imprisonment and the Convention will soon be in a similar situation if it should meet in this capital.'[3] On 31 August Gower reported the failure of the Assembly's attempt to suppress the Communes (on 30 August) and its aftermath. The municipality, 'having abrogated to themselves more power than is allowed them by the constitution', ordered the War Office to be searched and, as a result, brought all business there to a halt.[4]

Monro made some very critical judgements of the Sections and their henchmen:

> The ministers of every department are complaining of being unable to carry on the routine of their different offices for the interference of people who are ignorant of the nature of them; in short they all wish to be directors, but except the poor people that have been compelled to go to the army, none wish to be actors.

> The Marseillais still remain in Paris ... there is not the smallest doubt but they are Genoese assassins, hired for that purpose.[5]

(It would be open to question whether Monro could have distinguished between Provençal and Italian.)

Gower summed up the situation as he saw it: 'as the multitude are perfect masters, everything is to be dreaded'.[6]

Proscription of the Aristocrats

The work of August after the 10th was to round up all the potential sympathizers with the monarchy. This was both to eliminate them as a potential 'Fifth Column' and to gather evidence to be used against the king and queen in their forthcoming trials. Gower predicted that the outcome of the king's trial would be his imprisonment for life and the declaration of a republic. In the process of the gathering of evidence, 'many hundred people connected with the court and the aristocracy have been thrown into prison'.[7]

Morris's account of these days was more brutal: 'Another man is beheaded this evening for the crime *de lèse-nation*. He published a newspaper against the Jacobins.'

Morris managed to involve himself personally in the proscription of the aristocrats: 'I find company at home, which stays late. One of them, St-Croix, comes after I am in bed, to ask asylum. The municipality are in pursuit of him.' Morris agreed to shelter him, and hid him well enough to escape discovery by the next day's search party.[8]

Morris was surprised on 30 August to be able to have a civilized conversation about the situation in Paris with a representative from the Section: 'The *Commissaire de Section* called on me this morning, and behaved very well ... I learn that many people have been taken up last night. There was a general search throughout the town for arms, and I presume for people also. It still continues.'[9]

Gower, however, believed that most of those for whom the Sections were searching had escaped: 'since the Revolution of 1789, the political sentiments of almost every individual are pretty generally known, and the best informed people agree that almost all the aristocrats or friends to the old despotic form of government [have emigrated]'.[10]

The Approach of the Austrians and Prussians

With the Duke of Brunswick's Manifesto (received in Paris on 28 July 1792), Prussia had allied with Austria to attack France, and the Duke of Brunswick had assumed the role of Allied Commander-in-Chief. The Prussians were the most feared army in Europe. It was, therefore, with some surprise that Gower recorded on 27 August: 'it is however equally true and unaccountable that the approach of the Duke of Brunswick does not excite that alarm which might be expected'. (And which historians have tended to attribute to it.)

He went on, in the same despatch, to describe the only optimistic feature of the war from the French side: 'It is thought that if the Duke of Brunswick winters in France, his army will be enervated and lose its discipline, and if he returns to the frontier he will be obliged to begin everything again on the opening of a second campaign.' In terms of the fate of the Prussians after Valmy this was prophetic, as Europe's premier army did indeed fall apart.

Gower quickly reverted to the more immediate reality of Brunswick's advance: 'They say it is very possible he may penetrate to and conquer Paris, but in that case the Convention will remove to the south, where the enemy will find much difficulty in following them.'[11] (Gower was speculating on the situation a month hence when the 'National Convention' would have been sitting.)

To meet the threat to Paris, Danton put himself at the head of its defences.[12] On 2 September Gower broke off his despatch: 'While I am writing, my Lord, the alarm guns are firing, the Tocsin is ringing, and drums beating to arms all over the town.'[13]

Monro was much closer to the events: 'About one o'clock on Sunday forenoon three signal guns were fired, the Tocsin was rung, and one of the municipality on horseback proclaimed in different parts of the city, that the enemy was at the gates, Verdun was besieged, and could only hold out a few days.' The population *en masse* were ordered to the Champs de Mars to raise an army of 60,000: 'The Assembly applauded their conduct, and immediately passed a decree' – of death to all those who did not help the war effort and that all non-essential (i.e. carriage) horses be seized.[14]

The September Massacres
The massacre of prisoners in Paris's jails during 2–6 September 1792 was probably well planned and reflected the temper of some Revolutionary leaders, but it was actually occasioned by the immediate fear of a Prussian occupation of Paris.

On 2 September Morris linked the two events, reporting that 'the enemy are at the gates of Paris ... this proclamation produces terror and despair among the people. This afternoon they announce the murder of priests who had been shut up in the Carmes. They then go to the Abbaye, and murder the prisoners there. This is horrible.'[15]

Monro determined to establish exactly what was happening. He had heard that murders were being committed in the prisons by 'a large number of *sans-culottes* attended by a number of Marseillais and Brestois, the hired assassins of [the Jacobins]'. (This is the first use of the term *sans-culottes* by any of the commentators.) Monro continued: 'To be convinced of what I could not believe, I made a visit to the prison of the Abbaye ... a single file of men armed with swords, or pikes, formed a lane of some length ... and when I saw them seemed much fatigued with their horrid work.'

To quote Monro's very long despatch in full would confirm the brutality of the massacres but would not shed much light on their political context or importance. To précis what he saw: an impromptu court was set up in a room in the prison where 'defendants' were arraigned and interviewed briefly on their crimes against the Revolution. Most were found guilty but then told

they could go. Believing they were being set free they gratefully stepped into
the next room where the *sans-culottes* and *Fédérés* were waiting with swords
and pikes. They were hacked to pieces and the bodies flung outside the prison
to await the next victim. Monro watched the proceedings in both rooms.
Among the prisoners thus treated, Monro recognized two members of the
municipality.[16]

On what was to be the last day of the massacres Morris wrote: 'There is
nothing new today. The murders continue.' Summing up for Jefferson he
said: 'We have had a week of unchecked murders.'[17]

The Defence of Paris
The Prussians did not appear in the first week of September, but the need to
defend Paris in the face of their continuing advance was as pressing as ever.
The panic measures of 2 September – the raising of 60,000 volunteers and
the impressing of all carriage hourses – has been noted, as has Danton's
assumption of leadership. Monro had little faith in the military capabilities of
the Sections' levies: 'I have no doubt, were a Prussian army once to appear
before Paris, that many of the king's friends, who are either quiet or concealed
citizens that want peace, and a vast number of people that are averse to the
Jacobin principles, would readily declare themselves for the royal party.'[18]

Desperate measures were being followed by the Parisians, who 'are giving
in their iron pots to supply the place of shot, and are depriving the dead of
their coffins to make musquet balls, and it has even already been proposed
to kill all the dogs in the capital as so many useless mouths'.[19] The levy had
produced a 'prodigious' number of men under arms – 70,000 from Paris
alone, and 'Horses and waggons have been impressed in vast numbers today
to carry provisions.'[20] All movement in and out of Paris was regularly halted.
On 7 September Morris reported a scare that the royal family and government
might be trying to escape and that the gates were locked to keep them inside
Paris.[21]

Internal Dissension
The strain of continuing military defeat seemed to be opening up cracks in the
Revolution, which, again, subsequent historians have been able to interpret as
manifestations of rivalries between deputies and factions, but which the
commentators could only take at face value. The steady alienation between
the Brissotins and Jacobins since the early summer was not properly understood by the commentators as an underlying political reality.

On 10 September 1792 Monro detected 'a want of confidence in their
generals', and the 'greatest confusion and agitation' was being shown in the
defence of cities such as Longwy, Verdun, and Châlons, where 'there was
only one good patriot in the whole place'. On 12 September he continued: 'The

interior dissensions amongst the people in power seem daily increasing.'[22]

It may have been on reading this despatch that Burges commented to Auckland: 'Providence seems to have decreed that [the Jacobins] shall mutually immolate each other.'

Relying on information clearly not supplied by Monro, and picking up the theme of the effect on public morale of Paris being isolated, one of Auckland's correspondents relayed a report received from an agent who had left the city on 17 September. The report stated that

> they were preparing to shut the barriers, and a dismal and silent consternation seemed universally to prevail, though nothing more than the ordinary murders and robberies had happened, except indeed that the *garde-meuble* at the Tuileries had been broken open, and all the crown jewels had been carried off.

Monro added the detail that *the* diamond from the Affair of the Diamond Necklace had been among the gems stolen.[23]

Monro described the collapse of law and order:

> The want of police has got nearly to the height I expected it would; the blackguards of Paris have begun this day to stop people publicly in the streets, and take their watches and buckles from them; they have even taken the ladies' rings from their fingers and from their ears; my *traiteur* was obliged to bring me metal spoons for fear of the others being taken.

> I myself never move out but with pistols in my pocket, as I find them more necessary here than in Turkey.[24]

Huber, in part of his last despatch to Auckland to be quoted in this study, referred to France as 'That doomed country!'[25]

Valmy

The news from the front was, as ever, detailed but confused. The first hint that the unbroken run of defeats might be about to end came from Monro reporting that Dumouriez (now commanding at the front after his resignation from the ministry in June) had taken possession of 'a very advantageous piece of ground'. Two days later

> there was a report in the streets that General Dumouriez had killed four thousand Prussians, and that the king himself was besieged in Verdun; but this was all nonsense; I therefore understand that the whole advantage was that General Chazot stood his ground the first attack, which was perhaps more than was expected.[26]

Then on 22 September came Monro's report of the 'Cannonade of Valmy' (actually fought on 20 September). The news reaching Paris was that Dumouriez had fallen back 'after an action of twelve hours'. In other words, yet another French defeat.[27]

The importance of the events at Valmy took several days to be appreciated. Morris first became aware of them circuitously, on 26 September. 'I am told that the king of Prussia has made overtures for accommodation with the Assembly. This is, I presume, a military trick.' On 3 October the true situation was confirmed: 'This morning I have details respecting the retreat of the Prussians.' He refused, however, to give the French army any credit: 'Great sickness and the crafty policy of Austria account for it.... The rainy weather is very unfavorable to the sickly troops under the Duke of Brunswick.' At the same time Morris was having to admit that French arms were carrying all before them in Nice and Savoy and on the Rhineland front.[28]

Auckland passed the following judgement on the battle, once its implications had become apparent: 'It will be resounded through France (and through other parts of Europe) that a mere horde of undisciplined freemen has been able to foil the efforts of a combined army of veterans, greatly superior in numbers and appointments, and directed by the best commanders in Europe.'[29] The battle had saved the Revolution, and Morris was forced to conclude his review of the military situation: 'Everything looks favorably to the cause of the new republic.'[30]

(It is fair to observe as a footnote to Morris's ostensibly carping attitude to Valmy that no other commentators even began to assess the battle, or the campaign generally, in the light of what is clear to historians: that the Austrians and Prussians were indeed pulling their punches in this theatre in order to keep a strong military presence in eastern Europe, where Russia was triumphing over Poland and Turkey and upsetting the balance of power.)

Abolition of the Monarchy and the Trial and Execution of Louis XVI

The abolition of the monarchy had taken place *de facto* on 10 August 1792, but it still remained formally to adopt a republican constitution. Hand in hand with the process of turning France into a republic went the process of trying and judging the king and queen. The first part of that process had been the rounding up of royalist suspects for interview during August 1792.

The momentum for the death of the king was such that by early September 1792 British intelligence reports from Paris indicated that there were 'well-grounded fears for the safety of the royal family'.[31]

On 20 September Monro reported that Danton and Thomas Paine were well advanced in their preparations to give France a new republican constitution.[32] The actual abolition of the monarchy was recorded sardonically by Morris: 'Nothing new this day, except that the Convention has met and declared they will no king in France.' He was equally terse on 3 December

1792, when 'The Convention this day determined to try the king.'[33]

The decision to try one Bourbon led the Convention to appraise the situation of other members of that family in France, with a side-swipe (by Brissot) at the Jacobins:

> I am told this day that the committee think they have been pushed too far against the king, by the Orléans faction. The Convention banish the Bourbon family.

> a decree will soon be passed entirely to expel all Princes of the Blood royal from France; this blow is intended at the Duke of Orléans, who is the soul of Robespierre's party.[34]

In the event it did not prove possible to make this decree, and Orléans remained active in the Revolution.

On the first day of the trial Monro wrote: 'the *sans-culottes* it is said are determined either to have him acquitted or condemned at the sitting of that day'. He described the proceedings that day. Louis XVI was taken to the National Convention 'as fast as the coachman could drive'. The debates that followed were accompanied by 'the most extreme violence and confusion'. The Jacobins – perhaps fearing that a majority of the deputies were still sympathetic to the king – refused to allow a vote to be taken.[35]

Morris wrote at some length on the personal and political position of the king in the period between his trial and execution. To anyone not familiar with the history of the Revolution,

> it would seem strange that the mildest monarch who ever filled the French throne, one who is precipitated from it precisely because he would not adopt the harsh measures of his predecessors, a man whom none could charge with a criminal act, should be prosecuted as one of the most nefarious tyrants that ever disgraced the annals of human nature ... I think it highly probable that he may suffer [execution], and that for the following causes: The majority of the Assembly found it necessary to raise against this unhappy prince the national odium, in order to justify the dethroning him ... and to induce the ready adoption of a republican form of government.... The rage which has been excited was terrible; and, although it begins to subside, the Convention are still in great straits – fearing to acquit, fearing to condemn, and yet urged to destroy their captive monarch.

Morris believed that all hands were now turned against Louis, and that he would be of more value to the Counter-Revolution as a martyr than he ever could be as a prisoner:

The monarchic and aristocratic parties wish his death, in the belief that such a catastrophe would shock the national feelings, awaken their hereditary attachment, and turn into the channels of loyalty the impetuous tide of opinion. Thus he has become the common object of hatred to all parties, because he has never been the decided patron of any one.

Louis XVI's most dangerous enemy, however, was still the Duc d'Orléans who was acting as the tool of the Jacobins. Morris thought he had detected in the 'violent party' (i.e. the followers of Danton and Robespierre)

the design to restore royalty in the person of the Duke of Orléans. This man's character and conduct give but too much room to suspect him of criminal intentions. I have many particular circumstances which lead me to believe that he has from the beginning played a deep and doubtful game; but I believe, also, that on the present occasion ... he is the dupe. ... The *Cordeliers* (or privy council which directs the Jacobin movements) know well the design of inverting the order of succession. They know how to appreciate the fluctuating opinions of their countrymen, and, though they are very willing to employ the Duke of Orléans in their work, I am much mistaken if they will consent to elevate him to the throne.

The king's fate is to be decided next Monday the 14th. That unhappy man, conversing with one of the Council on his own fate, calmly summed up the motives of every kind, and concluded that a majority of the Council would vote for referring his case to the people, and that in consequence he should be massacred.[36]

Monro called the decision itself to execute the king an 'unjust and iniquitous judgment'.[37] The National Convention were aware and prepared for others to share this view: 'it is generally reported that ... no less than 100,000 men will be in this capital from the Departments prior to Monday (the 14th); and it is generally supposed that these men are intended to protect the decision of the National Convention whatever it may be'.[38]

The actual vote on the 14th for execution represented a volte-face by a great number of deputies, so that 'The king's friends were confounded.' Monro attributed the vote to pressure from the mob: 'The day I left Paris there were some thousands of armed men parading in different parts of the city ready to commit any sort of riot, and threatening destruction should the king not be put to death.'[39]

Monro said of Louis XVI after receiving his sentence: 'The king is perfectly reconciled to his fate.' He predicted – as had Morris's royalist friends – that insurrection would follow the execution. Morris wrote of the event: 'The late king of this country has been publicly executed. He died in a manner becoming his dignity.'[40]

Marie-Antoinette

While the queen's fate was inextricably linked to the king's, her trial was separate and her execution took place at a much later date (16 October 1793). The Revolution saw her crimes and trial as a different issue to the king's, and in August there was a suggestion that she might even be tried before her husband. On 27 August Gower reported that she 'is regarded as the cause of all the late misfortunes'.[41]

Nothing more is recorded of her until a most unexpected and melodramatic report was forwarded to Auckland, shortly before her execution, saying that 'an English Gentleman' had managed to see her in the Concièrge prison:

> He was admitted to see the Concièrge, and upon expressing a wish to see the unfortunate queen, was told it would be readily granted if he showed no signs of compassion, but that if he did, he must not think of ever going out of that place again; ... he was led into the room in which the poor queen was sitting, on an old worn-out chair made of straw.[42]

Morris gave an ambiguous account of her execution, and suggested that, like her husband, she was, perhaps, more useful to the Counter-Revolution dead than alive. He used the occasion of her death as an opportunity to comment more generally on the state of the Revolution:

> The queen was executed the day before yesterday. Insulted during her trial and reviled in her last moments, she behaved with dignity through-out. This execution will, I think, give future hostilities a deeper dye, and unite more intimately the Allied Powers. It will silence the opposition of those who would not listen to the dismemberment of their country, and therefore it may be concluded that the blow by which she died was directed from a distance. But whatever may be the lot of France in remote futurity, and putting aside the military events, it seems evident that she must soon be governed by a single despot.[43]

Conduct of the Revolutionary War

With success on all fronts after Valmy the regime issued regulations for the administration of conquered territories. They were noted on their publication by Monro without specific comment but as indicative of the changed times.[44] Morris described the surge of Revolutionary armies into *ancien régime* Europe: 'the Declaration of rights produces an effect equal at least to the trumpets of Joshua'.[45]

Morris reported extensively on the war, and on the reactions of other

European powers to it. This was partly because it was not a subject to which the authorities would take exception when they intercepted his despatches. On 7 March he wrote an illuminating account of the problems which had been created by victory, and showing the difficulties the Revolution was experiencing in mobilizing France's resources prior to Carnot's organization of the *levée en masse* in August 1793:

> It now appears that there is a real scarcity of *men*, and that the supposition that this country would procure five hundred thousand men required arose from little circumstances of dress and flattery calculated to catch idlers. The losses of the last campaign are sensible in the mass of population, so that, notwithstanding the numbers thrown out of employ by the stagnation of some manufactures and the reduction of private fortunes, the want of common laborers is felt throughout the whole country. Already they talk of drafting for the service, but if delayed it would not, I believe, go down, and at any rate would not produce in season the required force.[46]

War with Britain

As seen earlier, Britain was the one *ancien régime* power with which France desperately wished to remain at peace, but Gower's departing message to the new regime had been to ensure that they understood that Britain would regard the execution of Louis XVI as a *casus belli*. Thus as the National Convention lurched from trying to sentencing the king, the Revolution was caught on the horns of a dilemma.

The mere threat of war with Britain had an unfortunate effect for Thomas Paine, and Morris probably enjoyed reporting that 'Today all accounts from England show a design to engage in the war.... Paine looks a little down at the news ... he has been burned in effigy.'[47]

In France, the quest for peace became more frantic, and Morris reported that 'Count d'Estaing told me this morning that a majority of the Convention would give Mr Pitt the French West Indies to keep him quiet.'[48]

Monro reviewed the internal reactions to the fast approaching war:

> The prospect of a war with England of course creates a good deal of conversation here, the people speak for and against it according to the party they are of. The king's friends of course wish it, in hopes of creating a counter-revolution; and the Republicans sensible how materially it may affect their strange constitution wish by every means to avoid it, though at the same time they talk exceeding big, and even seem to threaten England.[49]

(In the event, it was the French who declared war on Britain in January 1793.)

Factions and Politics: Autumn 1792 to Summer 1794

Having taken the commentators' narrative through the abolition of the monarchy, the executions of the king and queen, the war (and its internal ramifications) up to Valmy and its extension to Britain, the story can now be told of the main and continuing business of the politics of the Revolution in terms of the struggle between *Feuillants*, Brissotins, and Jacobins, and between the Jacobin leaders. In this account the commentators were not able to perceive the falling out of the Jacobins and *sans-culottes* – even though foreseen by Gower in August 1792 – as something separate from the factional fighting within the Jacobins, but they could shed flashes of illumination on the movement towards the Terror and then (Morris above all) the experience of living under the 'Republic of Virtue'.

Only Morris was able to write throughout this period, but Monro's sketches of factions and leaders in late 1792 serve as a dramatis personae for the politics of the next two years. It is possible that he compiled these reports in order to keep a record of the men who might in the future be judged the leading regicides and face retribution from the allies. As mentioned earlier, Morris was not able to write freely, except on rare occasions and there is, therefore, no scheme or pattern to those of his despatches which make real political comment. He also could not report as closely on the men in power as Monro had done, and his comments tend to be more in the nature of general and critical surveys. But his despatches, for all that they make a disjointed narrative, heavily biased against the Brissotin and Jacobin regimes and highly moral in tone, are a unique record of a free-thinking man chronicling from within the progress of what he perceived as a tyranny.

Monro was able to attend the meetings of both the National Convention and the Jacobin Club. He gave cogent analyses of the state of politics in December 1792, with its three-way struggle between the *Feuillant* ministry, and the Jacobin and Brissotin oppositions:

> Robespierre's party is still strong.... Ministers I understand have been privately threatened by Robespierre's party, and Marat is suspected to be on the eve of deserting it.

> Rolland and Brissot's party are certainly struggling to save the king in order to humble Robespierre's party.[50]

Morris confirmed this political manoeuvring in his account of the politics of the king's trial: 'The Brissotins, finding themselves hard pushed towards killing the king, and apprehensive, not without reason, that this might be a

signal for their own destruction, determined on a measure not a little hazardous, but decisive. This was the expulsion of the Bourbons.'[51] As a personality
Robespierre never really emerges, in either Monro's or Morris's descriptions,
from behind the façade of the misnomer of the 'Sea-green Incorruptible'.
Monro must have met him and often seen him at close quarters in the Jacobin
Club. He repeated a slander about Robespierre, drawing in other Jacobins, in
a remark which suggests he must have disliked him: 'In short Robespierre,
the nephew of Damiens, who attempted to assassinate Louis xv, with his
bosom friends Marat and Egalité, will stop at nothing to assassinate those
who wish to save the life of Louis xvi.'[52] The interpretation of eighteenth-
century French history in terms of a family of regicides from Arras is a novel
one. (In fact Robespierre was not related to Damiens.)

Monro dredged up one anecdote about Robespierre, acting in this instance
in a personal capacity, which was obviously meant to show him in a poor
light: 'Robespierre made a trial of his strength last night at the *Comédie
Française*', when he tried unsuccessfully to have the performance of a royalist
satirical play stopped.[53]

At the height of Robespierre's power, Morris penned this description of
him:

> He is one of those of whom Shakespeare's Caesar speaks to his frolicsome
> companion, 'He loves no plays as thou dost, Antony.' There is no impu-
> tation against him for corruption. He is far from rich, and still further
> from appearing so. It is said that his idol is ambition, but I think that the
> establishment of the Republic would (all things considered) be most
> suitable to him.[54]

Morris meant by this that Robespierre was not seeking supreme dictatorial
power, but wished to operate as one of many political figures in a constitutional framework.

To return to the factional politics and the Jacobin Club in late 1792, Morris
described its position in these terms in December in a further extract from a
despatch previously referred to:

> You will have seen that the Jacobin Club is as much at war with the
> present government as it was with the preceding. Victory or death is
> the word with both parties. Hitherto the majority of the Convention have
> had rather the advantage, although they frequently decree what they
> do not wish. The ministers, possessing far more patronage than any
> monarch since Louis xiv, secured by that means the influence of the
> majority, their friends and the Jacobins, who, backed by the Parisian
> populace, have been several times within an inch of ruin. Luckily for

them their adversaries are many of them timid, while the Jacobin leaders are daring and determined.[55]

One of the most 'daring and determined' of the Jacobin leaders was Danton. He has already been seen through Monro's eyes as the self-proclaimed leader of the Parisians at the storming of the Tuileries and the defence of Paris against the Prussians. Morris, as quoted above in the context of the storming of the Tuileries and the king's trial, believed he had encouraged Orléans in the belief that he could become regent or even king if Louis XVI were removed from the scene. Morris persisted in this belief throughout Danton's career. He concluded Danton's career with another allusion to Shakespeare:

> Danton, when condemned, or shortly before it, told his judges that he had observed in reading history that men generally perished by the instruments of destruction which they had themselves created. 'I' (says he) 'created the *Tribunal Révolutionnaire* by which I am shortly to be destroyed.' Shakespeare had made Macbeth pronounce the same dreadful sentence on the wickedly ambitious long ago.[56]

Monro was able to fill in some greater detail of the often conflicting leading personalities in the Jacobin Club. Marat's first mention came in a despatch on 12 September 1792 describing him as 'a violent man laying himself out for whatever party he shall find best'. Monro fixed him firmly in the Jacobin camp on 20 September and identified his political style: 'Marat the associate of Robespierre ... had stuck up hand bills in every place they could be stuck, abusing as before most of the National Assembly and generals, and exciting the people in the plainest terms to punish the traitors.'[57]

On 22 September Monro made a somewhat cryptic report: 'Marat has begun to attack M. Pétion in *affiches*; Robespierre has as yet not opened his mouth.' If the implication here was a split between Marat and Robespierre, it was further suggested in December in another account: 'ministers I understand have been privately threatened by Robespierre's party, and Marat is suspected to be on the eve of deserting it'. By the end of the month, however, Marat was Robespierre's 'bosom friend' again.[58]

Morris did not mention Marat at all, and there is no comment to be recorded on his assassination. Orléans (or Philippe Egalité as he was by now known) has been seen in the context of the Jacobin and Brissotin factions, and as the Jacobins' ally in the prosecution of Louis XVI, but both Morris and Monro wrote of the odium he attracted as an individual.

Morris predicted his position if he were perceived to be playing a leading role against the king: 'for his share of the guilt, he may probably be rewarded with the shame of it, and the mortifying reflection that, after all the conflicts of his political ware, he has gained no victory but over his own conscience'.[59]

Monro wrote of the reaction to Orléans' vote for Louis XVI's execution: 'I cannot express the horror that was painted even in the countenance of every individual in the National Convention where the very worst of mankind are assembled, when Egalité gave his vote for the death of His king and relation.'[60]

Morris reported his subsequent imprisonment: 'The Duke of Orléans is in the way of reaping the fruits of his conduct, being ... sent a prisoner to Marseilles.' He did not, however, report on his eventual execution.[61] Collot d'Herbois was recorded only once, by Monro, when he was calling for 'a declaration they could not dispense making that night, which was the abolition of royalty'.[62]

Saint-Just also rated only one mention – again by Monro – as one of the deputies most vociferous in demanding the immediate death of the king.[63] Before the Brissotins and Jacobins could confirm their grip on the Revolution and then dispute its mastery they had to face the threat of military dictatorship and specifically of a *coup d'état* by the former Brissotin minister and now successful general, Dumouriez. On 1 January 1793 Morris linked the likely war with Britain with the mounting fear of political action by the army, *'En effet, tout décèle une disposition, de leur part, d'établir en France un despotisme militaire.'*[64] Dumouriez had been one of the leading lights of the Revolution in the summer and autumn of 1792. He had been the prominent minister and then the country's military saviour. He harboured, however, personal ambitions akin to Lafayette's. Huber had the measure of him as early as October 1792: 'My own private and secret opinion is, that Dumouriez is watching for an opportunity of giving a heavy blow to his present party, and that the Jacobins have not a cleverer nor a more dangerous enemy,'[65]

In January 1793 Monro noted that Dumouriez was in Paris and with the intention of rescuing the king.[66] Nothing, of course, came of this.

On 6 January 1793 Morris wrote in a despatch:

> As I have good reason to believe that this letter will go safely, I shall mention some things which may serve as a clue to lead through mysteries.... You know something of Dumouriez. The Council distrusted him. Westermann was commissioned to destroy him should he falter. The commission was shown to the general. It became the bond of union between him and Westermann. Dumouriez opened treaty with the king of Prussia.

Morris described how Dumouriez had been unable to surrender various cities under siege by the Prussians, who, in their turn, felt betrayed and had to retreat. At the same time Westermann had come under suspicion. Against this background 'Vergniaud, Guadet, etc., are now, I am told, the intimates of Dumouriez, and that the present administration is to be overturned, beginning with Pache, the Minister of War.'[67]

He followed up this report on 7 March 1793:

Already they begin to cry for a dictator.

> Great exertions are being made here ... to bring about a new revolution,
> whose effect, if successful, would be, I think, the destruction of what is
> called here the faction of the Gironde, and which calls itself the republican
> party, qualifying its enemies by the term anarchists.... Opinions seem
> to set very strongly against the Convention. They are supposed to be
> incapable of steering the state ship in the present rough weather; but it
> must blow yet a little harder before they are thrown overboard.[68]

In the context of these rumours of Dumouriez's *coup d'état* one of Miles's
British agents in Paris managed to smuggle out a (premature) despatch on
his defection and the (accurate) news of the first Austrian victory since Valmy.
This despatch illuminates the mood of fear, despair and Revolutionary passion
engendered in Paris by rumours of defection and of danger to the Revolution:

> The Austrians are said to be at Valenciennes, and Paris seems to be in
> a convulsion of despair.... The report of the day is that Dumouriez has
> emigrated, but I do not believe it. The *Tribunal Révolutionnaire*['s decree]
> is the object of much terror, and if the barriers of Paris be shut I dread
> the consequences.... The misery of Paris will soon be equal to its
> turpitude ... I write this at an *hôtel*, within hearing of a dozen drums
> and the noise at the *table d'hôte* of the full chorus of the 'Marseillaise'.[69]

Dumouriez's plans for a *coup d'état*, of course, came to nothing when the
army in the Austrian Netherlands would not follow him, and he was forced
(on 27 March 1793) to flee to the Austrian camp. With his disappearance
from the scene the commentaries narrow down almost exclusively to Morris's
infrequent unguarded despatches. What remains, therefore, is to tie up the
loose end of Monro's other work in and departure from Paris, present the
last report of note from Auckland's correspondents, and to follow Morris's
chronicle of his life under the Terror.

Monro's Work in and Departure from Paris and Auckland's last Report

Monro had to spend most of his time in autumn 1792 carrying out the
embassy's political intelligence work, but he still managed to send back some
detailed reports on the British, Irish and American Jacobins in Paris. He
was living as an English Jacobin in an *hôtel* which housed the expatriate
revolutionaries.[70] His work ended abruptly when a London Jacobin bookseller
newly arrived in Paris recognized him, knew him to be a secret agent, and
passed the word round in cafés.[71]

Monro stayed in Paris for a week after this – in what circumstances he does not mention – and arrived safely back in London on 21 January 1793. This left Morris as the only regular commentator still in Paris.

Except for the previously quoted report on Marie-Antoinette, Auckland received only one account of the situation in Paris which was of real insight during the rest of 1793 and 1794. This one (second-hand) despatch dealt with the mood in the capital in March 1794, when an eyewitness had reported rumours that Danton had poisoned Robespierre and that 'the people are sometimes very tumultuous and, in one of their late riots, threatened, if not speedily supplied, *"de manger les cadavres des membres de la Convention"* '.[72]

Morris's Experience of the Revolution and the Terror, August 1792–July 1794

Although the Terror strictly dated lasted from 2 June 1793 to the fall of Robespierre in July 1794, for Morris personally the fear and uncertainty engendered by being an active enemy of the Revolution had started in August 1792, when, as seen above, he first befriended an aristocratic fugitive from the Sections.

To set the scene for his embassy during this period, he wrote on 14 November 1792 of his relations with the war debts committee: 'the whole council are personally my enemies'. On 13 February 1793 he added 'some of the leaders here who are in the Diplomatic Committee hate me cordially'.

The problem lay not just in Morris's known royalist and aristocratic views, but in the Revolution's insistence that if Morris could not actively supply American help it must be because of his personal obstructiveness.[73] The Revolution recognized no neutrals, only friends or enemies, and in this atmosphere of paranoia Morris could conduct little of the government to government business of former times. The easy informal relations with ministers and deputies which he had enjoyed in earlier years were entirely absent after August 1792.

On 24 December 1792 Morris relayed an anecdote designed to illustrate the mood of the times:

> Some days ago a man applied to the Convention for damages done to his quarry. The quarries are deep pits, dug through several feet of earth into the bed of stone under the surface. The damage done to him was by the number of dead bodies thrown into his pit, and which choked it up so that he could not get men to work at it.[74]

On 5 January 1793 Morris felt he could no longer keep a diary: 'The situation of things is such that to continue this journal would compromise many people.'[75] He commented in a similar vein in late summer to other American consuls in Europe: 'My letters, even between Paris and Sainport, are delayed. The *Comité de Surveillance* have done me the honour to peruse some of them.... It is also impossible to commit anything to paper without great risks.' One of his couriers was stopped and

[my] letters taken from him, broken open, and sent to the *Comité de Surveillance*. He was detained two days.... To write in cipher is the sure way to have the letter intercepted.... Pray tell your French friends not to name anyone in their letters, for they will bring their friends to the guillotine.[76]

The precariousness of his position is revealed by his wry observation on 15 March 1793: 'I am told, that the London gazeteers have killed me, besides burning my house and other little pleasantries of the same kind ... they were not true at the time of publication.'[77]

On 13 August 1793 Morris wrote:

There exists a tyranny alike cruel and capricious, and restrained neither by shame nor principle. The body of the people long for the restoration of their former government. The exterior is more formidable in show than in substance.... As for what passes in our armies we are ignorant.... Hence it happens that good patriots see great victories and small checks where the other party behold slight skirmishes and dreadful defeats.[78]

In mid-October 1793 he commented in the aftermath of the purge and execution of the Brissotins:

The present government is evidently a despotism both in principle and practice. The Convention now consists only of a part of those who were chosen to frame a constitution. These, after putting under arrest their fellows, claim all power, and have delegated a greater part of it to a Committee of Safety.... It is an emphatical phrase in fashion among the patriots, that terror is the order of the day.[79]

On 12 March 1794 he commented on the atmosphere of the Terror in Paris: 'At present the people are restrained by fear from showing any sentiment unfavorable to the existent authorities. But, as is usual in like circumstances, should that fear be removed it will be succeeded by sharp resentment.'[80]

On 28 March he reported various experiences at the hands of the Sections and of municipalities outside Paris:

Yesterday afternoon I was arrested in the street and conducted to the *Section de la Butte des Moulins* because I had not a *carte de citoyen*. Fortunately a person who knew me, having heard what had passed, came to my rescue, and brought me out of the affair on his own responsibility.... Armed men came into my house yesterday, and although I have every reason to be satisfied with their conduct (for they went away as soon as I convinced them of the impropriety of their proceedings), yet I think that when general orders are given for these visits such houses ought to be excepted as are under the protection of the law of nations.... In the month of January it happened to me to be arrested and sent back to Paris under pretence that the passport [given me by the Foreign Ministry] was out of date.[81]

On 18 April 1794 Morris was able to write:

both the Dantonists and Hébertists are crushed. The fall of Danton seems to terminate the idea of a triumvirate. The chief who would in such case have been one of his colleagues has wisely put out of the way a dangerous competitor. Hence it would seem that the high-road must be laid through the *Comité de Salut Public*, unless, indeed, the army should meddle. But as to the army, no character seems as yet to have appeared with any prominent feature.... It is a wonderful thing, sir, that four years of convulsion among four and twenty millions of people has brought forth no one, either in civil or military life, whose head would fit the cap which fortune has woven. Robespierre has been the most consistent, if not the only consistent.[82]

On 25 April he added, on the occasion of the demise of Danton and his faction:

there have been abundant executions at Paris, and the guillotine goes on smartly. It was a matter of doubt before the blow was struck which party was the strongest. Perhaps the victory depended on the first stroke.

God only knows who is next to drink out of the same [poisoned chalice], but, as far as I can judge, there is no want of liquor.[83]

In July 1794 Morris exerted himself dangerously, but successfully, on behalf of Madame de Lafayette. He argued that so many of the family had taken up residence in America – with which they had such close historic links – that he felt she should be treated as an American citizen and not as just one more French aristocratic enemy of the Revolution.[84]

In Morris's last despatch as ambassador he gratefully handed over to his successor and passed one very fleeting comment on the situation following the (unreported) *coup d'état* – in the National Convention – of Thermidor, which ousted Robespierre from power: 'I am preparating for my departure, but as yet can take no step, as there is a kind of interregnum in the government.'[85] This one remark is, though, instructive of the political ambiguity at the time of Thermidor. It would not be clear for some time if it heralded an end to the 'Terror' and the 'Republic of Virtue' or marked their intensification.

In a later despatch, concerning his embassy, Morris put his work into a wider perspective, adding an incident which he had been unable to report at the time:

> I had stayed at some risk after the 10th of August [1792], because I thought the interests of America required it ... I saw misery and affliction every day and all around me, without power to mitigate or means to relieve, and I felt myself degraded by the communications I was forced into with the worst of mankind, in order to obtain redress for the injuries sustained by my fellow-citizens. During that state of things I was grossly insulted by the arrest of a lady in my house, by order of the Committee of General Safety. I could not resent this as I ought to have done, by quitting the country, because a great number of our citizens were then detained in France, with much of their property, and I knew the violences which those who administer the government were capable of.[86]

Morris was relieved of his post in July 1794 just after Robespierre's fall. He gratefully left the country and returned eventually to America. With his departure from the scene the last strand of continuity in this English and American commentary on the Revolution is broken, and the Revolution, under the Thermidor regime would revolve around themes already established in earlier years before evolving into the First Empire in 1799.

Conclusion

'This revolution thunder-strikes the keenest-sighted men.'

THROUGH the commentators' eyes, an impression has been gained of men and women who were engaged in politics and who could predict and understand the sometimes dizzying pace of the events of the French Revolution. Between them they give the Revolution the opportunity to speak for itself, conveying a very real sense of French men and women struggling with their own political destiny. Their understanding of, and frequent sympathy with, events act as guiding lights through a storm. If any one remark captures this it is Huber's in June 1789 that 'This revolution thunder-strikes the keenest-sighted men'.[1]

The commentators had a great deal to say about the Revolution, in terms of their own accounting for it and reactions to it. Much of this is best termed as 'philosophizing', and it is to their credit that they kept their personal feelings separate from their work of reporting as accurately as they could on the events and personalities they encountered. The questions to address to the objective factual content of their reportage are: what did they think caused the Revolution?; how did they perceive its eventual outcome and aims?; and how does their assessment on the spot match up to the historiography of the period?

Jefferson ascribed the causes of the Revolution to the combined effects of the Enlightenment preparing the intellectual ground and then of the outcome of the due constitutional processes forced on the *ancien régime* by its fiscal crisis. Morris, too, blamed the *philosophes* for providing the philosophical and political tools with which to dismantle a traditional social and constitutional order. The British embassy never felt the need for such profound speculation, but took the view that the *ancien régime* was too riddled with abuse to survive indefinitely, and that the French would inevitably – sooner or later – have to follow England's path towards a constitution and civil liberties. Arthur Young developed this theme in some detail, and had no doubts that the cumulative failures of the *ancien régime*, above all its inability to create an environment where agriculture could develop its full potential, made the Revolution both inevitable and – initially – desirable, once a national assembly of some kind had been permitted to meet. Morris, again, put the blame for the way in which, after the States-General had assembled, events moved inexorably towards democracy and egalitarianism, on Louis XVI's failure ever to give a firm or credible lead. He believed that, had the monarchy shown resolution at any point, the fickle French populace would have rallied to it and halted the Revolution in its tracks. The British embassy's reports provide a consistent account of a king probably clinically depressed, and this would in itself explain much of his, and the government's inertia in 1789. It would explain why he was incapable of taking the kind of lead Morris hoped for.

Their consensus view, therefore, was that the *ancien régime* and the monarchy had contained within themselves the seeds of their own destruction. None of the commentators defended the *ancien régime* until the Revolution was well under way and had started to threaten the lives of the royal family. The British embassy never condemned the Revolution unequivocally, and not even the royalist Morris's support for a restoration of the old order was whole-hearted.

The commentators each had to break off their narratives at some arbitrary point as duty or other commitments called them away. With the exception of Jefferson, however, they were united in their assessment of the future of the Revolution. Jefferson alone kept faith with the Revolution, and welcomed its progression towards an egalitarian and democratic (in the modern sense) republic. This he saw as its destiny, and pledged his faith in the Revolution, even after the September massacres, to William Short:

> In the struggle which was necessary, many guilty persons fell without the forms of trial, and with them some innocent. These I deplore as much as any body, and shall deplore some of them to the day of my death. But I deplore them as I should have done had they fallen in battle. It was necessary to use the arm of the people, a machine not quite so blind as balls and bombs, but blind to a certain degree.... The liberty of the whole earth was depending on the issue of the contest, and was ever such a prize won with so little innocent blood? My own affections have been deeply wounded by some of the martyrs to this cause, but rather than it should have failed, I would have seen half the earth desolated. Were there but an Adam and Eve left in every country, and left free, it would be better than as it now is.[2]

By contrast, Young, Miles, Morris, the British embassy, Monro, Short, and the correspondents with the British Foreign Office all predicted various permutations of anarchy, tyranny and civil war. Monro was alone in predicting that the monarchy could be restored. His speculation on how the French would suddenly discover a political moderation and affection for the monarchy if a victorious foreign army occupied Paris was an accurate forecast of how the Restoration eventually did take place in 1814.

All the commentators predicted the emergence of some great figure in the guise of a military dictator in the mould of Oliver Cromwell, or, as many Americans had (unfairly) feared, George Washington, if unrestrained by a Congress. They were disappointed in Lafayette and Dumouriez, disbelieving of Robespierre (Miles excepted), and would have been surprised by having to wait until 1799 for Napoleon. On the progress of the Revolutionary wars, Lord Gower assessed that France would be more than a match for the rest of *ancien régime* Europe combined, so long as Britain did not join a coalition against the Revolution. Thus the pattern of the Revolutionary and Napoleonic wars was sketched out, even if not their scope or duration. They all appreciated the potential of a reformed and united France; Jefferson perhaps expressed it best in the phrase 'This nation is rising from the dust.'[3]

Arthur Young, in his comparative analysis of the petitions of grievance as against the National Assembly's legislative programme, best outlined the general view of the aims of the Revolution at its beginning. This analysis has been quoted in full (see chapter 4), but, in summary, Young believed and hoped that the regime which would emerge would be a limited monarchy, with a written constitution and regular meetings of a sovereign national assembly elected by a rational representative suffrage based on property or income qualifications. Social and fiscal privilege would be abolished but social distinctions retained. The economy would be liberalized and restraints on trade, manufacture, and agriculture removed. The population as a whole would enjoy civil liberties such as habeas corpus, the abolition of *lettres de cachet*, and trial by jury. With the exception of its republicanism, the Thermidor regime in its conservative phases approximates to this model. That the Revolution was fulfilled in the Thermidor regime is a view taken by many subsequent historians.

This leads on to dealing with the third question – how the commentators' views match the historiographical and ideological interpretations of the Revolution. As just seen, they can reflect the essentially liberal school of thought that the Revolution was fulfilled in Thermidor, but they are less easy to match up to perspectives wholly reliant on hindsight. They do not, for example, share de Tocqueville's (non-ideological) outlook, that, however hard the Revolution tried to be different, it still succeeded in creating institutions analogous to those of the *ancien régime*. The commentators caught up in the Revolution could not see beyond the novelty of it. This serves as a useful reminder that primary sources, however useful, do have their limitations.

So far as the more political approaches to the Revolution are concerned, the commentators serve on the whole to confirm the bona fide nature of the Revolution's intentions and of the motives of most of those participating in it (e.g. in their vouchsafing the authenticity of the *poissardes* on the march to Versailles). Historians seeking to discredit the Revolution in general would find little favourable evidence in these commentaries. Royalist historians, in particular, could take little comfort, as no martyr king or queen emerged from the commentators' observations of the royal family. The commentators did not believe that plots or conspiracies had to be invented to account for events.

They were, though, unequivocal about the role played by Orléans in facilitating the radicalization of the Revolution. They despaired of the Jacobins' capture of the Revolution, whilst admiring them for being the only actors on the political stage with any real acumen or long-term plan and purpose. Conversely – and this is to be expected from men of their background and position in their own societies – they roundly condemned the Sections and *sans-culottes*, perceiving them as forces of anarchy and tyranny. Only Arthur Young paid more than the most cursory attention to the peasantry, and his work has proved seminal for the study of the late eighteenth-century rural economy, supplying the information not included in other sources.

Setting aside an over-emphasis on the power of the intellectual opposition to the *ancien régime*, the commentators' observations of the Revolution as it happened are consistent with Alfred Cobban's interpretation (and its restatement by François Furet). (For the most up-to-date account of the historiographical debate on the Revolution, readers should see the work of William Doyle and T. C. W. Blanning.)[4] This account, briefly, holds that the Revolution was occasioned by the cumulative effect of the coinciding disaffection of all social groups and institutions in the *ancien régime* during the pre-Revolution. The final blow was the defection of the peasantry, which eroded the bedrock on which the regime was based.

The Revolution was neither instigated, fuelled, nor led by discontented would-be capitalists (and even less by nascent proletarian social forces), but was driven by the class of professionals who felt they had the least to gain from a continuance of the *ancien régime* as it stood. These people were typified by the 'pettifogging' 'country attorneys' identified by the commentators themselves as forming the backbone of the Third Estate in the States-General and subsequently the deputies elected to the Legislative Assembly. Their apotheosis was in Robespierre.

Glossary of Terms Used*

Absolutism Rule by a monarch within a recognized legal framework but without any effective institutionalized limitation.

Abuse A **privilege** which has decayed away from its original intention.

Affair of the Diamond Necklace A **court** scandal in 1785 centred on a fraud to obtain a diamond necklace. A vital document purported to bear Marie-Antoinette's signature, and several of her friends were implicated.

Aides Duties on basic commodities whose collection was accountable to the *parlements*.

Anarchy Absence of law and order and recognized social structures – not to be confused with the yet-to-be-invented political philosophy of anarchism.

Arrêt Ruling by the crown or by a law court, which could be **registered** if needed or desired, having the force of precedent for future cases. An *arrêt* had to deal with a matter on which an **edict** had previously been **registered**.

Arrêté Legal or administrative ruling not serving as precedent, but otherwise similar to an *arrêt*.

Aristocratic(al) Party Those deputies in the **National** and **Legislative Assemblies** wishing to restore the full social structure of the *ancien régime* and monarchy.

Assignat A government 'I.O.U.' paid against the credit of church, royal, and *émigré* assets. These credit notes quickly became a paper currency in their own right.

Attroupement Armed illegal gathering usually to take action against high food prices. Under the *ancien régime* it was a specific capital offence to be a ringleader of an *attroupement*, but – so long as no actual violence were done – participation was generally not treated as a criminal offence.

Bailliage Jurisdiction subordinate to a **parlement**. The **States-General** constituencies were the *bailliages*.

Barrier A (lockable) iron gate with a customs post outside a town to charge duty on goods – especially foodstuffs – entering it. The **barrier** could also be used to stop movement in or out of a town. The **barriers** around Paris were thrown down in July 1789, but then restored, and not finally abolished until 1791. The customs houses were rebuilt by Louis XVI as part of the architectural embellishment of the capital, and hence had much royal prestige invested in them. They were owned privately and collection of the dues 'farmed out'.

Bonification Anodyne reform, especially in the fisc, whereby additional revenue was raised without offending vested corporate interests or addressing fundamental administrative issues.

Bourgeois A town dweller from the **Third Estate** who worked for a living, but not with his hands.

Brissotin A member of Brissot's faction in the **Legislative Assembly**. The term is broadly synonymous with **Girondin**. Their position was to favour a republic

---

* This is not a general glossary of terms used under the *ancien régime* and Revolution, but only of those used specifically within this study. Terms in bold type are defined in the glossary.

and war with Austria and Prussia, but not to intensify the Revolution to the extent desired by the **Jacobins** or *sans-culottes*. They were effectively the dominant group from March 1792 to May 1793.

Cahier de Doléance See **Petition of Grievance**.

Caisse d'Escompte Literally: discount bank. In the context of this study it was an institution equivalent to the Bank of England.

Capitainerie The exercise of feudal rights – especially hunting – over land whose freehold was owned by someone else.

Château A royal residence or the seat of a seigneurial jurisdiction. The actual building could range from a farm house to a palace (e.g. Versailles).

Citizen Under the *ancien régime* the term was restricted jurisprudentially to those invited by the crown to advise on political, administrative or legal matters. Under the Revolution it was – like the title of 'Monsieur' – extended to all (male) subjects. The Revolution believed that all men (the position of women, despite the example of groups such as the *poissardes*, remained ambiguous) had a duty to participate in the political process. Citizenship was, however, divided between 'active' (those above a certain level of income with the right to stand for election and exercise a vote) and 'passive' (those who were not, who included the poor, women, the insane, criminals and the royal family).

Civil Oath Public act of allegiance to the king, **National Assembly**, and constitution after 1790. All citizens – including the clergy – were expected to swear it.

Class(e) Sub-division of a juridical **Order** of society not necessarily related to wealth or profession.

Cockade Literally a bunch of chicken feathers. More usually coloured ribbon attached to a hat-band, the colours indicating political allegiance to the Revolution as a whole or a particular aspect of it.

Committee of Public Safety The **Revolutionary Tribunal** charged with protecting the state from internal threats to its security.

Committee of (General) Security (Surveillance) The **Revolutionary Tribunal** set up by the **National Assembly** in August 1792 to oversee the protection of the Revolution. It changed its name to the Committee of General Safety and then to the **Committee of Twenty-One**. Although its most important internal functions passed to the **Committee of Public Safety** it continued in existence.

Committee of Twenty-One See **Committee of Security**.

Comtat The area around Avignon was one of extraordinary historical and political complexity. The city of Avignon was held by the Papacy as a legacy of the Great Schism in the Middle Ages. In response to the Revolution the city rebelled against the Pope and called on France to invade and annex it. The Comtat (of Venaissin) was administered separately but also by the Papacy. Its response to the Revolution was to call on the Papacy for protection and to resist both the Avignonois and the Revolution. As an enclave within an enclave, the County of Orange was already under French rule, having been taken under the crown's protection after 1715. Troops were ordered into the area by the National Assembly in October 1790 and the Comtat and Avignon were formally annexed in September 1791.

Controller-General   (Director-General)

Head of the Control-General, the Department of State responsible for all fiscal and much other domestic administration. The Controller-General had the effective status of the most junior of the Secretaries of State, and was not guaranteed a place on the **Council** of State. He did, however, have the widest scope for independent and reforming action of any minister, hence the post attracted men of talent and/or ambition.

Cordeliers A political club (founded in 1790 and suppressed in 1795), more closely associated than the **Jacobins** with the *sans-culottes* and **Sections** in Paris, and often exhorting more violent action than the **Jacobins**.

Corporation A body enjoying the **privileges** of controlling its own membership, assembling at the times of its choice, and exercising autonomy in the regulation of its internal affairs without recourse to outside or higher authority.

Council Under the *ancien régime* the term **council** meant any group of men (women were specifically excluded) with the duty (but not the right) to advise the king; in practice they controlled the management of the executive arm of government and advised on legislative matters. Under the Revolution the Council was charged solely with executive functions. An *ancien régime* council could only meet with the king or his representative presiding. The **Council** was composed of most – but not necessarily all – of the Secretaries of State and the **Controller/Director-General of Finance**. (The ministers on the Council were members neither of the States-General nor of its successor bodies.)

Court 1. The ceremonial assemblage of the king, royal family, and courtiers; 2. The king and his ministers taking decisions influenced by the rest of the royal family (Marie-Antoinette especially), court officials and personal friends; 3. Those of the nobility prepared physically to stand by the royal family after their virtual imprisonment in the Tuileries.

Coutume An unwritten local 'customary' legal code.

Dantonist A follower of Danton in the **National Convention**. Danton's power was based more on personal charisma than on a coherent political programme. He did not wish to follow the same degree of state intervention as Robespierre.

Decree A ruling or instruction on administrative matters made by the **National Assembly** or its successors.

Democracy In the context of this study the term implies rule by mob.

Democratical (or Popular) Party The republicans in the **National Assembly**.

Despotism Rule by a single person without regard for law or custom with the implication of efficient and consistent rule.

Edict An *ancien régime* legislative proposal, requiring no precedent, issued by the crown and needing **registration** in the *Parlement* of Paris or local *parlements*. Only the crown could issue **edicts** with their power of political initiative, but only the *parlements* could **register** them and give them force of law.

Emigré Anyone leaving France after July 1789 as a gesture of defiance against the Revolution.

Enragé Contemporary translation: 'madman'. This term was used by the commentators as a synonym for **Jacobin**, but historians have seen the term as having a wider and more populist meaning and the *enragés* as precursors of the *sans-culotte* movement.

Estate See Order.

Extraordinary Any *ancien régime* fiscal measure not having the authority or time-honoured consent of the **States-General.** This covered the basic personal taxes of the regime. Extraordinary fiscal measures could only be implemented for limited periods and required **registration**.

Family Compact The Bourbon dynastic alliance between France and Spain, negotiated in 1761.

Faubourg Literally: suburb. One of the sub-divisions of Paris, administered by a **Section**, and noted for being able to field a politically active crowd at very short notice.

Federalism The movement to make Revolutionary France a federal state without close direction from the centre.

Fédéré Provincial delegate to a *Fête de la Fédération* often staying on in Paris. The *fédérés* gained a reputation for ruthless republicanism.

Fête (de la Fédération) Celebration of the anniversary of the storming of the Bastille, and of national unity and loyalty to the **National Assembly** (and its successor bodies).

Feuillant A member of the faction of deputies to the **Legislative Assembly** who met at the *Feuillant* church initially in summer 1791 and were prepared to work within a limited monarchy but wished to pursue an aggressive but realistic foreign policy. They were the dominant faction at the opening of the **Legislative Assembly,** and up to the formation of Dumouriez's **(Brissotin)** ministry in March 1792. The society was abolished in August 1792 by the **Brissotins**.

Gabelle A universal tax on salt levied through a tax farm, whereby its collection had been contracted out. This tax was perceived as the single most unjust and onerous of the *ancien régime*.

Girondin See **Brissotin**.

Governor The most senior provincial functionary appointed by and directly answerable to the king. The governor was always a courtier and had command over local troops and over any part of the administration not entrusted to the *Intendant* or other local agencies, on occasion he was given a special brief to act against local **corporations** or to impose and administer martial law.

Hébertiste Follower of Hébert in the **National Convention.** Hébert wished to follow policies which could be described as more 'socialist' than those of the **Jacobins**.

Hôtel de Ville The seat of municipal government and of martial law when in force after July 1789.

Intendant The *ancien régime*'s most senior civilian provincial functionary answerable to (and a member of) the royal **Councils.** The *Intendant* had wide legal and administrative powers, which did vary from province to province and were in decline towards the end of the regime. They were (perhaps wrongly) perceived as the heavy-handed representatives of royal power outside Paris and Versailles.

Jacobin The Jacobin Club was originally founded by a group of deputies to the States-General from Brittany who met in a disused church of the 'Jacobin' order. They lobbied hard to create the **National Assembly** and to sustain the gains made by the Revolution. The commentators used the term generically to denote any radical deputy as well as specific members of the Club and its provincial corresponding societies. They failed to make a full distinction between **Jacobins** and

Brissotins even in 1792. The Club's general policy was of an aggressive foreign policy (except under Robespierre), an intensification of the domestic Revolution through state control of society and the economy, and outright republicanism.

Lanterne In the 1780s Paris became the first major European city to have comprehensive street lighting. This was rigged up on iron brackets fixed to buildings. The brackets were strong enough to take the weight of one or more bodies hung from them. They served as extemporary gibbets – always on hand when needed – during the Revolution and the term *Lanterne* became synonymous with summary justice.

Legislative Assembly The name given to the successor body to the **National Assembly**. It met from October 1790 to September 1792.

Lettre de Cachet Under the *ancien régime* these were sealed orders bearing the authority of the crown and signed by the Secretary of State for the King's Household. At their most abusive they might carry only the signature, leaving someone else to fill in the name, the desired use of the *lettre*, and the duration of the instruction. The *lettres* were patently open to the gravest abuse (e.g. life imprisonment with no appeal for an innocent victim of mistaken identity), but were most often used for purposes such as instructions to deputies to provincial assemblies of **States**. The ultimate purpose of using a *lettre de cachet* was to put its contents beyond legal challenge.

Levée en Masse The conscription of all able-bodied men to assist the war effort.

Livre (Tournois) The basic accounting unit of the *ancien régime* and early part of the Revolution. (The actual currency

often went by different local names.) It is notoriously difficult to give workable present-day equivalents to former currencies, but the best guide to value is the figures on comparative wages researched by Arthur Young. A skivvy would have earnt in a year 70 *livres*, a basic labouring wage was 90 *livres*, while a skilled craftsman could command 300 *livres*. (*Livre* was usually abbreviated to *l*.)

Loi A new legislative proposal promulgated by the **National Assembly** (or its successors). Unlike an **edict** a *loi* did not have to go through any intermediary bodies before becoming law.

Maire du Palais Derogatory term from the early Frankish monarchy to indicate an official exercising (and by implication preventing the king from exercising) the powers of the monarchy.

Métayer Literally: share-cropper. This class of farmer was reckoned the backbone of the *ancien régime* economy, but it was upon them that the weight of inequitable taxation and feudal dues fell most heavily.

Militia (*Milice Bourgeoise*) Local embodiment of the **National Guard**. The militia under the Revolution acted under the control of the **municipality** rather than on royal authority.

Municipality During July 1789 every town and city in France appointed an assembly, whose members were elected without regard to juridical Order, to run local administration. These assemblies reported to the **National Assembly** and acted separately from – and often in opposition to – the still extant royal *Intendants* and **Governors**. Over the late summer elections (held on a non-juridical basis) regularized the membership of the municipalities. These jurisdictions frequently abrogated to themselves very wide extra-constitutional powers and put local above national interests.

National Assembly or **Constituent Assembly** The name given by themselves to the deputies of the **States-General** meeting as a single chamber without regard to juridical **Order**. The assembly under that name sat from June 1789 to September 1791.

Notables Representatives of the **privileged** Orders specifically representing landed interests. Notables were assembled in 1787 on a national basis to advise informally on fiscal matters.

Office A position in a **parlement** or some other part of *ancien régime* administration bought and owned (and protected) as personal private property.

Orders (or Estates) *Ancien régime* society was divided into three legally enforceable Orders. The first was the clergy, the second the nobility, and the third the common(er)s. Each Order had rights and priviliges appropriate to its role. By the Revolution the system had come to be perceived as institutionalized protection of the first's and second's privileges.

Palais-Royal As well as being the town house of the Dukes of Orléans, the Palais-Royal constituted a separate jurisdiction within the city of Paris outside the reach of the normal police authorities.

Parlement A sovereign law court, able to control its own membership and regulate its own internal affairs. A *parlement*'s functions were to act as a court of appeal for ordinary law suits, to oversee some aspects of administration, and to **register edicts**. Membership of a *Parlement* was owned as an **office** conferring nobility. The *Parlement* always refers to the senior court

in Paris. *Parlements* were composed of a number of different chambers, one of the more important being the Court of Aides.

Pays d'élection and *pays d'états* Under the *ancien régime* approximately three-quarters of the provinces fell under the direct central administration from Paris and Versailles. These were the *pays d'élection*. The remaining quarter of the provinces retained local administrative machinery – particularly fiscal – which was interposed between the province and the crown. These were the *pays d'états* and their machinery usually took the form of an assembly of **States**. The *pays d'états* were a byword for more efficient and equitable fiscal administration.

Pension A payment from royal (i.e. government) funds in recognition of services rendered to the monarch or the payee's intrinsic merit. Almost all *pensionnaires* were noble and most pensions were distributed as political patronage or to courtiers to sustain their life-style as companions to the royal family. The system became very unpopular when Marie-Antionette made undue demands on it for her friends.

Petition of Grievance On being summoned to elect deputies to an assembly of **States** (provincial or **General**) the three **Orders** had the right to petition the crown on matters related to administration. These were formalized in the *pays d'états* into professions of loyalty followed by horrific accounts of natural disaster and adverse climatic conditions preventing the full payment of taxes demanded from the province. With no current usage to draw on, the petitions for the **States-General** sometimes covered very wide constitutional social and economic issues and were highly critical of the regime and of fiscal **privilege**.

Physiocrat Physiocracy (literally: rule by nature) was the leading politico-economic theory of the late *ancien régime*. It held that all wealth ultimately derived from agricultural production, and that nothing must be allowed to interfere with this. In practice this meant a free-market economy in food and an anti-colonial policy.

Poissarde Literally: fishwife. A term of abuse adopted as a title for a woman of Paris taking direct political action (also occasionally *Dame de la halles*).

Princes of the Blood The members of the extended Bourbon dynasty. They enjoyed special **privileges** under the *ancien régime* including automatic membership of the *Parlement* of Paris and direct informal access to the king. They were automatically members of the **States-General**, but subsequently under the Revolution were made 'passive' **citizens** and effectively excluded from politics. Only the Duc d'Orléans capitalized on his position during the Revolutionary period.

Privilege Usually a dispensation (e.g. from needing special authority to assemble) or an exemption (e.g. from the *taille* or some obligation such as billeting soldiers) enjoyed by someone on the strength of their birth or membership of a particular **corporation**. Most **privileges** were confined to the First and Second **Orders** and were perceived as having to be paid for by the **Third**.

Quatre-Vingt-Neuf Constitutional club, initially rivalling that of the **Jacobins**, favouring a limited monarchy. (Its full name was *Society de la Constitution de 1789*.) It was founded, largely by Lafayette, at the beginning of 1790, and was always more of an exclusive

'gentleman's club' than a political party. It could not survive the discredit of the flight to Varennes and merged with the *Feuillants*.

Red Flag The symbol of martial law – to counter either internal or external (*La Patrie en Danger*) threats – when flying from the *Hôtel de Ville*.

Registration The procedure whereby **edicts** and some *arrêts* were scrutinized prior to be being publicized and given the force of law through the *parlements*. The *parlements* could refuse to *register* and *edict*, which set in train a complex process of dialogue between the courts and the crown which the crown on occasion chose to end by '**despotically**' exiling the magistrates and setting up alternative structures.

Revolutionary Tribunal Generic term for a body set up by the **National Assembly** or **Convention** with special executive powers to protect the Revolution. The best known was the **Committee of Public Safety**.

Royalists Either those deputies wishing to preserve the position of the monarchy, or those aristocrats prepared to go to any lengths to overthrow the Revolution.

Sans-Culotte Literally: one not wearing breeches (but the socially inferior garment of trousers). A term of abuse adopted with pride by the non-**bourgeois** working population of Paris to indicate a man or woman from that background taking direct political action – usually through the **Sections**.

Séance Royale A session of the **States-General** or successor body with the king present in person. Until June 1789 it had been unthinkable that the king's will would be challenged in his physical presence – to do so would be treason.

Section The Revolutionary governing

body of a *faubourg* or *arrondissement* existing informally by autumn 1789 and given formal recognition after May 1790.

Seigneur Literally: lord of the manor. The *seigneur* owned and exercised judicial and feudal rights in the *seigneurie.*

States (General) The three *Orders* of society when invited to form political assemblies by the crown to advise on administrative matters. The States-General was this institution operating at national level. It was not convened between 1614 and 1789.

Taille The basic ordinary flat-rate poll tax levied on all members of the Third Estate.

Tax farm A consortium of financiers who had bought (by competitive tender) the right to levy a particular tax under the *ancien régime*, and retain any 'profit' made over the contract.

Terror That period between June 1793 and July 1794 when the Revolution enforced the 'Republic of Virtue' with the guillotine and the government took a firm grip on all aspects of political, social and economic life.

Thermidor Literally: the hot month in the Revolutionary calendar. Used conventionally to indicate the *coup d'état* in the National Convention which removed Robespierre from power, and, by extension, to the regime which followed from July 1794 to November (Brumaire) 1799.

Third Estate (or Commons) The vast majority of the population (probably 96 per cent). This Order had no objective reality and embraced people from the richest financiers to the poorest beggars. In 1788–9 it discovered an identity as the embodiment of the political nation in opposition to the self-interested owners of privilege in the other Orders.

Tocsin Literally: alarm bell. The *tocsin* acquired a special significance in the Revolution as a call to arms and direct political action (often against the National Assembly or Convention) by the *Sans-Culottes* and Paris Sections.

Tribune Literally: a representative of a Revolutionary Tribunal. In the context of this study it implies a Revolutionary activist claiming to speak on behalf of the 'people' and usurping extra-constitutional power, usually at the expense of the Legislative Assembly or National Convention.

Tyranny Despotism without consistency.

Notes

Introduction

1 Gordon Wright, *France in Modern Times from the Enlightenment to the Present*, Stanford 1981 (3rd edn), p. 41.
2 Norman Hampson, *The French Revolution, a Concise History*, London 1975, p. 174.
3 A. de Tocqueville, *The Ancien Régime and the French Revolution*, Manchester 1966 (Fontana edn), p. 33 (first published 1856).

1 The Commentaries and Commentators

1 Unless otherwise specified, the general biographical information about the commentators is drawn from the appropriate national dictionary of biography, or from *Historical Dictionary of the French Revolution 1789–99*, edited by Samuel F. Scott and Barry Rothaus, 2 vols, Westport 1985.
2 *The Correspondence of William Augustus Miles on the French Revolution 1786–1817*, edited by the Rev. Charles Popham Miles, 2 vols, London 1890, I, pp. 171–2 (Miles to Sir Edward Newenham, 27 November 1790).
3 *The Journal and Correspondence of William, Lord Auckland*, edited by the Bishop of Bath and Wells, 4 vols, London 1861 (vols I and II) and 1881 (vols III and IV), II, p. 379 (Mr John Thomas Stanley to Lord Auckland, 7 December 1790).
4 *The Despatches of Earl Gower, English Ambassador at Paris from June 1790 to August 1792 . . .*, edited by Oscar Browning, Cambridge 1885, p. 13. (The despatches from Colonel George Monro are appended to Gower's papers, and references to these will carry Monro's name.)
5 Gower, pp. 213 (27 August 1792), 225 ff. (4 September 1792).
6 Ibid., pp. 77–8 (footnote to a despatch on 8 April 1791).
7 Biographical details on Colonel Monro from *Gower*, introduction (to Gower's despatches) and references throughout Monro's letters on his instructions and past career.
8 *The Papers of Thomas Jefferson*, edited by Julian P. Boyd (to 1986) and Charles Cullen (thereafter), 22 vols (still in publication), Princeton 1956– . These papers incorporate the official despatches written by William Short to Thomas Jefferson as Secretary of State after Jefferson's departure from France in October 1789, and references to Short's despatches will carry his name. Jefferson, 14, p. 420 (8 January 1789).
9 *The Diaries and Letters of Gouverneur Morris*, edited by Anne Cary Morris, 2 vols, New York 1888, vol. I, p. 94 (30 May 1789).
10 Ibid., p. 96 (3 June 1789).
11 Ibid., p. 100 (12 June 1789).
12 Ibid., p. 138 (22 July 1789).
13 Jefferson, 15, p. 243 (4 July 1789).
14 Quoted in *The Founding Fathers, Thomas Jefferson, a Biography in his own Words*, edited by the editors of Newsweek Books, New York 1974, p. 242.
15 Morris, I, p. 394 (25 March 1791).
16 Ibid., p. 358 (18 November 1790).

17 Jefferson (Short), 22, p. 194 (6 October 1791).

2 The Context for the Commentaries and Jefferson's Account of the Pre-Revolution

1 Two examples from works which were influential in their day are: S-H-N. Linguet, *Annales Politiques, Civiles, et Littéraires du Dix-huitième Siècle*. The Hague 1777–90, I, p. 445; and '*Pièces Détachées Relatives au Clergé Seculier et Regulier*', Marquis de Puységur, 3 vols, Amsterdam 1771, I, p. 21. This analysis is also given in *The Ancien Régime*, C. B. A. Behrens, London 1967, p. 16.

2 The scope of Necker's proposed provincial reforms has not often generally been recognized. Necker announced it as a manifesto for transforming the social and political structure of the regime in *Mémoire de M. Necker au Roi sur l'Etablissement des Assemblées Provinciales* and in subsequent subsidiary documents proposed their creation in a total of eight provinces. These memoirs are held in the *Collection Castries* (Bibliothèque Nationale, Manuscrits français 7059). Calonne's proposals in 1787 were more general but less radical, and had none of Necker's social engineering ambitions.

3 H. Méthivier, *L'Ancien Régime*, Paris 1964, pp. 5–7.

4 Archives of the Order of St John of Jerusalem, Series 3 (Liber Consigli di Stato), vol. 272, p. 213 (14 December 1770, Duc de Choiseul to the Chevalier de Justice).

5 Morris, I, p. 382. (Written on 15 February 1791).

6 See A. Lemaire, *Les Lois Fondamentales de la Monarchie Française*, Paris 1907.

7 Public Record Office, State Papers, Series 78 (France), vol. 292 p. 169 (Lord Harcourt to Foreign Secretary 15 June 1774).

8 Ibid., 280 p. 65 (February 1770).

9 Jefferson, 14, p. 212 (19 November 1788).

10 G-F. Letrosne, *De l'Administration Provinciale* ..., Basle 1779, Part I, p. 151.

11 V. de Mirabeau, *Mémoire concernant l'Utilité des Etats Provinciaux*, Rome 1750 (the year of publication is in itself significant). (Note: de Tocqueville devoted a separate study to the States of Languedoc in *L'Ancien Régime et la Révolution Française*, Paris, 1856.)

12 Jefferson reckoned the tax revenue at 600,000,000l. on 20 August 1788. Jefferson, 13, p. 530. Calonne's figures quoted in M. J. Sydenham *The French Revolution*, London, 1965, p. 27. The figure of 1,000,000,000l. is a generalization drawn from the writings of G-F. Letrosne, and principally, *De l'Administration Provinciale* ..., which synthesized all the provincial and fiscal reform schemes up to that date, and is based on Letrosne's calculation of the costs to the Control-General of existing 'abuses' and the additional revenue which could be realized by a reformed devolved fiscal structure still allowing some fiscal exemptions to the privileged Orders.

13 Quoted Sydenham, p. 28.

14 The single most important of the publications emanating from this circle for the eighteenth century was H. de Boulainvilliers, *L'Etat de France*, 3 vols, London, 1727. This work was based on a survey of the realm carried out in 1698, was very complimentary to the provinces retaining their assemblies of States, and advocated the summoning of the States-General.

15 References to the States-General and their prerogatives are scattered throughout the jurisprudential writings of the *ancien régime* – the prerogatives more often being described implicitly than explicitly. The fullest account of them was given in Piganiol de la Force, *Nouvelle Description de la France*, 15 parts, Paris 1752–4; in vol. I, part I, pp. 529–49 he detailed the arrangements for the elections to them.

16 Jefferson, 14, pp. 420–2 (8 January 1789).

17 The first, fullest, and most definitive statement of the *Parlement* of Paris's position with regard to the States-General was in *Remonstrance de la Cour des Aides* in May 1775, drafted by

Guillaume-Chrétien Lamoignon de Malesherbes and published in Paris in 1775.
18 Many books have been published on the 'pre-Revolution', but the seminal one, from which
   the chronology and nomenclature of the period have been taken by subsequent historians,
   is Jean Egret, *La Pré-Révolution Française*', Paris 1962

3 From the Declaration of Bankruptcy and the Summoning of the States-General to its Assembly

1 Arthur Young, *Travels in France during the Years 1787, 1788, and 1789* (first published Bury
   St Edmunds 1792), ed. Constantia Maxwell, Cambridge 1929, pp. 98–9 (13 August 1788).
2 Jefferson, 13, pp. 538–9 (23 August 1788).
3 *London Historical (Camden) Society*, 'Despatches from Paris 1784–1790', Camden Third Series,
   Vol. XIX, ed. Oscar Browning, Vol. II (1788–90) London 1910, p. 84 (7 August 1788). (Vol.
   I (1784–1787) published in Camden Third Series Vol. XVI, London 1909). (Referred to
   subsequently as 'Despatches, Paris').
4 Ibid., p. 86 (14 August 1788). (The *arrèt* was in fact published in late July, but did not pass
   into public debate until August.)
5 Jefferson, 13, p. 538.
6 'Despatches, Paris', p. 102 (11 September 1788).
7 Ibid., p. 86 (14 August 1788).
8 Jefferson, 13, pp. 529–30 (20 August 1788), 564 (3 September 1788), 14, p. 212 (19
   November 1788).
9 Ibid., 13, p. 564 (3 September 1788).
10 'Despatches, Paris', p. 95 (28 August 1788).
11 Ibid., pp. 92 (26 August 1788), 96 (28 August 1788), 99 (11 September 1788), 101 (11
   September 1788).
12 Ibid., p. 96 (28 August 1788).
13 Ibid., p. 105 (25 September 1788).
14 Jefferson, 13, p. 642 (29 September 1788).
15 Jefferson, 14, p. 671 (17 March 1789).
16 Jefferson, 13, p. 422 (8 January 1789); Auckland, II, p. 249 (Huber to Eden) (15 November
   1788).
17 'Despatches, Paris', p. 107 (9 October 1788).
18 Ibid., pp. 112–13 (13 November 1788).
19 Ibid., pp. 113–14 (13 November 1788).
20 Jefferson, 14, pp. 186 (18 November 1788), 329 (4 December 1788).
21 Auckland, II, p. 249 (Huber to Auckland) (28 November 1788).
22 'Despatches, Paris', pp. 121 (27 November 1788), 126 (11 December 1788), 127 (18
   December 1788), 129 (18 December 1788), 138 (1 January 1789), 139 (8 January 1789),
   146 (22 January 1789).
23 Auckland, II, p. 250 (Dorset to Eden) (29 November 1788).
24 Jefferson, 14, p. 656 (14 March 1789).
25 Ibid., p. 216 (19 November 1788).
26 Ibid., pp. 212–13 (19 November 1788).
27 'Despatches, Paris', pp. 116 (20 November 1788), 119–20 (27 November 1788).
28 Jefferson, 14, pp. 212–13 (19 November 1788), 276 (21 November 1788), 277 (22
   November 1788), 304 (29 November 1788), 343 (8 December 1788), 376 (23 December
   1788).
29 Ibid., pp. 376 (23 December 1788), 423 (8 January 1789).
30 See chapter 3, note 14.
31 Auckland, II, pp. 312–13 (Huber to Eden) (7 April 1789).

32 'Despatches, Paris', p. 148 (22 January 1789); Jefferson, 14, p. 653 (13 March 1788).
33 Jefferson, 14, p. 638 (11 March 1789).
34 'Despatches, Paris', pp. 169 (12 March 1789), 174 (19 March 1789), 189 (2 April 1789).
35 Jefferson, 15, p. 97 (6 May 1789).
36 Ibid., 14, p. 437 (12 January 1789).
37 Auckland, II, p. 281 (Huber to Eden) (16 January 1789): 'Despatches, Paris', pp. 151 (29 January 1789), 158 (12 February 1789).
38 'Despatches, Paris', p. 174 (19 March 1789).
39 Auckland, II, p. 305 (Huber to Eden) (18 March 1789).
40 'Despatches, Paris', pp. 189 (30 April 1789), 176 (26 March 1789).
41 Auckland, II, p. 305 (Huber to Eden) (18 March 1789).
42 Jefferson, 14, p. 330 (4 December 1788).
43 Auckland, II, p. 275 (Huber to Eden) (16 January 1789).
44 Young, pp. 348–9 ('The Revolution in France 1791, Future Effects').
45 'Despatches, Paris', pp. 138 (1 January 1789), 152 (29 January 1789), 165 (26 February 1789), 172 (12 March 1789), 190 (30 April 1789).
46 Ibid., p. 191 (7 May 1789).
47 Jefferson, 15, p. 104 (8 May 1789).
48 'Despatches, Paris', p. 188 (general description of riots pp. 186–8) (30 April 1789).
49 Jefferson, 15, p. 100 (8 May 1789).
50 Morris, I, p. 54 (17 April 1789).
51 'Despatches, Paris', p. 155 (5 February 1789).
52 Ibid., p. 164 (26 February 1789).
53 Ibid., p. 191 (7 May 1789).
54 Morris, I, pp. 21 (3 February 1789), 26 (February 1789).

4 From the Opening of the States-General to the Storming of the Bastille
1 Morris, I, pp. 73–7 (4–5 May 1789).
2 Jefferson, 15, pp. 104–5 (8 May 1789).
3 Young, p. 140 (12 June 1789).
4 'Despatches, Paris', p. 195 (14 May 1789).
5 Auckland, II, pp. 321–3 (Huber to Eden) (12 May 1789).
6 'Despatches, Paris', pp. 195–6 (14 May 1789).
7 Jefferson 15, pp. 104 (8 May 1789), 111 (9 May 1789), 136 (19 May 1789).
8 Ibid., pp. 136 (19 May 1789), 140, 141 (20 May 1789 – two despatches).
9 'Despatches, Paris', pp. 199 (21 May 1789), 202, 204–5 (28 May 1789), 206 (4 June 1789).
10 Young, pp. 132–5 (8–9 June 1789).
11 'Despatches, Paris', p. 210 (11 June 1789).
12 Young, pp. 136, 138 (11 June 1789).
13 'Despatches, Paris', pp. 215–17 (18 June 1789).
14 Jefferson, 15, p. 188 (17 June 1789).
15 Morris, I, p. 101 (19 June 1789).
16 'Despatches, Paris', p. 210 (11 June 1789).
17 Young, p. 139 (13 June 1789).
18 'Despatches, Paris', pp. 202 (28 May 1789), 210 (11 June 1789).
19 Young, pp. 142–4 (15 June 1789).
20 'Despatches, Paris', pp. 209–10 (4 June 1789).
21 Ibid., p. 219 (25 June 1789).
22 Jefferson, 15, p. 206 (24 June 1789, but written earlier).
23 Ibid.

24 'Despatches, Paris', p. 220 (25 June 1789).
25 Young, pp. 149–50 (20 June 1789).
26 Jefferson, 15, p. 206 (24 June 1789, but written earlier).
27 Young, p. 150 (22 June 1789).
28 Ibid., p. 152 (23 June 1789).
29 Jefferson, 15, p. 207 (24 June 1789).
30 Morris, I, p. 106 (27 June 1789).
31 Young, p. 154 (24 June 1789).
32 Jefferson, 15, p. 208 (24 June 1789).
33 Ibid.
34 Young, p. 157 (25 June 1789).
35 Jefferson, 15, p. 208 (24 June 1789).
36 Young, p. 157 (25 June 1789).
37 Ibid., p. 158 (26 June 1789).
38 Jefferson, 15, p. 223 (29 June 1789).
39 Young, pp. 159–62 (27 June 1789).
40 'Despatches, Paris', p. 223 (25 June 1789).
41 Ibid., p. 225 (28 June 1789).
42 Auckland, II, p. 326 (Huber to Eden) (5 July 1789).
43 'Despatches, Paris', pp. 208 (4 June 1789), 220 (25 June 1789), 229 (2 July 1789), 232 (6 July 1789).
44 Young, pp. 159–60 (27 June 1789).
45 'Despatches, Paris', pp. 229 (2 July 1789), 232 (6 July 1789).
46 Young, pp. 139–40 (13 June 1789).
47 Jefferson, 15, p. 190 (17 June 1789).
48 Young, pp. 154–5 (24 June 1789).
49 Ibid., p. 156 (25 June 1789).
50 'Despatches, Paris', p. 222 (25 June 1789).
51 Ibid., p. 233 (9 July 1789).
52 Ibid., p. 237 (12 July 1789).
53 Jefferson, 15, p. 273 (13 July 1789).
54 Morris, I, pp. 120–1, 122 (12 July 1789).

5 The Fall of the Bastille and the Burning of the Châteaux

1 Morris, I, pp. 123, 124, (13 July 1789).
2 Auckland, II, pp. 330–1 (Huber to Eden) (14 July 1789).
3 Jefferson, 15, p. 268 (11 July 1789).
4 Auckland, II, pp. 328–30, 332 (Huber to Eden) (14 July 1789).
5 'Despatches, Paris', p. 237 (12 July 1789).
6 Jefferson, 15, p. 267 (11 July 1789).
7 'Despatches, Paris', pp. 229–30 (2 July 1789), 233, 235 (19 July 1789).
8 Morris, I, p. 128 (15 July 1789).
9 Jefferson, 15, pp. 267–8 (11 July 1789).
10 'Despatches, Paris', pp. 232–3 (9 July 1789).
11 Ibid., p. 238 (16 July 1789).
12 Ibid.
13 Ibid., p. 239 (16 July 1789).
14 Ibid., pp. 240, 241, 243 (16 July 1789).

15 Auckland, II, pp. 337 (17 July 1789), 334, 333, (16 July 1789), 337 (17 July 1789) (all Huber to Eden).
16 'Despatches, Paris', p. 241 (16 July 1789).
17 Jefferson, 15, pp. 279 (17 July 1789), 289 (19 July 1789).
18 Auckland, II, pp. 335–6 (Huber to Eden) (16 July 1789).
19 'Despatches, Paris', pp. 244, 245 (19 July 1789), 246 (22 July 1789).
20 Morris, I, pp. 130, 131 (17 July 1789).
21 Auckland, II, p. 337 (Huber to Eden) (17 July 1789); 'Despatches, Paris', pp. 245, 246 (17 July 1789); Morris, I, p. 136 (17 July 1789).
22 Jefferson, 15, p. 290 (19 July 1789).
23 'Despatches, Paris', pp. 246 (22 July 1789), 250 (27 July 1789).
24 Morris, I, p. 136 (21 July 1789).
25 Jefferson, 15, pp. 301 (22 July 1789), 301 (23 July 1789).
26 Morris, I, p. 137 (22 July 1789).
27 Auckland, II, pp. 342, 341 (Huber to Eden) (28 July 1789).
28 Jefferson, 15, pp. 301 (23 July 1789), 305 (25 July 1789).
29 Young, pp. 180–1 (19 July 1789).
30 Ibid., pp. 182–3 (21 July 1789).
31 Ibid., p. 186 (25 July 1789).
32 Ibid., pp. 186–8 (26 July 1789).
33 Ibid., p. 188 (27 July 1789).
34 Ibid., pp. 192–3 (30 July 1789).
35 Ibid., pp. 194–5 (31 July 1789). (See Young p. 204 for further comment on the press.)
36 Ibid., p. 205 (6 August 1789).
37 Ibid., pp 215–16 (19 August 1789).
38 Ibid., p. 226 (30 August 1789).
39 Ibid., p. 228 (1 September 1789).

6 From the Fall of the Bastille to the March of the Women on Versailles

1 Jefferson, 15, pp. 268–9 (11 July 1789). (The declaration was ratified on 26 August 1789.)
2 Ibid., p. 334 (5 August 1789).
3 Ibid., p. 425 (13 September 1789).
4 Ibid., p. 365 (28 August 1789).
5 Ibid., pp. 458–9 (19 September 1789).
6 Ibid., p. 366 (28 August 1789).
7 Morris, I, p. 143 (end of July 1789).
8 Auckland, II, p. 348 (Huber to Eden) (17 August 1789).
9 'Despatches, Paris', p. 259 (3 September 1789).
10 Ibid., pp. 259–60 (10 September 1789).
11 Auckland, II, pp. 353, 355 (Huber to Eden as Lord Auckland) (26–7 September 1789).
12 Morris, I, p. 154 (13 September 1789).
13 Jefferson, 15, pp. 458–9 (19 September 1789).
14 Morris, I, pp. 162–3 (26 September 1789).
15 One of the fullest accounts of the *Assignat* system is in S. E. Harris, *The Assignats*, New York 1969, but Harris does not devote very much attention to their *ancien régime* proponents. They were specifically proposed in several *philosophe* and anti-clerical works, most specifically in a pamphlet published anonymously but allegedly written by Voltaire, *Les Récits de Frère Ecoute*, Paris (?) 1776.
16 Morris, I, pp. 162–3 (26 September 1789).

17 Jefferson, 15, p. 366 (28 August 1789).
18 Auckland, II, p. 365 (Huber to Auckland) (15 October 1789); 'Despatches, Paris', p. 267 (15 October 1789).
19 Jefferson, 15, p. 364 (28 August 1789).
20 Ibid., pp. 459–60 (19 September 1789).
21 Morris, I, pp. 142–3 (31 July 1789), 156 (17 September 1789).
22 Ibid., p. 170 (4 October 1789).
23 Jefferson (despatches now being written by William Short), 15, pp. 511 ff. (8 October 1789).
24 'Despatches, Paris', p. 263 (7 October 1789).
25 Auckland, II, p. 361 (Garlicke to Auckland) (6 October 1789).
26 Morris, I, p. 172 (4 October 1789).
27 'Despatches, Paris', pp. 263–4 (7 October 1789).
28 Morris, I, p. 176 (6 October 1789).
29 Jefferson (Short), 15, p. 531 (3 November 1789).
30 Ibid., pp. 177 (7 October 1789), 183 (11 October 1789).
31 'Despatches, Paris', p. 265 (8 October 1789).
32 Morris, I, p. 143 (31 July 1789); 'Despatches, Paris', p. 265 (8 October 1789).

7 From the King's Arrival in Paris to the End of 1789

1 Auckland, II, p. 365 (Huber to Auckland) (15 October 1789).
2 Morris, I, p. 195 (18 October 1789).
3 Jefferson (Short), 15, p. 532 (3 November 1789).
4 Morris, I, p. 233 (18 November 1789).
5 Jefferson (Short), 15, p. 533 (3 November 1789).
6 Ibid., 16, p. 46 (25 December 1789); 'Despatches, Paris', p. 285 (15 January 1790).
7 Morris, I, pp. 192 (16 October 1789), 197–8 (18 October 1789).
8 Ibid., p. 215 (3 November 1789).
9 'Despatches, Paris', p. 277 (6 December 1789).
10 Ibid.
11 Jefferson (Short), 16, pp. 44–5 (25 December 1789).
12 Jefferson, 15, p. 358 (27 August 1789).
13 'Despatches, Paris', pp. 267 (15 October 1789), 268, 271 (22 October 1789).
14 Ibid., p. 276 (6 December 1789).
15 Jefferson, 15, p. 266 (8 July 1789), and see deaths of Foulon and Bertier de Sauvigny in previous chapter.
16 Jefferson (Short), 15, p. 533 (3 November 1789); Morris, I, pp. 200, 201 (21 October 1789).
17 'Despatches, Paris', p. 277 (6 December 1789).
18 Ibid., pp. 274 (29 October 1789), 276 (6 December 1789).
19 Jefferson (Short), 15, p. 535 (3 November 1789).
20 Young, pp. 250–1 (10 January 1790).
21 Ibid., p. 256 (13 January 1790).
22 Jefferson (Short), 15, p. 534 (3 November 1789); 'Despatches, Paris', pp. 275, 274 (29 October 1789).
23 Jefferson (Short), 16, p. 3 (30 November 1789).
24 Morris, I, pp. 212 (1 November 1789), 267 (10 January 1790).
25 Ibid., pp. 230 (17 November 1789), 238 (28 November 1789).
26 Ibid., pp. 188 (13 October 1789), 234 (20 November 1789).
27 Ibid., p. 251 (16 December 1789). Jefferson (Short), 15, p. 534 (3 November 1789).
28 Jefferson (Short), 16, p. 3 (30 November 1789).

29 Jefferson (Short), 15, p. 535 (3 November 1789).
30 'Despatches, Paris', pp. 267–8 (15 October 1789).
31 Jefferson (Short), 16, p. 3 (30 November 1789).
32 Ibid., p. 50 (25 December 1789).
33 Young, p. 241 (25 December 1789).
34 Ibid., pp. 242, 244 (28, 29 December 1789).

8 From 1790 to the Fête de la Fédération
1. Auckland, II, p. 366 (Sheffield to Auckland) (8 January 1790).
2 Morris, I, pp. 276, 280 (late January 1790).
3 Young, p. 247 (4 January 1790).
4 Jefferson (Short) 16, pp. 121 (23 January 1790), 200 (3 March 1790).
5 Young, pp. 258 (15 January 1790), 251 (10 January 1790).
6 Ibid., pp. 261–2 (18 January 1790).
7 Jefferson (Short), 16, p. 133 (28 January 1790). (Huber was also a member of this club.) Miles, I, p. 205 (Miles to Mr Pye) (30 January 1791).
8 Gower, p. 9 (2 July 1790).
9 Young, p. 255 (12 January 1790). Miles made an almost identical observation in August, Miles, I, p. 159 (Miles to Lord Rodney) (23 August 1790).
10 'Despatches, Paris', p. 293 (12 February 1790).
11 Young, pp. 252–3 (11 January 1790).
12 'Despatches, Paris', p. 320 (9 April 1790).
13 Ibid., p. 293 (12 February 1790).
14 Jefferson (Short), 16, p. 219 (9 March 1790).
15 Young, pp. 259–60 (16–17 January 1790).
16 'Despatches, Paris', pp. 288–9 (1 and 5 February 1790).
17 Jefferson (Short) 16, p. 160 (10 February 1790).
18 Morris, I, p. 291 (3 February 1790).
19 Jefferson (Short), 16, p. 160 (10 February 1790).
20 Morris, I, p. 280 (26 January 1790).
21 'Despatches, Paris', pp. 292–3 (19 February 1790).
22 Young, p. 256 (13 January 1790).
23 Morris, I, p. 280 (26 January 1790).
24 Jefferson (Short), 16, pp. 571–2 (25 June 1790).
25 Ibid., pp. 404 (1 May 1790), 425–6 (11 May 1790), 430 (16 May 1790).
26 Ibid., p. 438 (23 May 1790).
27 Young, pp. 260–1 (17 January 1790).
28 'Despatches, Paris', p. 293 (19 February 1790).
29 Young, pp. 260 (17 January 1790), 252 (11 January 1790).
30 'Despatches, Paris', p. 292 (19 February 1790).
31 Gower, pp. 10 (2 July 1790), 12 (9 July 1790).
32 Morris, I, pp. 264–5 (4 January 1790).
33 Ibid., I, p. 280 (26 January 1790); Jefferson (Short), 16, p. 122 (23 January 1790).
34 Morris, I, p. 286 (26 January 1790); Jefferson (Short), 16, pp. 132 (28 January 1790), 403 (1 May 1790).
35 Jefferson (Short), 16, pp. 103 (12 January 1790), 131, 132 (28 January 1790).
36 Ibid., pp. 234 ff. (17 March 1790), 269–70 (25 March 1790), 374 (23 April 1790).
37 Ibid., pp. 371–3 (23 April 1790).
38 Ibid., pp. 507 (14 June 1790), 571 (25 June 1790); Morris, I, p. 335 (24 June 1790).

39 'Despatches, Paris', pp. 283 (1 January 1790), 296 (26 February 1790).

40 Jefferson (Short), 16, p. 161 (10 February 1790).

41 Ibid., pp. 219 (9 March 1790), 302 (4 April 1790).

42 Ibid., p. 420 (9 May 1790).

43 Morris, 1, p. 283 (26 January 1790).

44 Jefferson (Short), 16, p. 374 (23 April 1790).

45 Ibid., p. 373 (23 April 1790).

46 Young, p. 248 (4 January 1790).

47 Morris, 1, p. 286 (26 January 1790).

48 Jefferson (Short), 17, p. 27 (11 July 1790).

49 Gower, p. 14 (15 July 1790).

50 Young, pp. 246–7 (4 January 1790).

51 Morris, 1, pp. 276, 281 (26 January 1790).

52 Young, pp. 251 (10 January 1790), 252 (11 January 1790), 255 (13 January 1790).

53 'Despatches, Paris', pp. 285 (15 January 1790), 291 (5 February 1790).

54 Ibid., p. 287 (12 January 1790); Jefferson (Short), 16, p. 108 (12 January 1790).

55 Young, pp. 251 (10 January 1790), 252 (11 January 1790).

56 Morris, 1, p. 286 (26 January 1790).

57 Gower, p. 13 (9 July 1790). (The commentators did indeed report very many other plots (e.g. Favras'), but could not, in the circumstances, give more than partial accounts of them).

58 Jefferson (Short), 16, pp. 320–3 (4 April 1790).

59 'Despatches, Paris', p. 295 (26 February 1790).

60 Jefferson (Short), 16, p. 130 (28 January 1790).

61 Ibid., p. 202 (4 March 1790).

62 Ibid., p. 163 (10 February 1790).

63 Ibid., p. 506 (14 June 1790).

64 Gower, p. 8 (2 July 1790).

65 Jefferson (Short), 16, p. 586 (29 June 1790); Gower, p. 7 (25 June 1790).

66 Gower, p. 6 (25 June 1790).

67 Jefferson (Short), 16, p. 586 (29 June 1790); 17, p. 17 (7 July 1790).

68 Ibid., 17, pp. 212–13 (16 July 1790); Gower, p. 14 (15 July 1790).

69 Morris, 1, p. 337 (26 July 1790).

9 From the Fête de la Fédération to the Flight to Varennes

1 Jefferson (Short), 17, pp. 256–7 (22 July 1790); 18, p. 351 (23 December 1790); 20, p. 170 (8 April 1791).

2 Ibid., 17, pp. 393, 396 (15 August 1790).

3 Morris, 1, pp. 344 (14 August 1790), 345 (30 August 1790).

4 Ibid., pp. 358 (18 November 1790), 360 (23 November 1790).

5 Gower, pp. 93–4 (10 June 1791).

6 Miles, 1, pp. 171–2 (Miles to Sir Edward Newenham) (27 November 1790).

7 Ibid., pp. 160 (Miles to Lord Buckingham) (6 September 1790), 186–7 (Miles to the Rev. Howell H. Edwards) (24 December 1790), 154 (Miles to Lord Rodney) (23 August 1790).

8 Ibid., pp. 206 (Miles to Pye) (30 January 1791), 210 (Miles to Newenham) (16 February 1791).

9 Ibid., p. 230 (Miles to Mr T. Somers Cocks) (25 February 1791).

10 Ibid., p. 246 (Miles to Pye) (1 March 1791).

11 Ibid., e.g. p. 200 (Miles to Pye) (5 January 1791).

12 Ibid., p. 263 (Miles to Newenham) (18 March 1791).

13 Jefferson (Short), 18, pp. 84–5 (26 November 1790).

14 Gower, p. 46 (10 December 1790).
15 Ibid., pp. 45, 47 (3 December 1790).
16 Jefferson (Short), 18, p. 351 (23 December 1790).
17 Jefferson (Short), 17, pp. 311–12 (4 August 1790), Gower, pp. 18–19 (30 July 1790).
18 Ibid., 17, pp. 437–8 (27 August 1790).
19 Ibid., (Short), 17, p. 488 (5 September 1790); Gower, p. 29 (29 August 1790).
20 Gower, pp. 51–2 (23 January 1790).
21 Miles, I, p. 151 (Miles to Rodney) (23 August 1790).
22 Morris, I, pp. 353 (9 November 1790), 361 (25 November 1790), 376–7 (26 January 1791).
23 Jefferson (Short), 17, p. 504 (9 September 1790); 18, pp. 352 (23 December 1790), 511 (17 January 1790); 20, pp. 350–1 (2 May 1791), 384 (8 May 1791).
24 Ibid., 19, p. 533 (11 March 1791), Gower, p. 68 (4 March 1791).
25 Morris, I, p. 388 (2 March 1791).
26 Miles, I, p. 247 (Miles to Somers Cocks) (4 March 1791).
27 Morris, I, p. 404 (18 March 1791).
28 Jefferson (Short), 20, p. 259 (25 April 1791); Morris, I, p. 408 (21 April 1791).
29 Jefferson (Short), 20, pp. 259, 260 (25 April 1791).
30 Gower, p. 82 (29 April 1791).
31 Jefferson (Short), 20, pp. 532 (16 June 1791), 584 (29 June 1791).
32 Ibid., 17, p. 491 (5 September 1790); Gower, p. 31 (10 September 1790).
33 Gower, p. 51 (23 January 1791); Morris, I, p. 385 (24 February 1791).
34 Morris, I, p. 396 (2 April 1791).
35 Gower, p. 82 (29 April 1791).
36 Ibid., pp. 81–2 (22 April 1791).
37 Jefferson (Short), 20, p. 351 (2 May 1791).
38 Gower, pp. 31 (10 September 1790), 37 (8 October 1790).
39 Morris, I, p. 400 (8 April 1791); Gower, p. 102 (1 July 1791).
40 Morris, I, pp. 389, 390 (3 March 1791).
41 Gower, pp. 58 (11 February 1791), 67–8 (4 March 1791).
42 Gower, p. 76 (2 April 1791); Miles, I, p. 273 (Miles to Somers Cocks) (4 April 1791).
43 Jefferson (Short), 20, p. 171 (8 April 1791).
44 Morris, I, p. 398 (4 April 1791).
45 Gower, p. 77 (8 April 1791).
46 Jefferson (Short), 18, p. 84 (26 November 1790).
47 Gower, pp. 43, 44 (19 November 1790).
48 Auckland, II, pp. 378–9 (Mr John Thomas Stanley to Lord Auckland) (7 December 1790).
49 Jefferson (Short), 17, p. 491 (5 September 1790).
50 Ibid., p. 523 (26 September 1790).
51 Gower, p. 42 (12 November 1790).
52 Jefferson (Short), 19, p. 335 (25 February 1791).
53 Gower, pp. 55 (4 February 1791), 92–3 (3 June 1791), 79 (15 April 1791).
54 Ibid., p. 58 (11 February 1791).
55 Ibid., p. 75 (1 April 1791).
56 Ibid., p. 94 (10 June 1791).
57 Ibid., p. 42 (12 November 1790); Morris, I, p. 382 (15 February 1791).
58 Gower, p. 79 (15 April 1791).
59 Morris, I, p. 399 (8 April 1791).
60 Jefferson (Short), 20, p. 351 (2 May 1791).
61 Miles, I, p. 207 (Miles to Pye) (30 January 1791).
62 Ibid., p. 205.

63 Ibid., p. 245 (Miles to Pye) (1 March 1791).
64 Morris, 1, p. 396 (2 April 1791).
65 Gower, p. 79 (15 April 1791).
66 Jefferson (Short), 18, pp. 502–3 (10 January 1791), 605 (24 January 1791); 19, p. 635 (30 March 1791).
67 Jefferson (Short), 20, p. 258 (25 April 1791).
68 Ibid., 20, p. 368 (4 May 1791).
69 Morris, 1, p. 385 (23 February 1791); Miles, 1, p. 275 (Miles to Somers Cocks) (4 April 1791).
70 Gower, p. 25 (20 August 1790); Jefferson (Short), 17, p. 611 (21 October 1790).
71 Gower, p. 47 (17 December 1790).
72 Ibid., pp. 70–1 (11 March 1791).
73 Ibid., p. 86 (13 May 1791).
74 Morris, 1, p. 422 (17 May 1791).
75 Jefferson (Short), 19, p. 335 (25 February 1791).
76 Miles, pp. 177 (Miles to Mr Rose) (30 November 1790), 250 (Miles to Somers Cocks) (4 March 1791), 241 (Miles to Somers Cocks) (23 February 1791).
77 Jefferson (Short), 19, p. 634 (30 March 1791); 20 p. 549 (10 June 1791).
78 Ibid., 19, p. 534 (11 March 1791).
79 Ibid., p. 117 (28 January 1791); Morris, 1, p. 374 (22 January 1791).
80 Morris, 1, p. 382 (15 February 1791).
81 Jefferson (Short), 17, p. 441 (27 August 1790).
82 Jefferson (Short), 20, p. 364 (3 May 1791).
83 Gower, pp. 70 (11 March 1791), 88 (20 May 1791).
84 Jefferson (Short), 18, p. 605 (24 January 1791); 20, p. 170 (8 April 1791).
85 Gower, pp. 79–80 (15 April 1791).
86 Ibid., p. 88 (20 May 1791).

10 From the Flight to Varennes (and its Preludes) to the Dissolution of the National Assembly

1 Gower, pp. 25 (20 August 1790), 70 (11 March 1791).
2 Ibid., p. 69 (11 March 1791); Jefferson (Short), 19, p. 635 (30 March 1791).
3 Morris, 1, p. 400 (8 April 1791).
4 Miles, 1, p. 196 (Miles to Pye) (5 January 1791).
5 Gower, p. 59 (11 February 1791).
6 Ibid., p. 63 (20 February 1791 and 25 February 1791); Jefferson (Short), 19, pp. 362–3 (4 March 1791); Miles, 1, pp. 215–16 (Miles to Somers Cocks) (23 February 1791).
7 Jefferson (Short), 19, p. 533 (11 March 1791); Gower, pp. 66–7 (4 March 1791).
8 Gower, p. 67 (4 March 1791).
9 Ibid., pp. 80–2 (22 April 1791).
10 Miles, 1, pp. 225–7 (Miles to Somers Cocks) (25 February 1791).
11 Ibid., pp. 247–8 (Miles to Somers Cocks) (4 March 1791).
12 Gower, pp. 80–2 (22 April 1791).
13 Jefferson (Short), 20, p. 258 (25 April 1791).
14 Morris, 1, p. 415 (1 May 1791).
15 Jefferson (Short), 22, p. 194 (6 October 1791).
16 Morris, 1, p. 427 (25 June 1791).
17 Jefferson (Short), 20, p. 561 (22 June 1791).
18 Ibid., p. 562 (22 June 1791); Morris, 1, p. 428 (2 July 1791).
19 Gower, p. 96 (22 June 1791); Jefferson (Short), p. 561 (22 June 1791).
20 Gower, p. 100 (25 June 1791).
21 Gower, p. 99 (25 June 1791); Jefferson (Short), 20, pp. 578 (26 June 1791), 562 (22 June

1791); Morris, I, p. 429 (4 July 1791), Miles, I, p. 304 (Miss Miles to William Miles) (27 June 1791).

22 Jefferson (Short), 20, p. 574 (26 June 1791).

23 Miles, I, p. 302 (Miss Miles to Miles) (26 June 1791).

24 Jefferson (Short), 20, pp. 576-7 (26 June 1791), 585 (29 June 1791).

25 Morris, I, p. 429 (2 July 1791).

26 Gower, pp. 105 (8 July 1791), 106 (18 July 1791).

27 Jefferson (Short), 20, p. 609 (8 July 1791); Gower, p. 99 (25 June 1791).

28 Morris, I, pp. 431 (14 July 1791), 440-1 (6 August 1791) (and p. 507, 4 February 1792).

29 Jefferson (Short), 20, p. 609 (8 July 1791).

30 Ibid., p. 648 (20 July 1791); Gower, p. 106 (18 July 1791).

31 Jefferson (Short), 20, pp. 587 (29 June 1791), 610 (8 July 1791).

32 Ibid., p. 610 (8 July 1791); Gower, p. 105 (15 July 1791).

33 Morris, I, p. 429 (4 July 1791).

34 Gower, p. 108 (18 July 1791).

35 Morris, I, p. 449 (7 September 1791).

36 Jefferson (Short), 20, p. 650 (20 July 1791); Morris, I, p. 457 (30 September 1791).

37 Jefferson (Short), 22, p. 126 (4 September 1791).

38 Ibid., p. 145 (14 September 1791).

39 Morris, I, p. 257 (30 September 1791).

40 Jefferson (Short), 20, p. 672 (24 July 1792).

41 Morris, I, p. 432 (14 July 1791).

42 Ibid., p. 432 (15 July 1791).

43 Ibid., pp. 435, 434 (17 July 1791).

44 Jefferson (Short), 20, p. 649 (20 July 1791); Gower, p. 107 (18 July 1791).

45 Jefferson (Short), 20, p. 585 (29 June 1791), 610 (8 July 1791).

46 Morris, I, p. 430 (6 July 1791).

47 Jefferson (Short), 20, p. 649 (20 July 1791).

48 Ibid., pp. 649 (20 July 1791), 654 (21 July 1791).

49 Gower, pp. 108, 109 (22 July 1791). (Note, two despatches).

50 Morris, I, p. 491 (19 December 1791).

51 Jefferson (Short), 20, p. 673 (24 July 1791).

52 Gower, p. 107 (18 July 1791).

53 Jefferson (Short), 22, p. 106 (30 August 1791).

54 Comments on Condorcet and Brissot made in passing in a despatch on the National Assembly in Jefferson (Short), 20, p. 648 (20 July 1791).

55 Ibid., p. 610 (8 July 1791).

56 Morris, I, p. 457 (30 September 1791).

57 Jefferson (Short), 22, p. 106 (30 August 1791); Gower, p. 118 (26 August 1791).

58 Jefferson (Short), 22, p. 105 (30 August 1791).

59 Gower, pp. 102 (1 July 1791), 118 (26 August 1791).

60 Jefferson (Short), 22, pp. 107 (30 August 1791), 126 (4 September 1791).

61 Gower, p. 124 (16 September 1791); Morris, I, p. 457 (30 September 1791).

62 Morris, I, pp. 440 (6 August 1791), 457 (30 September 1791).

63 Jefferson (Short), 22, p. 19 (9 August 1791).

64 Ibid., pp. 19-20 (9 August 1791).

65 Ibid., p. 126 (4 September 1791).

66 Gower, pp. 122-3 (14 September 1791); Jefferson (Short), 20, p. 650 (20 July 1791).

67 Gower, p. 121 (9 September 1791).

68 Jefferson (Short), 22, pp. 130 (5 September 1791), 160 (22 September 1791).

69 Gower, pp. 123 (14 September 1791) 124 (23 September 1791); Morris, I, p. 452 (18 September 1791).
70 Jefferson (Short), 22, pp. 160–1 (22 September 1791).
71 Morris, I, p. 456 (30 September 1791).
72 Jefferson (Short), 22, pp. 145–6 (14 September 1791), 161 (22 September 1791).

11 **From the Meeting of the Legislative Assembly to the Storming of the Tuileries**
 1 Gower, p. 128 (7 October 1791); Morris, I, p. 461 (5 October 1791).
 2 Jefferson (Short), 22, p. 222 (22 October 1791).
 3 Ibid., p. 270 (8 November 1791).
 4 Gower, pp. 141–2 (16 December 1791).
 5 Jefferson (Short), 22, p. 222 (22 October 1791).
 6 Morris, I, p. 471 (26 October 1791).
 7 Gower, p. 135 (11 November 1791).
 8 Jefferson (Short), 22, p. 315 (21 November 1791); Gower, p. 136 (18 November 1791).
 9 Morris, I, p. 468 (22 October 1791).
10 Gower, pp. 139–40 (5 December 1791).
11 Jefferson (Short) 22, p. 270 (8 November 1791).
12 Gower, pp. 146 (6 January 1792), 147 (13 January 1792).
13 Ibid., pp. 130 (28 October 1791), 136 (18 November 1791).
14 Ibid., pp. 135 (18 November 1791), 159 (2 March 1792).
15 Ibid., p. 149 (20 January 1792) (see also a very similar report, p. 169, 2 April 1792).
16 Ibid., p. 145 (30 December 1792).
17 Ibid., p. 154 (10 February 1792).
18 Jefferson (Short), 22, pp. 270–1 (8 November 1791).
19 Gower, pp. 137–8 (25 November 1791).
20 Ibid., pp. 139 (2 December 1792), 141 (9 December 1791).
21 Ibid., pp. 155 (10 February 1792), 165 (30 March 1792).
22 Ibid., p. 140 (5 December 1791).
23 Morris, I, p. 511 (4 February 1792); Gower, p. 170 (11 April 1792).
24 Gower, p. 143 (23 November 1791).
25 Ibid., pp. 151–2 (27 January 1792).
26 Ibid., p. 154 (3 February 1792).
27 Ibid., pp. 157–8 (24 February 1792).
28 Morris, I, p. 524 (25 March 1792).
29 Gower, p. 164 (30 March 1792).
30 Ibid., pp. 175 (22 April 1792), 177 (27 April 1792).
31 Gower, p. 175 (3 May 1792); Auckland, II, p. 405 (Gower to Auckland) (4 May 1792).
32 Morris, I, pp. 530 (14 May 1792), 533 (14 May 1792).
33 Gower, pp. 177 (27 April 1792), 181 (4 May 1792).
34 Ibid., p. 186 (1 June 1792).
35 Ibid., p. 189 (8 June 1792).
36 Ibid., pp. 189–90 (8 June 1792).
37 Ibid., p. 190 (15 June 1792).
38 Ibid., pp. 159 (9 March 1792), 167 (2 April 1792), 173 (20 April 1792).
39 Ibid., p. 150 (27 January 1792).
40 Ibid., p. 154 (10 February 1792).
41 Ibid., p. 173 (20 April 1792).
42 Ibid., p. 184 (18 May 1792).
43 Ibid., pp. 142 (16 December 1791), 151 (27 January 1792).

44 Ibid., p. 153 (3 February 1792).
45 Ibid., p. 154 (10 February 1792).
46 Ibid., p. 156 (17 February 1792).
47 Morris, I, p. 535 (3 June 1792).
48 Gower, pp. 163 (23 March 1792), 187 (1 June 1792).
49 Ibid., pp. 190 (15 June 1792), 193 (22 June 1792).
50 Morris, I, pp. 544–5 (17 June 1792).
51 Gower, p. 193 (22 June 1792).
52 Morris, I, p. 546 (20 June 1792).
53 Ibid., p. 547 (26 June 1792).
54 Gower, p. 196 (29 June 1792).
55 Morris, I, p. 549 (29 June 1792).
56 Gower, p. 198 (6 July 1792).
57 Morris, I, pp. 566 (1 August 1792), 586 (12 September 1792); Gower (Monro), p. 251 (20 September 1792).
58 Morris, I, p. 549 (6 July 1792).
59 Gower, pp. 197 (29 June 1792), 198 (6 July 1792), 200 (13 July 1792).
60 Morris, I, p. 555 (22 July 1792); Gower, p. 205 (3 August 1792).
61 Gower, p. 198 (6 July 1792).
62 Morris, I, p. 563 (25 July 1792).
63 Gower, p. 199 (13 July 1792).
64 Ibid., p. 206 (3 August 1792).
65 Morris, I, p. 552 (10 and 11 July 1792).
66 Gower, p. 201 (20 July 1792).
67 Ibid., p. 203 (27 July 1792).
68 Morris, I, p. 567 (1 August 1792).
69 Gower, p. 203 (27 July 1792).
70 Ibid., p. 205 (3 August 1792).
71 Morris, I, p. 569 (5 August 1792).
72 Ibid., p. 570 (10 August 1792).
73 Morris, II, pp. 10–11 (21 December 1792), 26 (6 January 1793).
74 Auckland, II, p. 434 (Mr Burges to Auckland) (17 August 1792).
75 Gower, p. 208 (12 August 1792); Morris, I, p. 570 (11 August 1792).
76 Auckland, II, p. 433 (Burges to Auckland) (17 August 1792).
77 Gower, p. 209 (17 August 1792).
78 Ibid., p. 211 (23 August 1792).
79 Morris, I, p. 576 (22 August 1792).

Postscript 1792–94
 1 Gower, p. 215 (27 August 1792).
 2 Ibid., p. 213 (27 August 1792).
 3 Ibid., pp. 214, 219 (30 August 1792 – two separate despatches).
 4 Ibid., pp. 219–20 (31 August 1792).
 5 Gower (Monro), pp. 231 (5 September 1792), 237 (8 September 1792).
 6 Gower, p. 223 (3 September 1792).
 7 Ibid., p. 214 (27 August 1792).
 8 Morris, I, pp. 578, 580 (25 and 29 August 1792).
 9 Ibid., p. 580 (30 August 1792).
10 Gower, p. 217 (29 August 1792). (This despatch was probably phrased with the censor in mind.)

11 Ibid., pp. 214–15 (27 August 1792).
12 Ibid., p. 216 (29 August 1792).
13 Ibid., p. 222 (2 September 1792).
14 Gower (Monro), p. 225 (4 September 1792).
15 Morris, I, pp. 581–2 (2 September 1792).
16 Gower (Monro), pp. 226–7 (4 September 1792).
17 Morris, I, p. 583 (6 and 10 September 1792 – two separate despatches).
18 Gower (Monro), p. 231 (5 September 1792).
19 Ibid., pp. 234–5 (6 September 1792).
20 Ibid., pp. 234 (5 September 1792), p. 238 (9 September 1792).
21 Morris, I, p. 583 (7 September 1792).
22 Gower (Monro), pp. 241 (10 September 1792), 244 (12 September 1792).
23 Auckland, II, pp. 443 (14 September 1792), (Burges to Auckland), 445 (21 September 1792) (forwarded by Burges to Auckland); Gower (Monro), p. 251 (14 September 1792).
24 Gower (Monro), pp. 246–7 (14 September 1792).
25 Auckland, II, p. 450 (Huber to Auckland) (4 October 1792).
26 Gower (Monro), pp. 245 (12 September 1792), 250 (14 October 1792).
27 Ibid., p. 254 (22 September 1792).
28 Morris, I, pp. 593 (26 September 1792), 594 (2 and 3 October 1792).
29 Auckland, II, p. 453 (Auckland to Sir Morton Eden) (9 October 1792).
30 Morris, I, p. 594 (3 October 1792).
31 Auckland, II, p. 442 (Burges to Auckland) (14 September 1792).
32 Gower (Monro), p. 253 (20 October 1792).
33 Morris, I, p. 589 (21 September 1792), II, p. 7 (3 December 1792).
34 Morris, II, p. 8 (12 December 1792); Gower (Monro), p. 259 (17 December 1792).
35 Gower (Monro), pp. 265 (24 December 1792), 267 (27 December 1792).
36 Morris, II, pp. 8–10 (21 December 1792), 27 (6 January 1793).
37 Gower (Monro), p. 279 (21 January 1793).
38 Ibid., p. 275 (10 January 1793).
39 Ibid., pp. 280–1 (21 January 1793).
40 Ibid., p. 284 (21 January 1793); Morris, II, p. 31 (23 January 1793).
41 Gower, p. 214 (27 August 1792).
42 Auckland, II, p. 517 (Miss Chowne to Auckland) (23 September 1793).
43 Morris, II, pp. 53–4 (18 October 1793).
44 Gower (Monro), p. 259 (17 December 1792).
45 Morris, II, p. 2 (5 November 1792).
46 Ibid., p. 39 (7 March 1793).
47 Ibid., p. 8 (19 December 1792).
48 Ibid., p. 19 (25 December 1792). (It would be open to doubt whether d'Estaing was still using his title at this date, even if Morris credited him with it, but Morris's reference to it is a useful reminder that a great many former nobles continued to be politically active in France throughout the Revolutionary period – some even serving on the Committee of Public Safety.)
49 Gower (Monro), p. 273 (7 January 1793).
50 Ibid., p. 258 (17 December 1792).
51 Morris, II, p. 9 (21 December 1792).
52 Gower (Monro), p. 270 (31 December 1792).
53 Ibid., p. 278 (13 January 1793).
54 Morris, II, pp. 61–2 (18 April 1794).
55 Ibid., II, pp. 8–9 (21 December 1792).
56 Ibid., II, p. 63 (25 April 1794).

57 Gower (Monro), pp. 244 (12 September 1792), 251–2 (20 September 1792).
58 Ibid., pp. 256 (22 September 1792), 258 (17 December 1792), 270–1 (31 December 1792).
59 Morris, II, p. 11 (21 December 1792).
60 Gower (Monro), p. 284 (21 January 1793).
61 Morris, II, p. 43 (19 April 1973).
62 Gower (Monro), p. 253 (20 September 1792).
63 Ibid., p. 259 (27 December 1792).
64 Morris, II, p. 23 (1 January 1793).
65 Auckland, II, p. 451 (Huber to Auckland) (4 October 1792).
66 Gower (Monro), p. 275 (7 January 1793).
67 Morris, II, pp. 26–7 (6 January 1793).
68 Morris, II, p. 40 (7 March 1793).
69 Miles, II, pp. 76–8 (A lady (pseud.) to Miles), (12 March 1793).
70 E.g. Gower, Monro, p. 260 (17 December 1792).
71 Ibid., p. 277 (10 January 1793).
72 Auckland, III, p. 192 (Mr Crauford to Auckland) (11 March 1794).
73 Morris, II, pp. 2 (14 November 1792), 35 (13 February 1793).
74 Ibid., p. 15 (24 December 1792).
75 Ibid., p. 24 (5 January 1793).
76 Ibid., pp. 52–3 (September 1793).
77 Ibid., p. 38 (15 March 1793).
78 Ibid., II, p. 51 (13 August 1793).
79 Ibid., p. 53 (mid-October).
80 Ibid., p. 59 (12 March 1794).
81 Ibid., p. 41 (28 March 1793).
82 Ibid., II, p. 61 (18 April 1794).
83 Ibid., pp. 62–3 (25 April 1794).
84 Ibid., pp. 63–6 (25 July 1794).
85 Ibid., p. 66 (14 August 1794).
86 Ibid., pp. 77–8 (30 December 1794).

Conclusion

1 Auckland, II, p. 324 (Huber to Auckland) (28 June 1789).
2 Thomas Jefferson, *The Founding Fathers*, pp. 242–3 (Jefferson to Short) (3 January 1793).
3 Jefferson, 13, p. 458 (2 September 1788).
4 Alfred Cobban, *Social Interpretations of the French Revolution*, Cambridge 1965; François Furet, *Interpreting the French Revolution*, London 1975 (Paris, 1974); William Doyle, *The Ancien Régime*, Basingstoke 1986; T. C. W. Blanning, *The French Revolution*, Basingstoke 1987.

Notes on the Descriptive Illustrations

Opening of the States-General

The States-General met formally for their inaugural session, in the presence of Louis XVI and Marie-Antoinette, on 5 May 1789 at the Palace of Versailles in the Salle des Menus Plaisirs.

This engraving shows the session at the point where Necker (standing to left of table) was delivering his three-and-a-half-hour-long speech on the nation's finances. The deputies of the First Estate (Clergy) are to the left, those of the Second (Nobility) are to the right and of the Third (Commons) at the back of the hall facing the king. It is only really clear for the clergy, but each Estate was wearing its prescribed ceremonial dress.

On the dais Marie-Antoinette sits below and to the right of Louis XVI (who has established by this time that he should be wearing a hat and the deputies not – see page 42 ff). Members of the royal family, court officials, and other dignitaries also sit on the dais, while the Keeper of the Seals presides over the session from the table in the body of the hall.

Behind the deputies can be made out the two levels of public galleries. Thomas Jefferson, Gouverneur Morris, and Lord Dorset were definitely present on 5 May (i.e. are in this picture). From their accounts of the day it would seem that Jefferson and Dorset were in an upper gallery and Morris in a lower one. Subsequently Arthur Young, William Short, and M. Huber all sat in these same galleries to watch proceedings. It is clear even from this representation of the States General in all its solemnity that the separation between deputies and public left much to be desired. Those in the public galleries learned very quickly how to intervene in the debates and bring business to a halt.

It was from the meeting room depicted here that the deputies were barred on 20 June 1789. This led to their reassembling in the nearby tennis court to swear their oath and to create the National Assembly, which, in turn, then also met in this hall until it transferred to Paris in the autumn of 1789.

The Sacking of the Hôtel de Ville in Strasbourg

On 21 July 1789 Arthur Young was in Strasbourg when news of the storming of the Bastille fell upon the city. The public response was to sack the town hall as their own repudiation of the *ancien régime*. Young was among those watching the incident from the roofs of the stables in the foreground, and there is no reason to doubt that he is indeed one of the figures shown – albeit unknown to the artist. Among the documents strewn on the ground were all the local tax and feudal rolls. Despite the apparent orgy of violence, Young recorded only one casualty – a boy killed by a falling sofa.

Hanging of the Baker François

This picture shows the actual hanging of the baker François (as described on p. 87). The National Guard are conspicuous by their absence. This incident was the high-water mark of 'lynch-law' on the streets of Paris in the early days of the Revolution, and provoked a strong (but belated in the eyes of the commentators) response from municipal and national authorities.

Lafayette

If any one French Revolutionary leader influenced the commentators' own appreciation of the Revolution it was Lafayette. He is shown here in an idealized official portrait as commander of the National Guard. Lafayette was a personal friend of Morris, Miles, and Jefferson from meetings with them in America 1777–81 and he welcomed all of them into his home. Short inherited easy access to him after Jefferson's departure for America in autumn 1789; M. Huber reported having informal conversations with him; and Young opened a correspondence with him. Monro, who was, of course, posing as one of his political enemies, did not enjoy a personal relationship with Lafayette, but he was close to some of his associates in the Legislative Assembly/National Convention. The other members of the British embassy knew Lafayette more distantly, but all saw him as one of the few elements of stability in the Revolution and hoped for his success. Without the entry at the highest level into the Revolution which Lafayette offered, the commentators' reports would have been very much the poorer. For all that, the commentators were not uncritical in their judgements of him, and ultimately they all found him wanting as the great leader he had hoped to be.

Political Clubs

The local political clubs were the power-houses of the Parisian Revolution. This scene shows one in session with the president (on the left) addressing the speaker at the '*tribune*'. The term '*tribune*' became widened to cover any activist. Morris chronicled the usurpation of power by the '*tribunes*' after 10 August 1792, and he also managed to enjoy very poor relations personally with representatives from political clubs, who, in their turn, had no compunction about violating his diplomatic immunity. There might well have been an equivalent women's meeting going on at the same time elsewhere in the same building.

Second Storming of the Tuileries

The second storming of the Tuileries on 10 August 1792 is the climax to the story of the Revolution as retold in this book. The view here is a panorama of the Palace and its garden at the height of the assault. Morris recorded hearing the canon and muskets shown in action and guessing that they signified a 'warm' day (see p. 168).

Marie-Antoinette

David drew this sketch of Marie-Antoinette on her way to the guillotine shortly after the time when Auckland would have received the report from 'an English gentleman' who had somehow managed to visit her in prison (see page 181). It shows her dignity in adversity but still conveys her '*hauteur*' which had made her so unpopular under the Revolution. David, by the time of this picture, was deeply involved in Revolutionary politics and went on to serve on a Revolutionary Tribunal – hence his ability to gain access to so high-ranking a prisoner. Under the Directory David recanted his Jacobinism and became the court painter for the First Empire.

Louis XVI

This was the last portrait of Louis XVI. It was drawn in the Temple prison by Joseph Ducreux three days before the king's execution on 21 January 1793. It tallies with Morris's and Monro's description of him as resigned to his fate (page 180). The image is of a sadder but wiser man, the would-be sober and conscientious ruler of a constitutional monarchy. He is dressed respectably but informally and is depicted as a man rather than a king. This is in great contrast to the flamboyant but distant iconography of the monarchy under the *ancien régime*. The picture only hints at his growing obesity, itself partly caused by the close confinement under which he was held after October 1789. The portrait confirms his lack of wit, compassion, and decisiveness – the absence of which qualities made him so ineffectual a leader and meant he inspired so little loyalty. This was the man whom, according to Miles and Morris, the Counter-Revolution would find more useful dead than alive and who, in Saint-Just's famous observation, had to be executed not for who he was but for what he was.

'Les Journées de Septembre' by J-L Prieur

This picture shows the massacre of prisoners in the Abbaye prison on the night of 2/3 September 1792. One of the figures in the background may well be the British secret agent Colonel George Monro.

Monro had infiltrated English, Irish, and American Jacobin groups in Paris. He was living in an *hôtel* with English-speaking republicans and reporting back to London on their activities. Ostensibly an active member of the Jacobin Club, his Revolutionary credentials enabled him to gain access to the prison while the executions were being carried out, and he witnessed the whole proceedings closely enough to recognize both victims and their executioners (see page 175).

The picture comes from a collection of engravings made in Paris during the Revolution by the artist J-L Prieur.* They are consistently accurate, printed near to the time of the events portrayed, and are based on Prieur's own eyewitness observation of the events (or on other first-hand accounts). They are in themselves an important source of documentary evidence on the Revolution. Prieur was an ardent Jacobin whose career paralleled that of the more famous artist Louis David. As the Revolution progressed he became ever more deeply involved in politics. This print is the last in the series as he subsequently became an active member of the Revolutionary Tribunal which tried – amongst others – Danton in 1793. He was arrested under the Thermidorean regime, refused to recant his Jacobinism, and was guillotined together with Fouquier-Tinville in 1795.

* Published as *'Tableaux de Paris pendant la Révolution Française'* edited by Pierre de Nolhac, Paris 1902. The originals are held in the Carnavalet Museum. For the purposes of this book Nolhac's interpretation of the print as authentically representing the September massacres is accepted: there is, however, some controversy about this.

The picture itself tallies with Monro's account of events in the prison except that artistic licence has led Prieur to locate all the action in a single room. According to Monro the interrogations, executions, and then disposal of the bodies took place in three separate but adjoining areas.

Gillray's Cartoons
The British popular press heaped ridicule and contempt on the Revolution from its earliest days. These images are the mirror to contemporary Revolutionary woodcuts in a primitive style meant to celebrate and exhort the Revolution. They mix political comment with social satire. In their depiction of the *sans-culottes* they probably reflect the British embassy staff's private views, and are wholly consistent with the comments made by Miles and Morris. The one aspect with which the commentators might have taken exception was the lack of any honest motivation attributed to the caricatures.

Bibliography

Primary Sources

The Journal and Correspondence of William, Lord Auckland, 4 vols, edited by the Bishop of Bath and Wells, London 1861 (vols I and II) and 1881 (vols III and IV).

The Despatches of Earl Gower, English Ambassador at Paris from June 1790 to August 1792 ..., edited by Oscar Browning, Cambridge 1885. (The despatches written by Colonel George Monro from September 1792 to January 1793 are incorporated in this volume.)

The Papers of Thomas Jefferson, edited by Julian P. Boyd (to 1986) and Charles Cullen (thereafter), 22 vols (still in publication), Princeton 1956–. (Vols 13–22 consulted for this study.) (William Short's correspondence *to* Thomas Jefferson after autumn 1789 is incorporated in these vols).

The Founding Fathers, Thomas Jefferson, a Biography in his own Words, edited by the editors of Newsweek Books, New York 1974.

Despatches from Paris 1788–1790, London Historical Society (Camden Third Series), vol. XIX, edited by Oscar Browning, London 1910.

The Correspondence of William Augustus Miles on the French Revolution 1786–1817, edited by the Revd Charles Popham Miles, 2 vols, London 1890.

The Diaries and Letters of Gouverneur Morris, edited by Anne Cary Morris, 2 vols, New York 1888.

Tableaux de Paris pendant la Révolution Française, J-L Prieur (edited for publication by Pierre de Nolhac, Paris 1902, pictures drawn 1789–92).

Travels in France During the Years 1781, 1788, and 1789, Arthur Young, edited by Constantia Maxwell, Cambridge 1929. (First published at Bury St Edmunds 1792.)

Other Primary Sources

Les Récits de Frère Ecoute, Anon., Paris (?) 1776. (Allegedly written by Voltaire.)

L'Etat de France, H. de Boullainvilliers, 3 vols, London 1727.

Collection Castries, Bibliothèque Nationale, Manuscrits français 7059. (This collection includes Necker's several memoirs on provincial administration.)

Remonstrance de la Cour des Aides, Guillaume-Chrétien Lamoignon de Malesherbes, Paris 1775.

De l'Administration Provinciale ..., G-F Letrosne, Basle, 1779.

Annales Politiques, Civiles, et Littéraires du dix-Huitième Siècle, S-H-N Linguet, The Hague 1777–90.

Despatches from Paris 1784–1787, London Historical Society (Camden Third Series), volume XVI, edited by Oscar Browning, London 1909.

Mémoire Concernant l'Utilité des Etats Provinciaux, V. de Mirabeau, Rome 1750.

Compte Rendu, J. Necker, Paris 1781.

Nouvelle Description de la France, Piganiol de la Force, 15 parts, Paris 1752–4.

Public Record Office, State Papers Series 78 (France).

Pièces Détachées Relatives au Clergé Séculier et Régulier, Marquis de Puységur, 3 vols, Amsterdam 1771.

Archives of the Order of St John of Jerusalem, Series 3, Liber Consigli di Stato.

Qu'Est Ce que le Tiers Etat, L'abbé Sieyès, (Paris) 1789.

The Times, 1789.

Secondary Works

(The books listed below should not be taken as a bibliography for the period, but include those few specifically mentioned in the text.)

C. B. A. Behrens, *The Ancien Régime*, London 1967.

T. C. W. Blanning, *The French Revolution*, Basingstoke 1987.

Alfred Cobban, *Social Interpretations of the French Revolution*, Cambridge 1965.

William Doyle, *The Ancien Régime*, Basingstoke 1986.

Jean Egret, *La Pré-Révolution Française*, Paris 1962.

François Furet, *Interpreting the French Revolution*, London 1975 (Paris 1974).

Norman Hampson, *The French Revolution, a Concise History*, London 1975.

S. E. Harris, *The Assignats*, New York 1969.

A. Lemaire, *Les Lois Fondamentales de la Monarchie Française*, Paris 1907.

H. Méthivier, *L'Ancien Régime*, Paris 1964.

Samuel F. Scott and Barry Rothaus (eds), *Historical Dictionary of the French Revolution 1789–99*, 2 vols, Westport 1985.

M. J. Sydenham, *The French Revolution*, London 1965.

A. de Tocqueville, *L'Ancien Régime et la Révolution Française*, Paris 1856.

Gordon Wright, *France in Modern Times from the Enlightenment to the Present*, Stanford 1981 (3rd edn).

Index